ROMANTICISM IN PERSPECTIVE:
TEXTS, CULTURES, HISTORIES

General Editors:
Marilyn Gaull, *Professor of English,*
Temple University/New York University
Stephen Prickett, *Regius Professor of English Language and Literature,*
University of Glasgow

This series aims to offer a fresh assessment of Romanticism by looking at it from a wide variety of perspectives. Both comparative and interdisciplinary, it will bring together cognate themes from architecture, art history, landscape gardening, linguistics, literature, philosophy, politics, science, social and political history and theology to deal with original, contentious or as yet unexplored aspects of Romanticism as a Europe-wide phenomenon.

Titles include

Richard Cronin (*editor*)
1798: THE YEAR OF THE *LYRICAL BALLADS*

Péter Dávidházi
THE ROMANTIC CULT OF SHAKESPEARE: Literary
Reception in Anthropological Perspective

David Jasper
THE SACRED AND SECULAR CANON IN ROMANTICISM:
Preserving the Sacred Truths

Malcolm Kelsall
JEFFERSON AND THE ICONOGRAPHY OF ROMANTICISM:
Folk, Land, Culture, and the Romantic Nation

Andrew McCann
CULTURAL POLITICS IN THE 1790s: Literature, Activism
and the Public Sphere

Ashton Nichols
THE REVOLUTIONARY 'I': Wordsworth and the Politics of
Self-Presentation

Jeffrey C. Robinson
RECEPTION AND POETICS IN KEATS: 'My Ended Poet'

Anya Taylor
BACCHUS IN ROMANTIC ENGLAND: Writers and Drink,
1780–1830

Michael Wiley
ROMANTIC GEOGRAPHY: Wordsworth and
Anglo-European Spaces

Eric Wilson
EMERSON'S SUBLIME SCIENCE

The Revolutionary 'I'

Wordsworth and the Politics
of Self-Presentation

Ashton Nichols

Associate Professor
Dickinson College
Carlisle, Pennsylvania

First published in Great Britain 1998 by
MACMILLAN PRESS LTD
Houndmills, Basingstoke, Hampshire RG21 6XS and London
Companies and representatives throughout the world

A catalogue record for this book is available from the British Library.

ISBN 0–333–71889–5

First published in the United States of America 1998 by
ST. MARTIN'S PRESS, INC.,
Scholarly and Reference Division,
175 Fifth Avenue, New York, N.Y. 10010

ISBN 0–312–21165–1

Library of Congress Cataloging-in-Publication Data
Nichols, Ashton, 1953–
The revolutionary "I" : Wordsworth and the politics of self
-presentation / Ashton Nichols.
p.   cm. — (Romanticism in perspective)
Includes bibliographical references and index.
ISBN 0–312–21165–1
1. Wordsworth, William, 1770–1850—Political and social views.
2. Politics and literature—Great Britain—History—19th century.
3. Revolutionary poetry, English—History and criticism.
4. Political poetry, English—History and criticism.
5. Romanticism—England.   6. Self in literature.   I. Title.
II. Series.
PR5892.P64N53 1997
821'.7—dc21   97–40501
                                                          CIP

This book is printed on paper suitable for recycling and made from fully managed and sustained forest sources.

10   9   8   7   6   5   4   3   2   1
07   06   05   04   03   02   01   00   99   98

Printed and bound in Great Britain by
Antony Rowe Ltd, Chippenham, Wiltshire

To Kimberley Anne Smith Nichols
il miglior fabbro

Contents

Preface
The Prelude as Prologue

Wordsworth's *Prelude* is a significant text for a number of reasons, not least because it bears the name of a person who has assumed a complex and often contradictory status in literary studies. William Wordsworth has long been viewed by many scholars, teachers, and readers as claimant of a place in a canonical firmament that includes only Chaucer, Shakespeare, and Milton. At the same time, however, he is described by other commentators as a pretender to such a role: a pompous, overbearing composer of simplistic ballads and Miltonic blank verse who lacked a consistent voice or a coherent philosophy. Recent criticism has sought to connect him with major cultural currents of the past two centuries while linking his work to the sources of modernism, postmodernism, and eco-criticism; or to chastise him for his lack of political engagement while relegating him to the role of reactionary pseudo-revolutionary.

The Prelude itself accounts for part of this uncertainty. It was composed in confusing drafts over a period of half a century, unpublished until after its author's death, and also related in complex ways to his major unfinished project: *The Recluse*. The text is currently available in four 'finished' forms (two-book, 13-book and 14-book versions) with a fourth 'complete' five-book text existing as a shadowy, but complete (now published) palimpsest. Not one of these editions was ever seen through the press by its author. As a supposed standard for 'Romantic' autobiography, the text was only available to a wide range of readers by the middle of the Victorian era. More importantly, autobiography as a literary form was suspect in Wordsworth's day and still occupies an uncertain position in our own critical canon. It currently holds an increasingly important status in literary study, but one that is complicated by recent theoretical critiques of the genre. This ambivalence arises partly out of our confused sense of the purpose of self-life writing. Is autobiography literature? Is it designed to explain the sources of personal 'greatness'? Is it intended to justify the action or inaction of individuals who feel a need for such justification? Is it a reply to its author's critics? Is it merely a rhetorical 'practice'? Is it an alternative to some more serious form of imaginative production? Are the claims made in autobiography true? Are they a tissue of lies and evasions?

Wordsworth's *Prelude* exists in the interstices between many of these questions. It helps us to understand why we are currently so interested in autobiography and why autobiographical writing became such a widespread and pervasive form of writing at a certain point in cultural history. The second generation of Romantics, Victorians, Modernists, Postmodernists, and our own literary moment (whatever we may call it) are all connected in important ways to the author who said that he began writing his own life story in Miltonic blank verse because he was, in his words, 'unprepared to treat any more arduous subject and diffident of my own powers' (*EY*, p. 586: 1 May 1805). *The Prelude* seeks to authorize and account for a new view of the 'self', or more precisely, to chart one version of the emergence of the concept of 'self' out of the earlier concept of 'soul'. To paraphrase Wittgenstein, the self – as Wordsworth understands it – is not a *something*, but it is not a *nothing* either. Personal identity becomes increasingly important at those moments in history when people are forced to account for their existence in radically new ways. For most of human history, the majority of individuals gave little thought to the need to 'define' their soul or to imagine what their 'personal' potential might be. Renaissance humanism, Enlightenment rationalism, and eighteenth-century skepticism profoundly altered this perspective. By 1770, at the latest, a modernized version of the 'soul' – called the 'self' – came to require just such forms of self-definition.

The French ideal of the 'citizen', for example – like the American ideal of an individual who is part of an informed electorate – requires members of a society who are not only willing to stand up and be counted, but also willing to declare their most heartfelt values and desires. Such declarations demand individuals who can say what they think, defend their own viewpoints, and offer explanations of the sources of their strength. Human weaknesses also need to be accounted for in new ways when they are no longer seen as the result of a divine destiny, but rather as confusing complexes of biology and social conditioning, apparent accidents of birth and circumstance. By the early nineteenth century, many self-aware individuals come to participate in the rhetorical processes of understanding by which they are to be known. For these reasons, the self-conscious and self-reflexive textual account of a mind

(Wordsworth's) that grew to maturity between 1770 and 1800 becomes a valuable cultural document for its time and for ours.

Wordsworth's texts on his own life are also increasingly important to our understanding of literary theory. This prototypical Romantic poet understands, from the earliest stages in his autobiographical project, that his activity is psychologically problematic, philosophically charged, and linguistically complex. He also reveals – in all of these texts – confusing interactions among speakers and the voices in which they speak, even when the speaking voice belongs to an ostensible 'self'. From Wordsworth's earliest lyrical fragments on his childhood, through the published text of 1850, the poet half-perceives and half-creates his own life story. He alters accounts of events from first-person to third-person or from third-person to first-person. He rearranges chronology, appropriates stories told to him by others as parts of his own story, and claims that events that happened to him actually happened to other people. In general terms, he reveals the problems attendant on turning human experience into a narrative. In more specific terms, the author of the texts that became known as *The Prelude* knows that his voice is not strictly his own. He also indicates that many uses of language are less stable than we often assume. But this does not mean that such ego-producing language-games are not useful, or that an imaginative writer is unable to tell the story of a personal self. *The Prelude* suggests, in complex ways, that the telling of any story, particularly one's own story, is culturally encoded even as it is personally controlled. Two centuries later, as we shall see, a contemporary poet like Derek Walcott can remind us of the ways a 'real' self can be textually constructed within the rhetorical riches of lyric poetry.

I have benefitted greatly, as will be evident in these pages, from critical and theoretical works by Bakhtin and Byron, Homans and Chodorow, McGann and Magnuson, Starobinski and Hartman, Wittgenstein and Wordsworth, among others. I include the details of this indebtedness in the endnotes to this volume. But like many members of my critical generation, I hesitate to assign a specific name to my methodological assumptions. Literary scholars laboring in the rarified air of textual research and traditional philology have just as much to answer for (in the minds of our wider culture) as subtle theorists whose ideology becomes a single-minded engine for whipping errant readers into shape. We need good texts to read and discuss, and we need interpretive strategies that help us to keep literary texts alive in the culture as objects of dialogue. At the same time, we should remind ourselves – particularly if we are engaged in the business of criticism – that poems, plays, novels, and short stories have always been experienced as objects of pleasure. And literature – however we define that category – is also employed by many readers whose main purpose in reading a text is the pleasure of reading: not studying, not teaching, not contextualizing, not critiquing, not promoting, not publishing. Part of the appeal of autobiography over the past two centuries is surely the extent to which the self-life writing of others helps us to fashion self-life readings of our own lives.

Like many of my colleagues, I have become skeptical of modes of interpretation that seek to totalize the experience of writing or reading. Culture, economics, psychology, material history, text, gender, literary history: all of these ways of reading bear on the production and interpretation of imaginative texts, but none of these categories can provide a complete analysis of any piece of writing. Writers write for as many different reasons as readers read. In what follows, I have sought to draw on a number of interpretive strategies that help me to make sense of the details of those writings we now call *The Prelude*. I cannot understand these texts without resituating them in some version (my own?) of the times in which they were produced. But no empirically based historical account can explain the complexities of the suppressed psychological materials that no doubt underlie Wordsworth's writing. Likewise, any reflections of mine on gender must acknowledge my own gender and the fact that the English language has conventions of pronoun use that are specific to our language. Nor does my own sense of history, my gender, or my pronoun-use necessarily correspond to any 'natural' state of affairs. All the manuscript research in the world will never explain precisely why Wordsworth conceived and re-conceived the boundaries of his autobiographical poem as often as he did and in the ways that he did. But none of this potential skepticism prevents a reader from making useful claims about these texts, their relation to the author named William Wordsworth, to the years between 1798 and 1850, and to the responses of individual readers of these influential literary documents over the past two centuries.

The past three decades of criticism have called into question the stability of all texts, arguing first – deconstructively – that all language uses are potentially equivocal, and more recently – new historically – that no text is less complicated than the cultural circumstances that gave rise to its production. My own view charts a middle ground, situating our lived experience of human agency somewhere between the semantic limitations of a purely textual meaning and the dizzying complexities of historical context. In each chapter I locate my argument within a range of theoretical assumptions: Chapter 1 analyzes Wordsworth's rhetoric and earlier criticism of the poems in order to reveal the multivocality of the Wordsworthian 'I'; Chapter 2 draws on the historiography of the French Revolution, as well as performance theory, to present Wordsworth's poetic voice by 1798 as a dramatized persona in a revolutionary literary performance; Chapter 3 links Bakhtinian dialogics with an analysis of the dramatic monologue to chart the emergence of the autobiographical 'Wordsworth'; Chapter 4 employs gift-exchange theory and letters of the Grasmere Circle to emphasize Coleridge as an important source of the therapeutic energy that helped to expand the brief text of 1799 into the book-length autobiography of 1805; Chapter 5 draws on recent feminist theory to place Dorothy at the silenced center of her brother's poetic voice by 1802; Chapter 6 concludes by linking Wordsworthian auto-biographical practice with another 'Romantic' autobiographer in our own era – Derek Walcott – a poet/dramatist whose 'Caribbean Prelude' reveals how cultural voices and personal identity can be linked through a textual 'I' when lives are told as stories, even within the genre of lyric poetry. Each chapter reveals different ways that voices can combine and modulate to produce an autobiographical 'I'.

This study avoids many of the most often discussed passages in *The Prelude*, in part because they often lead to the one-sided, monological view of Wordsworth I am trying to critique. *The Prelude* charts dialogic interchanges that produce a variety of positions for the Wordsworthian 'I' to occupy. Wordsworth's strategies of self presentation obviously produce a complex, polyvocal, and dramatized autobiographer. As autobiography, these texts do not record a search that leads to the discovery of a 'self', nor do they reveal the development of an isolated, unified individual. Rather, they record verbal processes whereby a self *becomes* itself in a text. The 'politics' of this position, in the strategic sense of 'politics', also emphasize the status of autobiography as a gift. In Wordsworth's case, *The Prelude* is a gift to Coleridge in hopes for the future, a gift to Dorothy in thanks for the past, a gift to Mary for her role in

William's adulthood, and a gift from an earlier version of Wordsworth's self ('some other being') to a subsequent self that hopes for 'future benediction'. For all of these reasons, the Wordsworthian 'I' is a multivalent speaker, culturally constructed but also 'self realized' in first-person literary texts.

My sense of the value of such emphasis in Wordsworthian studies is reflected in two recent books, both of which appeared as this volume was nearing completion. Sheila Kearns's *Coleridge, Wordsworth and Romantic Autobiography* offers perhaps the best analysis we have had to date of the challenges posed for critics of autobiography in the wake of poststructuralist theorizing. Authors are not 'dead' after three decades of literary theory; they are merely speaking in stranger ways than we had previously realized. More recently, Elizabeth Fay argues, in *Becoming Wordsworthian*, that the performance of the Wordsworthian 'I' was accomplished only by way of a complex personal and rhetorical interaction between William and Dorothy. Fay also argues for a concept of the 'feminine sublime' that should color all our future attempts at assessing male self-fashioning during the Romantic era. Both of these works link up at points with my argument to suggest important directions for future study of the rhetoric of first-person speakers in all literary texts.

Likewise, emphasis on the textual Wordsworthian 'identity' has connections to discussion currently under way about the relationship between text, hypertext, and the concept of a unitary self. The 'Wordsworth' I seek to describe in the following pages is a Wordsworth that might only be finally representable by reference to all of the texts he produced, those we possess and those we do not. This Wordsworth is, importantly, not 'a better poet' in his earlier texts and 'a lesser poet' in his later texts. He is more like the ever-changing identity that each of us can appreciate when we read our own letters written decades ago or meet people we have not seen in years and can not quite recognize as our former acquaintances. This is also a 'Wordsworth' who will probably be better understood when we have access to hypermedia versions of his textual productions. When the Norton Critical Edition printed facing page versions of the 1805 and 1850 texts of *The Prelude* in 1979, readers could 'see' a textual self changing on the page. The dynamic and malleable 'I' of all autobiographical writing will no doubt seem even more evident when we can observe multiple textual selves (as hypertext revisions) on quickly shifting screens in a very short span of time. Hypermedia editions of multiple texts will remind us how unstable was the Wordsworth who often sought to represent himself as a unified and unifying 'I'. My own goal is not so much to decenter the 'subject' Wordsworth as to reveal those forms of selfhood that are textually produced in the material drafts of those poems to which we have physical access. My conclusions, however, have important implications for our understandings of literary texts, electronic hypertexts, and a wide range of textual selves. Modern selves may make themselves textually out of complex cultural materials and many voices, but they can still represent themselves in printed, 'stable' texts.

I suggest that there is little need for a consistent theory of autobiography, since self-life writing contributes to a literary form defined more by its *purposes* than by its generic characteristics. Why did St. Augustine need to tell his story as he did? What was Rousseau setting out to accomplish by claiming merely to record the events of his own life? Why did John Stuart Mill write his life in a particular way: who was his audience, what were his goals? What caused Wordsworth to write about himself in the ways that he did? The answers to such questions are more important to our understanding of autobiography than are precise literary rules or generic constraints. Such a utilitarian, we might say pragmatic, view of autobiography reminds us that literature has *uses*, not just characteristics or meanings. Regenia Gagnier has recently advocated a 'pragmatics of self-representation'; my own study rests on a foundation well stated by Gagnier: 'instead of evaluating the truth of a statement, pragmatism considers what it does. Thus pragmatism seeks to locate the purpose an autobiographical statement serves in the life and circumstances of its authors and readers'.[1] A pragmatic criticism emphasizes our uses of literature rather than the search for definitive 'meanings' in our interpretation of texts. 'What does this text mean?' is replaced with 'What does this text do?' or 'What is this text good for?' To paraphrase Wittgenstein again, the meaning of a poem, text, or utterance is found in its use.

I should also explain the title of this volume. I claim that Wordsworth's 'I' is revolutionary because it does what all revolutions do; it ushers in a new way of thinking. In this case, rhetorically complex literary speakers – based on the 'I' of *The Prelude* – contribute to new ways of writing in the century after the 1850 publication of the poem 'on [Wordsworth's] own life'. Wordsworth's autobiographical texts define a 'politics' of self presentation if we see 'politics' broadly as the 'use of intrigue or strategy in obtaining any position of power or control'; my use of the term 'politics' is also closer to the nuances of 'politic', as in, '1. sagacious, prudent. 2. shrewd; artful. 3. expedient; judicious'.[2] On these terms, Wordsworth's 'politics' often seem most mysterious when his texts appear most transparent. Because he is so often overtly autobiographical, Wordsworth is one of the most teachable of poets; at the same time, he is one of the hardest poets to 'understand'. My students have helped me to see just how useful Wordsworth is as a paradigm for the way meaning emerges in all literary texts and also for the way our readings construct meanings at the same time that we are being constructed by them.

Finally, this work arises out of my contention – evident in my conclusion – that Wordsworth's autobiographical texts help us to reflect on powerful currents in contemporary critiques of literary meaning. In the words of Philip Lejeune: 'A person is always *several* people when he is writing, even all alone, even his own life', adding 'How can we think that in autobiography it is the lived life that produces the text, when it is the text that produces the life!'[3] By collapsing the apparent distinction between poet and critic in his own work, Wordsworth helps us to recognize the limitations of any viewpoint that sees poets, playwrights and novelists engaged in one discrete activity while scholars, critics, and theorists are engaged in a qualitatively different one. This book will have succeeded if it sends its readers back to *The Prelude*, back to Wordsworth's other writings, and back to their own lives. Our lives, and our senses of the lives of others, are themselves autobiographical acts. When we choose to write down any story at all, we are choosing one among a number of ways of becoming a self. Even if that self is a fiction, it is one of those necessary fictions by which we live.

Acknowledgments

This work originated in a series of conversations during an NEH Summer Seminar at Johns Hopkins University in 1989. I am grateful to the director of that seminar, Jerome Christensen, and to the participants, particularly David Collings, Anthony Tyler, and John Murphy for helping spark the ideas that led to this research and writing. My thinking was focused and clarified during a visit to the Wordsworth Summer Conference in Grasmere in 1990. During that conference I benefitted from conversations with Anthony Harding, Paul Magnuson, Nicholas Roe, Jonathan Wordsworth, and Duncan Wu. I also appreciate the assistance of library staffs at the Dove Cottage Library, the Eisenhower Library at Johns Hopkins, the Spahr Library at Dickinson College, and the Library of the University of East Anglia.

I am grateful for financial support from the NEH, the Dickinson College Research and Development Committee, particularly for a Board of Advisors Grant and for funds to support my travel to conferences in Oxford and the Lake District. A Mellon Grant provided additional funds and supported the work of Bronwyn Jones; her diligent research assistance and thoughtful writerly advice helped focus the project in important ways. I also thank my students, particularly fellow travelers in my seminar on 'Revolutionary Romanticism'; their careful readings and insightful questions as I completed this work fostered my own efforts to understand these texts.

I have also benefitted from the advice, counsel and comments of a variety of friends and colleagues who read drafts, answered questions, clarified my thinking, and often provided other less scholarly, but no less necessary, forms of support. Among this group I particularly thank Peggy Garrett, Sharon O'Brien, H. L. Pohlman, John Ransom, Thomas Reed, Michael Reid, Roger Thompson, and Robert Winston. I am grateful to Marilyn Gaull for her warm and supportive help throughout the editorial process and to Stephen Prickett for a generous reading of the work. Anne Rafique read the complete manuscript with a careful editorial eye. I have also benefitted from the assistance of Charmian Hearne and Julian Honer at Macmillan.

Parts of the work have already appeared in different forms in *The Bucknell Review* (36: 1, 1992) as 'The Revolutionary "I": Wordsworth and the Politics of Self Presentation' (pp. 66–84) and in *Imagination, Emblems and Expressions*, ed. Helen Ryan-Ranson (BGSU Press, 1993) as 'Colonizing Consciousness: Culture and Identity in Walcott's *Another Life* and Wordsworth's *Prelude*' (pp. 173–90). I am grateful to them for permission to reprint here. Excerpts from *Another Life* by Derek Walcott, copyright © 1973 by Derek Walcott. Reprinted by permission of Farrar, Straus & Giroux, Inc.

The dedication to this volume speaks for itself and suggests a debt beyond the reach of grace or art. My final thanks go to the people who continually help me to understand the sources of their identities and the limits of my own – my daughters: Amy Eliza, Molly MacKenzie, Elizabeth Ashton, and Tessa Brooks. The four of them have no problems with self presentation. They all know exactly who they are; they also know what they mean to me.

Abbreviations

The following works are abbreviated in references in the text:

BL   *Biographia Literaria*, Samuel Taylor Coleridge, ed. James Engell and Walter Jackson Bate, 2 vols. (Princeton: Princeton University Press, 1983).

CL   *Collected Letters of Samuel Taylor Coleridge*, ed. Earl Leslie Griggs, 6 vols. (Oxford: Clarendon Press, 1956–71).

Cornell   *The Prelude 1798–1799*, ed. Stephen Parrish, Cornell Wordsworth (Ithaca: Cornell University Press, 1977).

CPW   *Coleridge: Poetical Works*, ed. Ernest Hartley Coleridge (Oxford: Oxford University Press, 1911).

EY, MY, LY *Letters of William and Dorothy Wordsworth*, ed. Ernest de Selincourt. 2nd edn. *The Early Years, 1787–1805*, revised Chester L. Shaver (Oxford: Clarendon Press, 1967); *The Middle Years, 1806–11*, revised Mary Moorman (Oxford: Clarendon Press, 1969); *1812–1820*, revised Mary Moorman and Alan Hill (Oxford: Clarendon Press, 1970); *The Later Years, 1821–50*, revised Mary Moorman and Alan Hill (Oxford: Clarendon Press, 1979).

Gill   *William Wordsworth* [Oxford Authors], ed. Stephen Gill (Oxford: Oxford University Press, 1984).

Journals *Journals of Dorothy Wordsworth*, ed. Mary Moorman (Oxford: Oxford University Press, 1971).

Life   *William Wordsworth: A Life*, Stephen Gill (Oxford: Clarendon, 1989).

PL   *Paradise Lost*, John Milton, ed. Alastair Fowler (London: Longman, 1971).

Prelude   *The Prelude: 1799, 1805, 1850*, ed. Jonathan Wordsworth, M. H. Abrams and Stephen Gill (New York: Norton, 1979).

Prose   *Prose Works of William Wordsworth*, ed. W. J. B. Owen and Jane Worthington Smyser, 3 vols. (Oxford: Clarendon Press, 1974).

PW   *The Poetical Works of William Wordsworth*, ed. Ernest de
             Selincourt and Helen Darbishire, 5 vols. (Oxford:
             Clarendon Press, 1940–9).

Journals:

ELH   *English Literary History*
NLH   *New Literary History*
SIR   *Studies in Romanticism*
TSLL   *Texas Studies in Language and Literature*
TWC   *The Wordsworth Circle*
WLWE   *World Literature Written in English*

1

Silencing the (Other) Self:
Wordsworth as 'Wordsworth!' in 'There was a boy'

Amid the continuing conversation about Wordsworth's revisionary practices, we sometimes forget that Wordsworth's greatest revision was performed in a text but on himself. The constant writing and rewriting of poems with many titles over many decades was a textual act designed, at least in part, to create a version of the word 'Wordsworth' that would satisfy the poet's expectations and the expectations of his imagined, as well as real, readers. The Wordsworth(s) thus created, from the descriptive narrator of the 1790s to the autobiographer of 1805, are best understood as complex dramatized projections developed through a series of incomplete narratives, rather than as an authentic reflection of the historical William Wordsworth who grew to adulthood in the English Lake District between 1770 and 1790.

Wordsworth sets forth his textual identity in dialogical terms; he presents a poetic version of himself as a way of imagining an ennobling interchange from without and within. By seeing himself through a series of doubling oppositions – self then/self now, self to others/self to self, self to Coleridge/self to Dorothy, epic Miltonist/domestic rustic – he is able to produce a version of his identity that becomes the mask of a great poet. This is not to suggest that Wordsworth's creation of the 'I' of *The Prelude* is not a significant literary achievement. It is rather to argue that biographical and autobiographical terms may be among the most deceptive of all approaches to Wordsworth, and to suggest that he reveals their limitations in his own texts. By rhetorically dramatizing his voice in such complex ways, Wordsworth provides a key to his own subjective position and a warning to his readers about the dangers of associating poets with their poetic self-descriptions.

Jean Starobinski's comment about Rousseau applies in important ways to Wordsworth: He 'composes an image of himself,

1

which he intends to impose on others through the prestige of absence and the resonance of the written word'.[1] By 1798–9, Wordsworth has chosen a model of retirement – the conventional pose of a writer removed from society – as a means of writing his own great philosophical poem. But a series of tensions are thus created that lead the poet to seek textual resolution of a number of 'conflicting' Wordsworths: ventriloquist/lyrical 'I', Miltonic/domestic, urbane/rural, epic/lyrical, public/private, high philosophical/low narrative, Coleridgean/Dorothean. The creation of the Wordsworthian autobiographical narrator between 1799 and 1805 requires the suppression of a wide range of complex and multivalent voices. Wordsworth must silence, or seek to silence, a series of conflicting viewpoints within his texts. Like the narrator of 'The Thorn', he wants to reveal the authority of his own version of events. But also like that narrator, his own words suggest the difficulty, if not the impossibility, of justifying a single point of view. The illusion of an integrated, autonomous, autobiographical 'I' is a necessary fiction in the production of a unified version of the self. We can date the process of the emergence of this drama- tized Wordsworthian voice, and the concurrent suppression of other voices, from the Goslar writings of late 1798 to early 1799, particularly the fragment of lyrical narrative known as 'The Boy of Winander' or 'There was a boy'.

'There was a boy' is a powerful verbal vortex that draws in much that is significant in Wordsworth's poetry up to the time of the Goslar writings, while at the same time sending out radiating significance about the autobiographical figure first developed in Wordsworth's poetry between 1798 and 1799. For all of the commentary these lines have generated about hooting owls, a dialogue between human and inhuman voices, and a subsequent silence that leads to a powerful moment of imaginative 'apprehen- sion' (in both senses of the word), too little attention has been paid to the most significant aspects of this passage: the change of the subject from first person to third person between 1798 and 1800 and the exclusion of this most 'Wordsworthian' of narratives from the two-part *Prelude* of 1799.

Most commentators note the shift from first to third person between the draft of 1798 and the text of the 1805 edition of the poem that would become *The Prelude*. The seeming self-sufficiency of 'There was a boy' as a lyric was supported when Wordsworth included the lines in the 1800 edition of *Lyrical Ballads* as 'There was a boy' and subsequently as the first of the 'Poems of the Imagination' in all collected editions of his poetry after 1815. But the importance of the shift from a living 'I' in 1798 to a dead 'he' in 1800 has received surprisingly little comment. As for the exclusion of the incident from the two-part *Prelude*, Jonathan Wordsworth's comment is suggestive: 'probably written for 1799, but excluded on grounds no longer obvious' (*Prelude*, p. 492).[2] If not obvious, the exclusion of these lines nevertheless does reflect powerfully on the emergence of the first-person voice of the most autobiographical of English Romantic poets. At the same time, this exclusion suggests why Wordsworth's most recent biographer, Stephen Gill, stresses the perils of connecting the first-person subject of *The Prelude* with the flesh-and-blood William Wordsworth (*Life*, pp. 7, 9).[3]

The earliest known draft of 'There was a boy' reads as follows:

> There was a boy – ye knew him well, ye rocks
> And islands of Winander, and ye green
> Peninsulas of Esthwaite – many a time
> [   ] when the stars began
> To move along the edges of the hills,
> Rising or setting, would he stand alone
> Beneath the trees or by the glimmering lakes,
> And through his fingers woven in one close knot
> Blow mimic hootings to the silent owls,
> And bid them answer him. And they would shout
> Across the wat'ry vale, and shout again,
> Responsive to my call, with tremulous sobs
> And long halloos, and screams, and echoes loud,
> Redoubled and redoubled – a wild scene
> Of mirth and jocund din. And when it chanced
> That pauses of deep silence mocked my skill,
> Then often in that silence, while I hung
> Listening, a sudden shock of mild surprize
> Would carry far into my heart the voice
> Of mountain torrents; or the visible scene
> Would enter unawares into my mind
> With all its solemn imagery, its rocks,
> Its woods, and that uncertain heaven, received
> Into the bosom of the steady lake.

(*Prelude*, p. 492)[4]

Particularly striking given the subsequent shift to third person pronouns is the fact that this early draft – presumably the one read by Coleridge in late 1798 – presents the first and third person pronouns already vying for ascendancy. The personified rocks and islands and peninsulas know 'him'. 'He' calls to the owls, and they answer 'him'. Only with the 'pauses of deep silence' does the silence mock a skill described as 'my' skill, leading to another powerful silence, the third silence in the passage. It is in this third silence that a new 'I' suddenly hangs listening. This new 'I' marks the birth of the poetic speaker of the poem that will become *The Prelude*.

In these powerful lines we can chart the sacrifice of one version of the self to another. The child who once called to owls can now only be described in the third person because, by 1798, this child has to die if the adult Wordsworth is going to become the poet that Coleridge and Wordsworth want him to become. Ironically, the 'death' in this early draft is only recorded by a shift in pronouns. What looks like an authenticating autobiographical move – 'this actually happened to me', 'I waited in this silence', 'I hooted at these owls' – is, in fact, the imaging of the poetic figure 'Wordsworth' into the text. By 1798, Wordsworth needed an 'I' that could begin to validate the importance of his earlier experiences; this 'I' emerges in lines 16–17 of the 1798 draft of 'There was a boy', commenting not on the perceptual details of a conversation with owls, but on the psychological and aesthetic significance at the conclusion of the experience.

This new 'I' hangs listening and inactive (hangs 'dead'). At that same instant, a shock carries a natural voice into the heart of this listener. A visible scene enters into the mind of the narrator who is described significantly as 'unawares'. No child (conceived of as 'he') can evaluate the subsequent importance of such an experience; the child simply has experiences – like the leech-gatherer who neither stood, nor sat, but simply *was*. It surely takes a self-conscious and self-dramatizing adult poet (now conceived of as a dramatic 'I') to turn the accidents of experience into a meaningful narrative, to allow the boy William Wordsworth (b. 1770) to 'die' into the text and emerge as the verbal 'Wordsworth' for whom 'voices' and 'scenes' and 'images' – all obviously literary terms – are more important than stars and owls and lakes.

The adult can never return to the point when stars and owls and lakes were what they once were by just *being*. Now these objects must be conceived of in poetic and literary terms. They must become part of a text that is the story of a self. They must make sense as details in the story of the poet Wordsworth must become if he is going to write the poem that Coleridge wants him to write. It is as though Wordsworth is saying, in the fragments produced in Goslar: 'I will write a poem about the self I might be so that I can then proceed to write the great poem such a self might write'. In Wordsworth's own words to Coleridge: 'I am positively arrived at [the Poem on my own life]. When the next book is done ... I shall consider the work as finished ... I am very anxious to have your notes for the Recluse. I cannot say how much importance I attach to this' (*EY*, pp. 448–51, 52).

From the vantage point of adult life, as Wordsworth will later admit, childhood seems dead and gone. As adults 'We live as if those hours had never been' (1799, II, 387–8). The result of this distancing is a paradoxical doubling of the self:

> so wide appears
> The vacancy between me and those days,
> Which yet have such self-presence in my heart
> That sometimes when I think of them I seem
> Two consciousnesses – conscious of myself,
> And of some other being.
>
> (1799, II, 26–31)

These two consciousnesses are clearly reflected in the 'he' and 'I' of the earliest drafts of 'There was a boy'. Again and again, having excluded 'There was a boy' from the 1799 version of the poem on his own life, Wordsworth retains the pattern of this boy's experience as a paradigm for the most significant events in the formation of his youthful identity: sounds and language (human or otherwise) give way to stillness and silence that allow a visible scene or powerful voice to *enter into* an emerging consciousness. But this process is always described as though it happened to a character, a dramatized projection created for the purpose of unifying the otherwise disparate details of experience. The texts of 1799, 1804, 1805, and 1850, work to create a 'stable' 'Wordsworth' out of Wordsworth's own fears about the instability of his identity. The fragmentary bundle of perceptions (described by David Hume) that Wordsworth may dread is unified by becoming what Shakespeare's Hamlet is: an intended, complete, artistic creation.

Notice how often the Boy of Winander's psychic pattern recurs in the two-part *Prelude* of 1799. The river's murmurs blend with the nurse's song to send 'a voice' flowing into the infant's dreams (I, 3–6). The 'ceaseless music' of the 'beauteous stream' gives the child 'knowledge, a dim earnest, of the calm / Which Nature breathes' (I, 14–15). The wind blows as a 'strange utterance' that leads to an aestheticized sky ('not ... Of earth') and unforgettable clouds (I, 64–6). The clock tolls, the skate blades hiss, the precipice rings with a din, the trees and crags tinkle 'like iron', while the hills send an alien sound 'Into the tumult', leading to a static visual prospect: the stars 'sparkling clear, and in the west / The orange sky of evening died away' (I, 168–9). Cracking ice on the lake calls out like howling wolves. A 'whistling hawthorn', the 'bleak music' of a stone wall, and the 'noise of wood and water' unite to produce a sustaining image and powerful 'workings of my spirit', even when they are connected with the death of the father (I, 344, 364–74).

This often-repeated structural movement from sight or sound to aestheticized perception achieves its fullest statement – and closest parallel to the Boy of Winander – when Wordsworth places himself as an actor/observer in a powerful 'natural' drama, once again set on the shores of Windermere and Belle Isle. Playing idly for half an afternoon, a group of children has sent shouts that 'Made all the mountains ring'. Crossing the water at dusk, this troop has left one of their companions alone on a rock, blowing his flute out over the lake. At this moment the text repeats another version of the process first recorded in 'There was a boy':

> oh, then the calm
> And dead still water lay upon my mind
> Even with a weight of pleasure, and the sky,
> Never before so beautiful, sank down
> Into my heart and held me like a dream.

> (II, 210–14)

A variety of acts of submerging take place in this passage. The water is 'dead' still; it lies upon the boy's mind and hides the body of past experience like the subsequent body of the drowned man of Esthwaite or the buried body of the Boy of Winander. Here the sky, which was earlier received into the lake after the owls had hooted, sinks into the boy's heart, holding him as a dream holds one beneath the surface of waking consciousness. Again and again we find this image of a dramatized self submerged, held down, stopped dead in its tracks: stillness, silence, stasis and death become characteristics of a powerful self-creation that represents itself as self-recognition.

Wordsworth admits that he may be creating himself textually toward the close of the two-part *Prelude* when he imagines himself walking beside Esthwaite Lake years earlier with John Fleming. The lines that record this past event will, Wordsworth suggests, be a 'blank' to others who did not share the experience. Even between the adult Wordsworth and John Fleming, however, the past can only be associated with a silence that betokens death. The minds of the two former friends are now 'silent to each other' so that they 'live as if those hours had never been' (II, 387–8). The past self can die as many times as the present self can create versions of it in the text. The self as process submerges any stable identity that would represent itself as a finished product.[5]

The verbal re-creation of those morning walks with Fleming is important to the poet because these words produce a dramatized version of the passage from passive observer to active re-maker of the event. A prosaic adult, for whom the past years seem as if they had 'never been', is transformed into a poet who can use words to create something that does not really exist, a textual version of the past. In the 'utter solitude' of those childhood mornings Wordsworth says he was able to forget 'the agency of sight', so that what he saw then 'Appeared like something in myself, a dream, / A prospect in my mind' (II, 400–1). An unreal textual world comes to replace a real physical world as a way of transforming forgotten moments of silence into images preserved as marks on paper. But the image of the past self thus created is no more the *real* self than the dream in the mind is the *real* world. This is why the 'soul' – a word Wordsworth always uses in confusing ways in the early drafts of his autobiographical poem – remembers 'how she felt' but not 'what she felt' (II, 364–6). The identity that the poet forges on paper is a textual creation out of emotional memory, not a literal re-membering of a past self.

II

The 'ghostly language of the ancient earth' (II, 358) is important to the Wordsworthian child because it is this language (not a literal 'language' at all?) that makes more sense than human language. The voice spoken by winds, owls and rain produces feelings, not rational understanding. This helps to account for the moaning winds, speaking rocks, muttering crags – and the hooting owls – scattered throughout the texts that create the dramatic character 'Wordsworth'. Rousseau sheds light on this potential genealogy for language when he claims that language emerged out of the passions, not out of reason. According to Rousseau, as language grows more complex, and more fully developed, it undergoes a process that is strikingly similar to the movement of Wordsworth's language between 1797 and 1814: 'it becomes more precise and less passionate; it substitutes ideas for sentiments; it no longer speaks to the heart but to the reason. As a result accent dies out and articulation becomes more persuasive; language becomes more exact and clear, but more sluggish, subdued, and cold' ('Essay on the Origin of Language', p. 249).[6]

In this verbal sense, Wordsworth kills off the Boy of Winander, Lucy, Matthew, the Danish Boy, and other characters in the text, so that he can speak for them instead of allowing them to speak for themselves. He does this, in part, because he senses that as soon as language becomes complex enough to be rendered as poetry it has lost some of its power as pure emotion. A cry of pain or a shout of ecstasy evokes more powerful emotions than a sonnet. By the time Wordsworth produces the 'I' of 1798–9, many of the dramatic voices of *Lyrical Ballads* and earlier are being submerged in a dramatized voice that becomes the Wordsworthian autobiographical speaker. Even in *Lyrical Ballads*, however, we find numerous cases where the actual language of another voice is presented as only a few words or phrases – Goody Blake, Harry Gill, Johnny, Martha Ray – at least in part as a way of retaining a direct connection between these utterances and a pure emotion: 'Oh misery! oh misery! / Oh woe is me! oh misery!' (*PW*, 2: 248).

Many of Wordsworth's poems suggest, as Rousseau had argued, that 'in all language the liveliest exclamations are inarticulate; cries, moans are nothing but utterings [*voix*]; mute, that is to say deaf persons, utter only inarticulate sounds' ('Essay on the Origin', p. 247). Vocative utterance is powerful in direct relation to its inarticulateness. The inability to speak a language – coupled with the ability to make sounds – seems to provide an index to the power and authenticity of all human sound. Authentic utterances may be those that need not be expressed in any particular language in order to convey their meaning, but only in a way that will be universally expressive. Hence all of the Wordsworthian emphasis on ghostly natural noises, animal sounds, and inarticulate human speech. Proximity to the 'passions', and to authentic emotion, may be a function of inarticulateness, not just an attempt to reproduce the common speech of ordinary people. Such common human speech, however, may often ally itself with inarticulateness and direct expressions of emotion: cries, groans, sighs, shouts. On such a continuum, the most artificial, least lively, and most subdued language of all would be the careful, articulate words of a self-conscious verbal artist: a poet. A woman crying out 'Misery!' conveys much more direct emotion than a sophisticated lyricist saying 'Her heart was heavy because the father of her child had gone'. The self, on what comes to be a widespread Romantic model, may be more itself when hooting to owls than when *writing about* hooting to owls; hence the emphasis on stillness and emptiness in the silence that leads to an aestheticized moment of imaginary calm during an otherwise dramatic moment. Of course, narrative also becomes part of this formula; we shape stories partly in order to make sense of details within those stories.

The imagined ideal of a stable self – an artistic creation that can represent the 'I' – is like the calm that follows the boy's verbal exchange with the owls; it is an illusion created to help preserve something that cannot be preserved. The 'truer' self may be the self in dialogue, the voice engaged in passionate and even inarticulate exchange in a language that is not really a language at all, sounds that have no meaning except the meaning that is imposed upon them. By 1805, of course, Wordsworth's fear that all language may be a version of hooting to uncaring – if emotion-producing – owls, leads him to bury that liveliest verbal version of himself in the text – 'This boy ... died / In childhood, ere he was full ten years old' – and replace him with an 'I' who can self-consciously meditate at the grave of another ('there / A full half-hour together I have stood'). This new 'I' then can evoke a muteness ('looking at the grave in which he lies') that belies and contradicts silence by being represented in words. The only inarticulateness worth its power is the one that lacks a determinate meaning. The only muteness worth its silence is the one that is never recorded, recounted, or told. Describing silence, like describing death, is one way of trying to gain ascendancy over it. The poet's frustration, like the frustration of any living speaker, is that words on a page are silent: silent like the literal silence that always, and finally, follows speech.

Of course, even the simplest human sounds represent an exchange, a dialogue, and thus motion of some sort. From the murmurs of the Derwent, which blend with the nurse's song and contribute to the infant's own first murmurings, to the hooting exchange with the owls, an extremely complicated evolution has occurred. The boy who calls to the owls, whether we call him 'Wordsworth', 'the Boy of Winander', or 'lines of text', has learned a sort of owl-language, or at least a complex verbal interchange. The boy must know what the owls sound like; he must also know when, where, and how to imitate their sound in order to stimulate their response. Implicit in this process is a powerful sense of the self defined by its auditory relatedness ('I am the voice to which these owls are responding'), and also a version of the dialogic and echoic aspect of all language use. If it is not fair to call an exchange with owls 'linguistic', we can still see this as an analogue for much verbal learning. We hear sounds, and make sounds, until our own sounds are responded to; only then do we produce a related emotion and, later on, meaning.

Echoing is, as John Hollander has noted, a central 'figure of representation', since all re-presentation involves re-production, the trope of copying from an original.[7] But if every original is itself a copy – what sense would it make to talk about the *first* hooting owl – then every utterance, no matter how seemingly autonomous, monological and lyrical, is always already part of a dialogue, an echo, a repetition and exchange. In Wordsworth's case, this dual-voiced aspect of language may be *represented* as a dialogue between nature and consciousness, but what is actually recorded in the poem are always rhetorical interactions among words. Even calling owl-sound a 'hoot' suggests that no letters could really reproduce the sound. The sound gains part of its lyrical power by being one of the purest paradigms for what we might imagine as the spiritual: it is substantial (it has intensity and duration) without actually being a substance; it is endlessly capable of repetition and recurrence without ever being self-originating.

Hollander quotes Ausonius (*c.* AD 3) on the representation of Echo as an invisible goddess who is nevertheless known to all:

> Daughter of aire and tongue: of judgment blind
> The mother I; a voice without a mind.

I only with another's language sport:
And but the last of dying speech retort.

(p. 9)

By the time Wordsworth composed the earliest draft of 'There was a boy', he had already indicated the beginning of his attraction to voices without minds. At the same time, he had – by 1798 – sported with 'another's language' in numerous experiments with the dramatic voices: Rivers and Mortimer in *The Borderers*, the story-teller of the Salisbury Plain poems, Margaret, the Recluse, and many others. Out of this sense of echoing back 'the last of dying speech' comes a double-edged and double-voiced desire. On the one hand Wordsworth longs for an authentically self-generating voice that is not dependent on the echoes of others. On the other hand, he seeks a silence that might stand for the permanence, stasis, and unchanging quality that language, by its very dynamism, denies.

The most affecting tombstone inscription, Wordsworth argues in his 'Essay on Epitaphs', would be the one that records an infant's name, with birth date and death date separated by only one day (*Prose*, 1: 370). On these terms, the state-of-being represented by Matthew, Lucy, and the revised 'dead' boy of Winander may be a state to be desired, though perhaps not in a literal sense. Wordsworth's monumentalizing ego tends always to deny the possibility of literal self destruction. But if language can be used to silence others (not only the boy, but also the owls, are silenced in 'There was a boy'), then language can also create the ultimate illusion: that monuments (in stones or pages) do memorialize (instead of being washed or shredded away). Silencing the dialogic voices of others allows the lyrical speaker to assert that words do come *from* the 'self' (instead of merely echoing the words and sounds of others), and that the language of poetry can re-present perma-nently stable forms of nature and human life, instead of simply tracing an ever-shifting, echoic dialogue of multiple sounds: 'quiv-ering peals, / And long halloos, and screams, and echoes loud / Redoubled and redoubled'. Again and again in the first draft of *The Prelude* Wordsworth returns to the pattern first established in 'There was a boy': sound conceived of as a 'voice' leads to stasis, silence, or stillness. Such events become source materials for narra-tives that radiate power; in these texts the self becomes a dramatic speaker placed verbally between natural sounds or sights and dreamlike mental images.

Equally significant in this regard is a passage from the 1805 *Prelude* in which the voices that lead to exaltation are the purely human voices of the Wordsworthian child and his friend (presumably John Fleming) reciting poetry. On the edge of the still lake they repeat 'favorite verses with one voice / Or conning more'; this poetic dialogue makes them 'as happy as the birds / That round us chaunted' (V, 588–90). The causes of such happiness are the 'airy fancies' of poetry which, although often 'false and in their splendour overwrought' are nonetheless able to trigger the most 'noble attribute of man' (V, 591, 594, 597). The claim made in this seldom-discussed passage is remarkable. Poetry, even though it may be about false objects and artificial splendor, has the power to awaken 'That wish for something loftier, more adorned, / Than is the common aspect, daily garb, / Of human life' (V, 599–601). On these terms, poetry is an act of self-dramatizing wish fulfillment. The creation, even of false (unreal) objects, has a power like the power of music, or drama, or carnival. It awakens our capacity to conceive something which does not exist, yet which is nevertheless able to inspire in us a sense of possible sublimity:

> What wonder then if sounds
> Of exaltation echoed through the groves -
> For images, and sentiments, and words,
> And every thing with which we had to do
> In that delicious world of poesy,
> Kept holiday, a never-ending show,
> With music, incense, festival, and flowers!

> (1805, V, 601–7)

The power of poetry lies in its ability to create a false world of imaginative fantasy which nevertheless leads the mind to experience powerful ideas and their related emotions. Coleridge admits a similar uncertainty about the relationship between poetry and its objects in 'To Nature': 'It may indeed be phantasy, when I / Essay to draw from all created things / Deep, heartfelt, inward joy that closely clings'.[8] And perhaps Byron is the Romantic master of the conceit that connects poetic imaginings with fanciful self-creation. As early as *Childe Harold* III he admits that poetic imaginings allow the poet to produce 'A being more intense that we endow / With form our fancy, gaining as we give / The life we image, even as I do now' (III, 6).[9] The Byronic self here claims to create its identity out of the ability to shape itself in a text. It is surprising to find Wordsworth, ostensible originator of the egotistical – 'Wordsworthian' – sublime, admitting that his own imagined self may be an earlier version of such a Byronic, and fanciful, identity.

Wordsworth's recollection of the power of 'false' poetry concludes a passage in which he compares poems that once fascinated him to vacant theaters. These formerly affecting poems are now as 'Dead in my eyes as is a theatre / Fresh emptied of spectators' (1805, V, 574–5). In assessing the autobiographical narrator of *The Prelude*, we would do well to consider at least the possibility that he too may be a 'false object' with 'splendour overwrought', nevertheless valuable for his ability to create a never-ending show that has the power to elevate readers into a realm more lofty and adorned than the common aspect of daily life. 'The poem on my own life' becomes, from this perspective, a textual stage on which Wordsworth presents the character 'Wordsworth'.

Such a recognition helps to explain why the Boy of Winander dies in the text between 1798 and 1800, and why Wordsworth revises that death carefully between 1800 and 1805. For in addition to dropping all of the first person pronouns from the 1798 passage, the mature poet adds lines that entomb the boy who had once been himself into the text:

> This boy was taken from his mates, and died
> In childhood ere he was full ten years old.
> Fair are the woods, and beauteous is the spot,
> The vale where he was born; the churchyard hangs
> Upon a slope above the village school,
> And there, along that bank, when I have passed
> At evening, I believe that oftentimes
> A full half-hour together I have stood
> Mute, looking at the grave in which he lies.

> (1805, V, 414–22)

The fictionalizing of the dead boy is also the figured projection of the adult poet. 'Together I have stood' may, in addition to connecting half an hour, signal Wordsworth's admission of the two-part aspect of this boy, 'myself and some other being'. The living boy described in the first-person draft of 1798 ('I') no more 'existed' than did the dead and buried boy of 1805 ('ten years old') and the revised boy of 1850 ('twelve years old'). All three versions of this 'self' reflect the desire to verbally create a stable version of personal identity. But all three textual boys reveal the ultimate impossibility of such stabilization.

The image of Wordsworth, standing mute at the grave of a former version of himself, is a perfect analogue for the dramatized Wordsworthian 'I' produced in the 1799 *Prelude*. The self-reflexive speaker can only speak in relation to someone else; such speech is at once an act of projection and sympathy. His affections are provoked to seek meanings for his experiences. But there is, at the same time, something fearfully isolating and solipsistic in this image. The boy who dies before he is 10 years old (1805) or 12 years old (1850, from 1816/19) is a version of Wordsworth's past self. The poet created by the text ('I') gazes on the dead earlier version of the self ('he'). Unable to speak any longer in the voice of that boy, the adult must recall that voice. Turning past experience into a text involves the production of a new self, reborn out of the grave of childhood identity. The epitaphic memorial – the grave – becomes a version of identity that will last, even though it is mute: entombed in silent words that are printed on a page, though still able to reflect an image, like the mirroring waters of a still silent lake.[10]

Consider the frequent Wordsworthian grammar: 'There was a boy', 'There was a time when meadow, grove and stream', 'There was a roaring in the wind all night', 'There is a thorn', 'There is a tree, of many one' (There is a *me*, of many one?). Again and again Wordsworth asserts: 'I would enshrine the spirit of the past for future restoration.' I would enshrine the dead boy in order to have him reborn into the text, to make him changeless. I would write an affecting epitaph, Wordsworth implies, which is possible only when the subject is dead. I would make the thorn (or my own life) as affecting in a text as that thorn (or life) seemed to me when I experienced it. No living subject can be fully memorialized, however, because the living person can change in such a way that the memorial might become inaccurate, or meaningless. Thus the most moving epitaph that Wordsworth can imagine records only the name and dates of a child who lived for one day: no chance for change, perfect stability, absolute stasis and stillness – but also gone forever.

The accidental continuity of conscious existence demands – at least for artists – a response to transience in acts of figuration that leave a permanent trace out of the living hand, as Keats clearly understood: 'This living hand, now warm and capable'. But the letter is dead as soon as the ink has dried on the page. Already the sentence I have just written may be something I want to change, to rewrite or revise. Already, the 'me' that wrote the word 'change' may want to change that word to 'alter'. The only way out of this fearfully echoic interplay of consciousness may be its opposite: still lakes, silent owls, inanimate rocks and stones, dead boys, dead girls, dead still water, dead silence. At the moment that the Wordsworthian self gives up the illusion of its independent exis- tence, it dies into the text to be reborn into something, as Yeats would later say, intended and complete. The Wordsworth who writes poems is no longer the Wordsworth who sits down to the breakfast table; rather, he is a new being – 'false' perhaps – yet aesthetically 'perfect', and, at least artistically, permanent.[11]

'There was a boy' is an epitaph for the child that fathered the poet Wordsworth. But in order to father 'Wordsworth' forth in a text that child had to die rhetorically – at 10 years old or 12 years old, it little matters which. Even these ages confer proximity to two other significant literal deaths: Wordsworth's mother before he was 10 years old, his father shortly after he was 12 years old. 'There was a boy' is thus an auto-epitaph (a record of a dead self), as is the two- part autobiography of 1799 and its subsequent revisions. The autobiographical, typically Wordsworthian, 'I' emerges most persistently at that biographical moment – during the Goslar winter – when the poet is concerned with the 'deaths' (or losses) to him of several other persons, textual and otherwise: Lucy, Matthew – and Annette? – and also with the fact that while there *was* a boy, there no longer *is* a boy.

III

Coleridge's 'The Nightingale' is an essential and overlooked source text for 'There was a boy'. Coleridge's poem was written in April 1798 and appeared in *Lyrical Ballads* as Wordsworth, Dorothy, and Coleridge were leaving together for Germany. 'The Nightingale' represents not only a poem with important intertextual connec- tions to 'There was a boy', but also an important clue to the role played by Coleridge in producing the mature, poetic voice of Wordsworth. Coleridge did not help Wordsworth *discover* himself in the texts that became *The Prelude*; rather, he showed Wordsworth what Wordsworth would have to *stop being* if he was going to fulfill his destiny as a great 'philosophical' poet. Coleridge, in this sense, fostered the silencing of Wordsworth as the Boy of Winander ('I') and the production of the Wordsworth who is the mute observer at the grave of that boy. In effect, Coleridge says to Wordsworth: 'You must stop ventriloquizing (hooting at owls, speaking for vagrant women) and start seeing your random, accidental experiences as part of something coherent that connects "Man, Nature, and Human Life". But in order to do that you must silence the numerous voices that echo in your verse (idiots, madmen, mad mothers, children) and produce a consistent (philosophical) version of your own voice'. 'The Nightingale' charts the failure of just this process in Coleridge's own poetical career, and reveals Coleridge's desire to see such a movement from ventriloquist to philosopher in the texts he will come to identify with the name 'Wordsworth!'

'The Nightingale' begins with an almost Wordsworthian silence, a silence with 'no murmuring', through which the sound of a nightingale is suddenly heard. The song tempts the poet to recall Milton's description of the same bird: 'Most musical, most melancholy'. But such an echoic temptation reminds the poet Coleridge that there is no melancholy but thinking makes it so. What we call the melancholy sound of a natural object (bird, wind, sea) is nothing more than the emotions of a melancholy person projected onto nature, the words of a 'poor wretch' who, in the absence of any real correlative to his state of mind, fills 'all things with himself' and thereby makes 'all gentle sounds tell back the tale / Of his own sorrow' (19–21). Once melancholy has been ascribed to nature by one poet, however, many a later poet 'echoes the conceit'. Coleridge connects such a dramatization of the self with Milton. Of his own appropriation of Milton's line of poetry, he says: 'This passage in Milton possesses an excellence far superior to that of mere description; it is spoken in the character of the melancholy Man, and has therefore a *dramatic* propriety' (Coleridge's note, *CPW*, p. 264). So Milton himself must have assumed the character of the melancholy person in order to describe such a bird's song as sad.

But no poet in 1798 should merely echo this 'conceit', according to Coleridge. Rather, the contemporary poet should engage in a mysterious process that sounds like a literal death-wish, not just a longing for communion with nature. The new poet, instead of 'building up the rhyme' out of lines from the past

> had better far have stretched his limbs
> Beside a brook in mossy forest-dell,
> By sun or moon-light, to the influxes
> Of shapes and sounds and shifting elements
> Surrendering his whole spirit, of his song
> And of his fame forgetful! so his fame
> Should share in Nature's immortality,
> A venerable thing! and so his song
> Should make all Nature lovelier, and itself
> Be loved like Nature!

> (25–34)

Die into nature and you will live forever, as nature does. Link your song and yourself with something lasting, and everlastingness will rub off on both your song and your self. Here in April of 1798 we find Coleridge offering a precise description of another poet who emerges in a series of autobiographical texts written between December 1798 and 1800: the poet that calls himself 'Wordsworth'. While other 'youths and maidens most poetical' are losing the 'deepening twilights of the spring / In ball-rooms and hot theatres' (35–7), this new poet will be surrendering his spirit to the nonhuman world of owls, and merging his fame not with worldly glory but with a natural version of immortality.

What a consoling philosophy for the young Wordsworth, who has presumably cut his ties with radical politics, abandoned his lover and daughter in France, and embarked on adulthood without any clear sense of a public calling or career. The disdain for 'hot theatres' reminds us that Coleridge and Wordsworth had been struggling, unsuccessfully, to see their dramas *The Borderers* and *Osorio* completed and acted on the London stage. 'Of his fame forgetful' reminds us that the true profession would be a literal vocation, a calling not from the mundane and fallen world of letters, but from the elevated world of spirit, here called 'Nature'. Coleridge's own creation of the category 'Nature', as he employs the term, has more to do with his perceived failures as a political writer and journalist than with any insight into metaphysical reality. Wordsworth's desire to run to the nonhuman in Nature – and hide? – likewise has much to do with the people and places he is running to and hiding from: his wider family, France, Annette? 'Nature', as an ideal and a precise locale (Cumbria), provides an excellent spot for both Coleridge and Wordsworth to 'retire' to in the years between 1798 and 1804.

It is therefore no surprise that the next stanza of 'The Nightingale' invokes 'My Friend, and thou, our Sister!' In Coleridge's poem, William and Dorothy are a 'youth and maiden' who will not 'lose the deepening twilights of the spring'. They have left false 'theatres' behind for the 'real' stage of the natural world. In a single word ('our') Coleridge is instantly able to form a family for himself: Dorothy is sister to both of them and, by extension, William is his brother as well. This new 'natural' family is also a literary family that has 'learnt / A different lore' from the lore of the city, knowledge that will send them out into the April night hearing, but not profaning, 'Nature's sweet voices, always full of love / And joyance!' (42–3).

Coleridge then goes on to invoke an auditory image of nightingales that directly anticipates the owls of 'There was a boy'. In a wild grove, near a 'castle huge', live 'So many nightingales' that when they sing

> They answer and provoke each other's song,
> With skirmish and capricious passagings
> And murmurs musical and swift jug jug,
> And one low piping sound more sweet than all –
> Stirring the air with such a harmony,
> That should you close your eyes, you might almost
> Forget it was not day!
>
> (58–64)

Coleridge does not need to make himself the active agent in this scene – as Wordsworth will when he calls to his owls – because Coleridge lacks the egotistical sublime he is ascribing to the 'superior' poet. The pathology by which Coleridge found a power for himself in the power he ascribed to others – particularly Wordsworth – is transposed in Wordsworth's poetry into the power that Wordsworth 'found' (should we say 'created'?) for himself in the powers he ascribes to nature. Wordsworth becomes for Coleridge what Nature is for Wordsworth, an inexplicable and superior master to whom the self does homage in order to gain authority by bathing in a powerful, if still reflected, light.

Coleridge invokes yet another Wordsworthian figure in the next stanza of 'The Nightingale'. A silent woman lives in the castle near the nightingale-infested grove, and she 'knows all their notes'. This unspeaking woman becomes the first-born twin sister of the Boy of Winander when Coleridge describes her experience of uncontrolled night-time birdsong:

> That gentle Maid! and oft, a moment's space,
> What time the moon was lost behind a cloud,
> Hath heard a *pause of silence*; till the moon
> Emerging, hath awakened earth and sky
> With one sensation, and these wakeful birds
> Have all burst forth in choral minstrelsy,
> As if some sudden gale had swept at once
> A hundred airy harps!
>
>   (75–82, italics added)

My italics indicate the precise verbal borrowing that Wordsworth will make from Coleridge's poem; the subsequent lines of both poems suggest a shift, from Coleridge anticipating Wordsworth in April 1798 to Wordsworth echoing Coleridge in December 1798. Coleridge begins and ends with birds. Wordsworth ends as he began, with a powerfully wish-fulfilling vision of himself calling to birds.

The Wordsworthian poet, described so well by Coleridge in the early lines of 'The Nightingale', must 'surrender' his 'fame' (public personality) so that he can share in 'Nature's immortality'. But this act of silencing the self in nature is actually a means of attaining textual power. By silencing the self, the poet's song will 'make all Nature lovelier, and itself / Be loved like Nature!' The poet's song makes Nature lovelier than it is and in so doing comes to be loved itself: people will love the poem (and the poet) that taught them how to love nature. The voice that is able to bestow 'new splendour' on the 'setting sun', make the 'midnight storm / [Grow] darker in the presence of [its] eye', and achieve psychic 'dominion' over birds, breezes, and fountains (*Prelude*, 1799, II, 417–23) will be loved as the voice that has intensified its emotions by representing nature as lovelier than it is. Coleridge leaves his silent maid rapt in the wanton songs of birds. Wordsworth leaves his silent boy with the aestheticized sound of mountain torrents carried '*into* his heart', a powerful scene entering '*into* his mind' (my italics). Soon Wordsworth will turn this overflowing Boy of Winander into an autobiographical 'I' who can write a book-length poem about just such a process of being filled up by nature.

The final parallel between Coleridge's 'The Nightingale' and Wordsworth's 'There was a boy' occurs when Coleridge imagines his own infant child. Such a child, 'Capable of no articulate sound / Mars all things with his imitative lisp' (92–3). The child does, however, find a way of communication through gesture: 'How he would place his hand beside his ear, / His little hand, the small forefinger up, / And bid us listen!' (93–5). In this folded hand we find the antitype of the woven fingers of the Boy of Winander. Coleridge's receptive image points us out onto the world (listening); Wordsworth's projective image folds us back on the self (calling). In both cases, however, the child makes 'an instrument' to allow for an exchange across a boundary that ordinarily separates human from nonhuman sound. The Coleridgean child fashions an ear trumpet; the Wordsworthian child forms a vocal trumpet for calling to owls. Coleridge sees his exchange in terms of human reception; Wordsworth emphasizes the productive and projective aspect of human voices. Wordsworthian sound, like Wordsworthian sight, is cast out onto the world, where it receives a response from nature that then leads to silence or stillness and produces a powerful, if illusory, moment of aesthetically stabilized consciousness.

Coleridge is much more naturalistic than Wordsworth in his depiction of this interaction, yet his lyric reveals an inverted version of the close of the earliest draft of 'There was a boy'. Coleridge ends 'The Nightingale' by recalling an occasion when he took his night-frightened child out in the orchard to see the moon. In lines that anticipate the close of 'Frost at Midnight' – and bear comparison with 'The Idiot Boy' – the young child gazing at the moon 'suspends his sobs, and laughs most silently'. Coleridge closes this address to William and Dorothy ('A Conversation Poem') by noting that if 'Heaven / Should give' him life he will insist that this same child grow up familiar with birdsong so that 'with the Night / He may associate joy'. Even the dreadful fear of night may be overcome if night can be associated with a pleasant sensation. It is not incidental that Coleridge ends the poem reflecting on the possibility of his own death. Coleridge has a natural desire; he wants to live long enough to influence the development of his child. In the 'unnatural' world of Wordsworth, this same desire to associate physical sensations with humans becomes an aesthetic image: 'that uncertain heaven received / Into the bosom of the steady lake'. These lines are the very lines that Coleridge will cite, in his famous letter of December 1798, as the most Wordsworthian of Wordsworth's utterances. By appropriating and transforming the aesthetic ideology of Coleridge's 'The Nightingale', Wordsworth is facilitating his textual evolution from William Wordsworth (b. 1770) into the poet 'Wordsworth' (b. 1798).

IV

The Wordsworthian texts that begin emerging during the Goslar winter of 1798–9 might best be seen, not as an autobiography, but as an 'autography'. We may need this new term to describe this sense of a self writing itself as a text rather than a self recording its past in words. Wordsworth does not so much start telling the story of his past life in 1798 as he starts writing a version of life that can become his story. Of course, producing a story that tells who you are also solves the problem of what you are going to do: I am going to tell the story of the person who is getting ready to tell a great story. This convoluted phrase, of course, describes the convoluted state of mind in which Wordsworth prepared, and unprepared, himself to write *The Recluse*. The Lucy poems, the Matthew poems, and the lyrical first-person fragments that would evolve into the 1799 'poem to Coleridge', begin to produce the personal identity that Wordsworth is seeking as a poet. That identity 'ends' only with the posthumous publication of the poem his wife would entitle *The Prelude*.

Until recently, the general assumption has been that we hear traces of Wordsworth in the Pedlar, the Wanderer, the Solitary, and the narrator of 'The Ruined Cottage', but that by the time we reach the 1805 *Prelude* we have achieved a more stable, authentic – and self-declared – auto*bio*graphical voice. But the 'autographical' Wordsworthian voice of 1798–9 is as much the voice of the kind of poet Coleridge wanted Wordsworth to become as it is an authentic version of the biographical William Wordsworth. Coleridge acknowledged the production of this self in the famous letter of 10 December 1798. Writing to Wordsworth and Dorothy in Goslar,

Coleridge admitted, for the first time, that the word 'Wordsworth' was now a term that referred to a particular kind of text rather than to a biological subject.

Coleridge quotes lines from the epistolary draft of 'There was a boy', and says, 'That "uncertain heaven received / Into the bosom of the steady lake", I should have recognised any where; and had I met these lines running wild in the deserts of Arabia, I should have instantly screamed out "Wordsworth"!'[12] At this point the self has become a text. If we can identify 'lines' (the diction suggests written rather than spoken language) as 'Wordsworth', then identity has been transferred from the person who can write into lines that have been written. What are these lines in the desert? – They are 'Wordsworth'. In order to know Wordsworth, we must now recognize him in the text. From now on Wordsworth is, in one sense at least, his text. He may not be *only* his text, but his text can be taken as standing for him, can represent him, can figure him forth in 'lines' that make someone else say, 'aha! there's "Wordsworth!"'.

This same poetic voice that Coleridge recognizes as Wordsworth is, as we have seen, already a dramatized and polyvalent speaker that wants to be and not be like Milton, to be and not be like Dorothy, to be and not be like Coleridge. In addition, we can assume that Wordsworth still wants to embody, in some sense, the numerous other voices whose stories he has been trying to appropriate: Simon Lee, the mad mother, the narrator of 'The Thorn', the idiot boy Johnny. These voices, along with those of Rivers and Mortimer in *The Borderers*, and even the loco-descriptive narrator of 'Descriptive Sketches' and 'An Evening Walk', modulate by 1799 into a dramatized projection that is a first person speaker, an 'I' that sacrifices an earlier version of itself (The Boy of Winander) in order to produce a textual self that is recognizable to others.

What Paul Magnuson has seen as a lyrical dialogue between Wordsworth and Coleridge is also, in *The Prelude*, a strategy for dialogizing the self.[13] Wordsworth had come to fear the autonomy and isolated authority represented by Humean, Hartlean, Godwinian, and revolutionary versions of identity. As a result, he sought to produce a poetic version of the self, an image of identity that would not be restricted to a monologic, and therefore debatable, stability. The result of this strategy is twofold: he desires to produce a self that is open, indeterminate, and constantly evolving; at the same time he wants to describe a self that can be in dialogue with itself, or with earlier versions of itself.

By the time he returned from Goslar, Wordsworth had begun to connect his poetics as social practice with a specific view of his profession as calling. His own account of the progress of his profession ('Preface' to *The Excursion*) recounts how the author of *The Excursion* had 'retired to his native mountains'; retirement becomes Wordsworth's means of beginning a career. He describes the genesis of the poem to Coleridge as an effort to review 'his own mind' in preparation for writing *The Recluse*, 'a philosophical poem, containing views of Man, Nature, and Society'. The principal subject of this great philosophical poem, however, is to be 'the sensations and opinions of a poet living in retirement'.[14] The striking circularity of this description places the literary construction 'Wordsworth' at the center of the entire project. The poet retires to the mountains in order to review his own mind so that he can write 'a literary Work that might live' about a poet living in retirement. Wordsworth's subsequent performance of the role of poet living in retirement becomes the controlling strategy that justifies the entire project.

In March and April of 1804 Wordsworth recorded the strains in his own commitment to a calling that seemed still to require public justification. He writes to De Quincey of the work on his 'own earlier life': 'This Poem will not be published these many years, and never during my lifetime, till I have finished a larger and more important work to which it is tributary' (*EY*, p. 454). He further devalues the autobiographical text by comparing it to the philosophical poem (*The Recluse*) and the narrative poem (never named), calling the autobiography the poem 'on my own life, the least important of the three' (*EY*, p. 454). Six weeks later he writes to Richard Sharp saying of the poem about himself: 'it seems a frightful deal to say about one's self, and of course will never be published, (during my lifetime I mean), till another work has been written and published, of sufficient importance to justify me in giving my own history to the world' (*EY*, p. 470). This last comment suggests a striking reversal of Wordsworth's priorities. At this point he argues that he must write a work of sufficient importance to establish a reputation that will warrant presentation of his 'own history to the world'. He does not need to survey his own mind in preparation for writing Coleridge's great philosophical poem; rather, to Sharp he suggests that he must write and publish an important work of poetry that will prepare the way for the publication of his own personal history.

The Recluse, according to Wordsworth, is to be a poem the 'principal subject' of which is 'the sensations and opinions of a poet living in retirement'. This description might just as easily be applied to *The Prelude* in the form in which it exists by 1805. In a sense, the 13-book poem of 1805 *is* the philosophical poem on 'Man, Nature, and Society'. The retired poet of 1799 had set out, as the 'Preface' to *The Excursion* would say, to review 'his own mind, and examine how far Nature and Education had qualified him for such employment'. He will review his mind by recording 'the origin and progress of his own powers'. Wordsworth claims a need to produce a version of a self that is worthy of a larger task; he has to see if he is good enough to write a great philosophical poem (in Coleridge's sense). But circularly again, the poem expressing his qualifications for employment becomes the poem that justifies his reason for retirement. His employment can be that of a poet living in retirement if he performs the role of a poet who retires in order to write a poem about why he has retired.

Wordsworth had sufficient reasons to be concerned about his profession and employment by 1804. His family and friends had expressed interest and concern for the past decade about his career intentions. As the similarly beleaguered 19-year-old aristocrat Byron would say in the 1807 preface to *Hours of Idleness*: 'I have not only to combat the difficulties that writers of verse generally encounter, but I may incur the charge of presumption for obtruding myself on the world, when, without doubt, I might be, at my age, more usefully employed'. Wordsworth's 1804 letters to De Quincey, Sharp, and George Beaumont, all indicate a comparable sense of the presumptuousness of a certain kind of poetic practice. The poem on his own life will be 'an alarming length! and a thing unprecedented in Literary history that a man should talk so much about himself' (*EY*, p. 586). Of course Wordsworth knows, and is almost quoting from, the opening lines of Rousseau's *Confessions*. There is, he claims, no precedent for so much talk about the self. His employment will be in doing what has not been done, the adding of a new kind of history ('my own history') to 'Literary history'.

At the same time, Wordsworth has a parallel need to justify the reasons for his specific retirement to the Lake District. There was perhaps ample precedent for the notion of the literary figure who retreats from the distractions of the urban or social world in order to achieve a contemplative perspective: Milton in the 1630s, Thompson, Cowper, Gray. But in Wordsworth's case we find a hitherto active young adult who decides by age 30 that his greatest contribution to society may be made by retiring to the place of his birth, by removing himself from the vagaries of the social world so that he may be reborn into stable poetic texts. His profession will be to profess his own version of his life; his calling will be to call out to nature and record nature's responses, even when, as is often the case, the most profound of nature's responses are inarticulate or silent.

By 1804 Wordsworth records a need to say, in effect, 'I am not just hooting at owls; I am not just talking to vagrants, insane women, and idiots. I am becoming a figure worthy of writing a great philosophical poem. I will show you the beginnings of that figure in the person that I *was* – like the leech-gatherer, not the person that stood, nor sat, but the person that simply *was*. That person was my "other" self, a self I have up until now silenced in the voices of Rivers, the Pedlar, the girl in "We Are Seven" and others. I will now recreate that silenced self into an avatar of poetic calling, a poet who deserves to retire to his native mountains in order to continue his break with poetic as well as social codes and conventions, and thereby to write a great poem'.

Of course in the process of allowing this 'other' self to speak, Wordsworth is actually producing a self that is as much dramatic performance as it is autobiographical voice. What sort of poet does he need to say he is in order to write the sort of poem he has described? Just such a poet is presented in the fragmentary lyrical texts that begin appearing in the Goslar winter of 1798–9. These same texts are then organized into a book-length dramatic lyric that performs itself as an autobiographical epic by 1805. In this sense, the speaker in the *Prelude* is more like a speaker in one of Browning's dramatic monologues than he is like the Augustine of *Confessions*. He is not so much explaining his past actions to his readers as he is presenting himself in a way that will lead his readers to have a certain view of him.

Equally revealing are the comments made by Wordsworth and others which suggest that 'the poem to Coleridge' was understood, even within the Wordsworth circle, to be a 'performance' rather than an accurate autobiography. In June 1805, announcing to Beaumont the completion of 'my Poem', Wordsworth sounds not like someone who has found his employment, but like someone who has lost a position he never really had:

When I looked back upon the performance it seemed to have a

dead weight about it, the reality so far short of the expectation; it was the first long labour that I had finished, and the doubt whether I should ever live to write the Recluse and the sense which I had of this Poem being so far below what I seem'd capable of executing, depressed me much.

(EY, p. 594)

Wordsworth connects this depressed state of mind with the recent death of his brother John and with his feeling that if he can add *The Recluse* and 'a narrative Poem of the Epic kind' to this work on his own life, he 'shall consider the *task* of my life as over' (*EY*, p. 594–5: his italics). The task – and the life? – will end when the poetry ends?

Three decades later, Isabella Fenwick connects this feeling of partiality and incompleteness with Wordsworth's pervasive sense of the failure of his own self-revelations: 'yet (as he said last night) how small a portion of what he has felt or thought has he been able to reveal to the world; and he will leave it, his tale still untold'.[15] *His tale still untold*: a strange comment coming from the most overtly autobiographical poet of the century. Fenwick had earlier referred to the drafts of *The Prelude* as 'that marvellous work of his which is to appear when he ceases to be'. A new version of himself will appear when 'he' ceases to be, but the work that purports to be *his* tale will still be a tale untold. One explanation for Wordsworth's unwillingness to publish this major work may be his sense that the poem was not what it represented itself as being.

Fenwick also connects Wordsworth's egotism with his lack of a profession. His persuasive sense 'of his own *greatness*', she wrote, 'maintained itself through neglect and ridicule and contempt' (*Prelude*, p. 538). While family and friends, and later readers and critics, are questioning Wordsworth's motives and intentions, he remains convinced of a personal greatness that does not need external justification. At the same time, however, the public profession of that greatness must walk a fine line between self-silencing (in Nature, through Dorothy, with Coleridge) and self-aggrandizement (as visionary, speaker for others, first-person autobiographer). Wordsworth ends up professing a self that flies in the face of almost all social expectations. By performing a self that defines itself as independent of social censure, he prepares the way for a career that appears to operate free from societal expectations. All the more interesting then, that after 1798, with the rise of his public reputation, Wordsworth became endlessly concerned with the details of publication, editions, and the textual presentation of his personal attitudes and opinions.

These reflections on Wordsworth suggest that we need to adopt a much looser way of talking about the relationship between biological subjects and their representation in literary texts. Just as editors can exhaust untold energies in search of a stable, authentic text, so critics can do the same in their search for an authentic writer within the written word. The self represented in an autobiographical text, however, is much more complicated than our naive readings often suggest. This is not to argue that a textual self is merely a tissue of lies and evasions, although those rhetorical practices may always enter into the process of self-figuration. More important is the sense in which the autobiographical self creates itself in part as a response to the needs of the specific autobiography: am I justifying my actions to others? am I replying to my critics? am I explaining myself to myself? In all cases where an author adopts an ostensibly self-conscious 'I', readers need to be as sensitive to the reasons for the adoption of that 'I' as they do to the claims made by the first-person 'I' that is speaking.

As readers, of course, we have perfectly legitimate reasons for being interested in the biography of William Wordsworth, the lakeland author who walked while he composed, fathered an illegitimate child, spoke with an accent, and seemed peculiar to the very Cumbrians he was inscribing himself upon. But as critics we should take an equal, if not greater, interest in the *autography* by which this historical subject performed a version of himself in a series of texts that became paradigms and prototypes for a vast amount of subsequent writing about the self. In this regard, the Wordsworth of *The Prelude* is not only a source for two centuries of autobiographical writing, he is also the literary ancestor of Robert Browning's dramatic speakers, W. B. Yeats's masks, and Ezra Pound's personae. It makes as much sense to say that Wordsworth is revealing a true self in *The Prelude* as it does to say that Byron *is* Childe Harold (originally 'Childe Byrun') or Don Juan, that James Joyce is Leopold Bloom, or that Thomas Pynchon is Tyrone Slothrop. The complex, polyvalent autobiographer of the Goslar manuscripts may best be understood in terms of literary ideas that take on meaning only later in the nineteenth and twentieth centuries: the dramatized lyric speaker, the mask, the persona.

From 'Descriptive Sketches' and 'An Evening Walk', through 'Salisbury Plain' and *The Borderers* to *Lyrical Ballads*, Wordsworth experimented with descriptive, dramatic, and dialogic voices. When the apparently single-voiced 'I' emerged in the first draft of 'There was a boy' and other narrative fragments that gave rise to *The Prelude*, Wordsworth had not turned his back on ventriloquized narrative voices; rather, he had silenced a series of potential selves as a way of creating a new voice of personal authority. The 'I' that cannot be bewildered because it only describes what it has felt and thought, the 'I' that finds his poem 'a frightful deal to say about one's self' (*EY*, p. 470), is best understood not as an authentic auto-biographical version of William Wordsworth. Rather, this 'I' is a complex figuration of the word 'Wordsworth', a name that can live forever in a text only by dying into the still silence of words on a page.

2

The Politics of Self-Presentation:
Wordsworth as Revolutionary Actor in a Literary Drama

In the winter of 1798–9, shut up in the frigid German town of Goslar, William Wordsworth began producing a series of lyrical fragments that appeared first in letters written to Coleridge and eventually emerged as source texts for *The Prelude*. What is revolutionary in these lyrics is their evolution of a new version of the autobiographical 'I'. The Wordsworthian first person, which becomes the prototype of so much subsequent writing about the self, emerges out of an interplay between complementary and conflicting discourses: the rhetoric of the French Revolution, eighteenth-century ideas about the profession of authorship, and Wordsworth's pronounced need to create an identity whose center is at once poetical (in Wordsworth's sense) and philosophical (in Coleridge's sense). Wordsworth's 'I' in *The Prelude* is revolutionary because it presents a dramatized cultural self rather than an authentic self-biographer. Wordsworth's 'I' also reminds us that autobiographical writing is always a discursive cultural practice, not merely a mimetic revelation of identity.

The discourses of the French Revolution help to provide support for this view of Wordsworth's originality. Lynn Hunt has argued that 'revolutionary political discourse was rhetorical; it was a means of persuasion, a way of reconstituting the social and political world'.[1] Just as the French nation needed to be reconstituted through 'language, images, and daily political activities', so Wordsworth felt a need to reconstitute the secular and postenlightenment view of the self out of the dissolving hierarchy that had represented the earlier idea of 'soul'. And like the human actors in the drama of the French Revolution, who often became performers on a public stage in order to stabilize new visions of political authority, Wordsworth felt a similar need to dramatize a version of himself that might solidify a new form of personal authority in the wake of the destabilizing effect of eighteenth-century anxieties about the 'soul' and the 'self'. Eighteenth and nineteenth-century literary constructions of personal identity (Rousseau, Wordsworth, Mill) are often tied to the need to re-imagine the 'I' as a rhetorical and biographical speaker who gains new power in light of emerging ideas about democracy, personal liberty, and artistic freedom.

The notion of needing to act or perform, so important to François Furet's critique of revolutionary history, shades over into the need to become an actor on the stage of history. This process is no less true for rhetorical and textual 'actors' than for political and social ones. For Furet, 'the act by which each individual citizen continually establishes the general will' is at the center of the revolutionary model of social order; or, as Hunt says of Furet's analysis of revolutionary language: 'Language becomes an expression of power, and power is expressed by the right to speak for the people'.[2] This view derives ultimately from Rousseau, whose own complex role-playing reminds us that dramatized 'selves', as actors, contribute to all revolutions. Every French baker, doctor, teacher, or seamstress who became a revolutionary had to, at some point, see his or her own role in dramatic terms: the individual assumes the mask(s) of the revolution in order to gain extraordinary authority that supersedes his or her ordinary role as a player in the drama of daily life. Likewise, American planters, printers, and merchants had to 'become' new selves in the early 1770s in order to enact their emerging roles as revolutionaries. For Wordsworth, the act of writing his identity in poetic texts becomes a similar way of regenerating himself and providing a model for the regeneration of others, perhaps particularly Coleridge. To live in a text, however, Wordsworth must present a dramatic character that fulfills the expectations of the story he is telling, an 'I' that will satisfy not only himself, but also Coleridge, Dorothy, and all of the other potential readers implied in the communal model for poetry first described in the 1800 'Preface' to *Lyrical Ballads*.

Hunt claims that language was fundamentally important to revolutionary action in France because it became a substitute locus for power that had previously resided in the now-silent (literally headless) king: 'charisma came to be most concretely located in words, that is, in the ability to speak for the Nation' (p. 26). There is a concurrent tension in all revolutionary rhetoric: it must be consistently dynamic, flexible, and capable of change in order to question the authority of the past; at the same time, such language must offer a form of stabilizing unity that can be seen as the center of a 'new' national identity. A similar problem confronts Wordsworth's attempt to forge a revolutionary poetic language that might critique the literary authority of the past while at the same time offering a new model of personal identity, a revived poetic 'nationhood' of the self. The poetic voice can help to create a wider, if dramatized, voice of personal authority.

Nicholas Roe places the young revolutionary Wordsworth in a 'complex psychic drama' with a cast of three crucial figures: the self-projected Wordsworth-as-Gorsas (journalist and delegate) clashes with Wordsworth-as-Robespierre (executioner and ruler). Complicating this opposition is the figure of Wordsworth-as-Beaupuy (patriot and philosopher/soldier). Roe asserts that these 'revolutionary selves' all contributed, in varying degrees, 'to the "devoted voice" of the poet' Wordsworth 'eventually became'.[3] Indeed, when Wordsworth recollects hearing Beaupuy – 'the voice / Of one devoted' (1805, IX, 406–7) – we see one first-person voice (Beaupuy's) creating a memory that becomes the performative source of the next voice (Wordsworth's) that will be able to speak; Wordsworth's memory now *is* the only voice that Beaupuy has left (because Beaupuy is literally dead). Likewise, Wordsworth's numerous poetic voices throughout the 1790s contribute to a unified 'Wordsworth' that will eventually (*c.*1798) speak for himself in the first-person, for 'poetry', for those sentiments and ideals with which he wants to be allied, and for a whole range of people (vagrants, mad mothers, idiot boys) who are otherwise silent. The process is complicated by the fact that *The Prelude* itself charts a clear change in first-person sensibility from the thieving rover of the early books, through the idealistic and then disillusioned young adult of the middle books, to the assertive poetic 'hero' of the later books. Wordsworth does not resolve the conflicting parts of these self-presentations so much as he reveals them to be contributors to the complex identity – like a personal version of a democratic nation? – that his adult self was eventually to become.

If the new 'revolutionary' version of a poet (*Lyrical Ballads* 'Preface') is going to create the taste by which he is to be enjoyed, then he will also need to *create* the voice in which he is speaking.

Instead of merely assuming a voice derived from earlier poetic models (the traditional bardic stance), the revolutionary Romantic speaker must construct a voice that is at once personal (his own authority is the best authority for these claims) and capable of participating in the language really used by men. At the same time, such a poet must help to create a new model for wider literary authority (the public taste by which such poetry is to be enjoyed). What evidence do we have that the 'I' of Wordsworth's lyrics is such a dramatized projection? Quite simply, Wordsworth often speaks as a revolutionary actor in a literary drama throughout the poetic texts of 1798–1805. He assumes roles, and their accompanying voices, in order to accomplish the personal and poetic tasks he has set for himself.

The ventriloquizing of *Lyrical Ballads*, which Coleridge would consistently criticize in *Biographia Literaria* and elsewhere, persists before, during, and after the fragments of autobiography that later evolved into 'the poem to Coleridge'. It is also significant that, throughout Wordsworth's maturity, ventriloquizing (speaking in a voice he claimed not to be his own) remains a powerful and consistent poetic strategy. By 1798, Wordsworth has spoken in at least the following voices: an aging sea-captain ('The Thorn') a mad woman ('Her Eyes are Wild'), Lucy's lover (the Lucy poems), a forsaken Indian woman ('The Complaint'), a once-wicked shepherd ('The Last of the Flock'), Betty Foy and Susan Gale ('The Idiot Boy'), 'Nature' itself ('Three years she grew'), a dead girl ('Lucy Gray'), a literalist father and his imaginative son ('Anecdote for Fathers'), a literalist adult and an imaginative girl ('We Are Seven'), and all of the cast of *The Borderers*. By 1802, additional Wordsworthian dramatic voices will have included a woman grieving for her dead son ('The Sailor's Mother'), a French woman ('The Emigrant Mother'), a gatherer of leeches, ('Resolution and Independence'), a knight ('Hart-Leap Well'), the Priest of Ennerdale and Leonard the mariner ('The Brothers'), Barbara's mourner ("'Tis said that some have died for love'), a penniless orphan ('Alice Fell; or, Poverty'), the shepherds James and Walter ('The Idle Shepherd Boys'), and Barbara Lewthwaite ('The Pet-Lamb'). I present this list not as a bibliographical review, but to remind us how many voices helped to shape the 1798–1805 speaker who is willing to refer to himself most often as 'I'.

In several revealing instances, Wordsworth admits that he is using his own voice to create the speech of another person; he speaks in words that are technically his own (he wrote them down on paper), but he places them into the mouth of another. In 'The Pet-Lamb', for example, the Wordsworthian speaker watches a young girl – unobserved – and describes one version of the process that leads him to speak in someone else's voice: 'from a shady place / I unobserved could see the workings of her face: / If Nature to her tongue could measured numbers bring, / Thus, thought I, to her lamb that little Maid might sing' (17–20).[4] The poem then presents 40 lines spoken in a 'poetic' version of the voice of the 'pretty Maiden'. The girl has only literally spoken four words from her own mouth in the poem – 'Drink, pretty creature, drink!' – and when the poet completes his imagined song for her, he reflects on the complex processes whereby one voice can appropriate another:

– As homeward through the lane I went with lazy feet,
This song to myself did I oftentimes repeat;
And it seemed, as I retraced the ballad line by line,
That but half of it was hers, and one half of it was *mine*.

Again, and once again, did I repeat the song;
'Nay', said I, 'more than half to the damsel must belong.
For she looked with such a look, and she spake with such a tone,
That I almost received her heart into my own'.

                                        (61–8)

My purpose is not to determine what precise percentage of the song was the poet's and what percentage the girl's, but to remind us how self-consciously Wordsworth reflects here on the literary strategy of ventriloquism. In 'The Pet-Lamb' a poet speaks in order to offer us four words spoken by a girl that then give rise to ten stanzas of imagined speech and conclude with a direct quote from the speaker within the speaker's own unquoted words ('"Nay", said I'). Of course, this final stanza also reminds us how complicated are the processes of self-ventriloquism: let me tell you what I said; here's what I say I said; here's what I have to say about what I said. Clearly, the poet often speaks as another person in order to speak for himself.

A similar process occurs in 'The Emigrant Mother', where a lyrical 'I' imagines words that might be spoken by a French immigrant woman to a local English child she treats as her own:

> This Lady, dwelling upon British ground,
> Where she was childless, daily would repair
> To a poor neighbouring cottage; as I found,
> For sake of a young Child whose home was there.
> Once having seen her clasp with fond embrace
> This Child, I chanted to myself a lay,
> Endeavouring, in our English tongue, to trace
> Such things as she unto the Babe might say:
> And thus, from what I heard and knew, or guessed,
> My song the workings of her heart expressed.

> (*PW*, 2: 56, 5–14)

Eight stanzas follow, in which the mother (by way of the poet's voice, of course) imagines the unrelated child into a position of psychic kinship with her own – abandoned? – child in France: 'His little sister thou shalt be; / And, when once more my home I see, / I'll tell him many tales of Thee' (94–5). Once again, it is the ability of one person's 'heart' to enter into another's that becomes the source of the parallel ability to speak for someone else. The mother speaks for the child much as the poet speaks for the mother (much as I am now speaking 'for' the poet in order to write this paragraph of critical interpretation). How audacious then, for either the poet or his subsequent critics (myself included), to make the ventriloquial assumption behind 'The Emigrant Mother': 'My song the workings of her heart expressed'.

Equally important, of course, are cases in which Wordsworth seems to have – or claims to have – spoken as 'himself'. In these instances we – as his readers – often recognize complex processes of figuration, transformation, emphasis, alteration, and fabrication involved in even the most seemingly straightforward statements of the form – 'this happened to me'. In numerous lyrics Wordsworth presents himself as a literal participant or a trustworthy observer (rather than as a calculating actor in a textual drama), but these utterances pose particular problems for any critique of the self-authenticating aspect of poetic voices, particularly autobigraphical ones. I will focus on only three examples of this process, all from 1802: 'The Sailor's Mother', 'Alice Fell', and 'Beggars'. In each of these cases, the first-person teller of a tale stresses the rhetorical complexity of the 'I' that is speaking, while also reminding us of the parallel complexity of the biographical figure behind (within? speaking for?) this 'I'.

'The Sailor's Mother' recounts a conversation which, according to Wordsworth's own testimony, occurred exactly as he describes it: 'I met this woman near the Wishing-Gate, on the high-road that then led from Grasmere to Ambleside. Her appearance was exactly as here described, and such was her account, nearly to the letter'.[5] What strikes a reader first about this claim is its palpable falsity, if for no other reason than that the woman in the poetic text speaks her 'account' in perfect rhyming stanzas: day/away, see/property, his/voyages, trim/him, behind/mind, care/there, fed/dead, wit/it. In addition, her lines are presented in regularly alternating tetrameter and pentameter, with a closing alexandrine. In what sense are we meant to see this as an accurate account of literally spoken words, 'nearly to the letter'? A ventriloquist is once again at work, manipulating the voice of another speaker.

The narrator of this metrically regular lyric also poses additional problems for readerly interpretation. While ostensibly recording a typical encounter with an ordinary Lakeland dweller, the 'I' in 'The Sailor's Mother' overlays his objective observation of humble and rustic life with a powerful simile that links this woman to an heroic classical past. The mother's 'mien and gait' is 'like a Roman matron's' (*PW*, 2: 54). Her mere presence (even before she speaks) convinces the narrator that 'The ancient spirit is not dead', although he never mentions what specific aspect of this ancient spirit he wants to emphasize: good, bad, or indifferent. She is majestic, strong, and dignified, but – if 'Old times ... are breathing there', we are also reminded that Roman matrons were not always deserving of unalloyed praise. In fact, the narrator admits the potential dangers of the kind of transformation he is working on this woman when he associates her with his own first response to her presence – pride: 'Proud was I', 'I looked at her again, nor did my pride abate'. Likewise he admits that he has to wake from 'these lofty thoughts' in order to actually converse with this woman.

Like the narrator of 'Resolution and Independence', the 'I' of 'The Sailor's Mother' hints that he may be placing too strong a metaphorical emphasis on the humble human subject before him. Indeed, the story told by this aging woman – and the fact that she has 'begged an alms' – stands in stark contrast to the imagined Roman heroism of the poet's 'lofty thoughts'. This woman has

gone to her dead son's lodgings, found the caged bird her child
left behind when he set out on a fatal ocean voyage, and now
carries this 'little Singing-bird' with her because her drowned son
'took so much delight in it'. She claims that this strange burden is
the result of her own 'little wit' and of this bird's ability to serve
as a reminder of her lost child. The text of the poem (provided by
our first-person narrator) thus produces a characteristically unre-
solvable Wordsworthian tension. The human figure described in
this poem can be seen as a majestic Roman matron, dignified and
strong, or as a witless old woman whose pathological grief over
the death of her son leads her to carry a caged bird wherever she
goes. As readers we are left to reevaluate our own interpretations
based on this woman's ability to represent or 'contain' such a wide
range of potential responses. Is this woman as noble as a Roman?
Maybe. Is she deserving of pity and help? Perhaps. Is she both?
How would we know except through our interpretation of a poet's
words, spoken by an authenticating 'I', perhaps, but by this stage
of interpretation far distanced from any precise biological subject
named William Wordsworth.

What the poem provides are not the historical words of a female
rural speaker transcribed by a faithful poetic narrator. Rather, 'The
Sailor's Mother' offers another case where Wordsworth's interest in
the actions of the human mind produces a powerful and resonant
lyric.[6] The poem records the narrator's own tendency to transform
this woman imaginatively into an heroic figure (although she may
not be heroic at all, but rather pitiful and in need of practical help:
'alms'). The text also records the process whereby the human mind
(woman's, poet's, or reader's) can transform a seemingly insignifi-
cant object (the bird) into a powerful symbol (representation) of
something else (the dead son). The speaker cares about this woman
primarily because she represents something in his mind (Roman
nobility), just as the woman cares for the bird primarily because it
is associated in her mind with her child, not for any natural or
intrinsic reason. She would not carry this bird around had it not
belonged to her son, nor would she carry any bird around simply
because it was a bird. She carries this particular bird for a very
specific psychological reason. Likewise, the poet speaks as and for
this woman because of what she is to him and does (psychologi-
cally?) for him.

'The Sailor's Mother' was the poem which, in Coleridge's
opinion, was 'the only fair instance that I have been able to

discover in all of Mr. Wordsworth's writings, of an *actual* adoption, or true imitation, of the *real* and *very* language of *low and rustic life*, freed from provincialisms'.[7] Coleridge's distinction between '*actual* adoption' and 'true imitation' is an important one. It reminds us that imitation is not only a sincere form of flattery but also a way of *becoming* the object that is being imitated. When I speak for you or as you, I am identifying myself with more than your words. When I speak for myself or as myself, I am acknowledging – to some extent – that my words are not strictly my own, but are bound up in complex ways with the words of others. I confirm, I respond, I answer, I reply, I cajole, I criticize, I argue, I plead: I never simply speak without reference to other language uses going on around me.

'Alice Fell' poses related problems for our understanding of the evolution of the Wordsworthian first-person narrator. In this case, the action of an 'I' is the rhetorical center of the poem; the narrator provides money for the orphaned Alice Fell to buy the cloak that makes her a 'Proud creature' in the penultimate line of the lyric. The first-person narrator claims to have met Alice when her old cloak became entangled in the wheel of the coach in which he was riding: 'I saw it in the wheel entangled, / A weather-beaten rag as e'er / From any garden scare-crow dangled' (*PW*, 1: 232, 27–9). The narrator gathers the child into the chaise, carries her to Durham, finds her lodgings, and gives the tavern-keeper money for a new cloak. All of this seems another straightforward case of the Wordsworthian poet recording a simple, subsequently moralized or psychologized, incident from his own life. But Dorothy's *Journal* (16 February 1802) attributes the 'I' narrator of 'Alice Fell' not to her brother William but to Robert Graham, a Glasgow solicitor: 'Mr. Graham said he wished Wm had been with him the other day – he was riding in a post chaise and he heard a strange cry that he could not understand, the sound continued and he called to the chaise driver to stop. It was a little girl that was crying as if her heart would burst. She had got up behind the chaise and her cloak had been caught by the wheel and was jammed in and it hung there ... Her name was Alice Fell'.[8]

Wordsworth takes Graham's account of this event and within a month transforms it into a lyric that places a powerful poetic 'I' at the center of the story: four-and-a-half of the stanzas are not about Alice at all, but about the speaker's response to the mysterious crying before the child is discovered. Wordsworth also alters the details of Graham's account just enough to complicate the 'meaning' of the story. Dorothy's version of Graham's account stresses the girl's plight and eventual return to safety; William's poetic version emphasizes the role of the speaker in turning Alice Fell from a disheveled sobbing mass of rags into a proud creature. In the process we are reminded that the teller of the tale (see also 'The Thorn') is often as important to the story's 'meaning' as the events being described. Does the text of the poem represent an accurate version of Alice's account of her condition? Graham's version? William Wordsworth's? His sister Dorothy's? Is the 'meaning' of the poem contained in my account of any of these other accounts? Is meaning dependent on your own account based on your reading? How would we distinguish among these various potential speakers and interpreters? Who, precisely, is speaking in a lyric like 'Alice Fell', and to whom, and for what purpose? Can we be sure?

'Beggars' presents a final example of the way the emerging Wordsworthian 'I' is complicated not only by the circumstances surrounding poetic composition, but also by the material text and by modulations in the voice of the speaker. The poem recalls a first-person speaker's encounter with three beggars. This speaker ('I') admits a serious problem with first-person objectivity in the poem's first stanza. He sees a tall woman who is covered in a cloak and, as a result, his vision is limited: 'What other dress she had I could not know' (*PW*, 2: 222: revised text). She might have a beautiful gown under her 'Mantle' – or, she might have rags. Like the woman in 'The Sailor's Mother', this figure strikes the speaker as representing more than is suggested by her outward appearance. He claims 'never' to have seen such a 'Figure' in all his walks; she is fit 'for a Queen', like an 'Amazonian' or a Greek 'Bandit's Wife'. With these dramatic and dramatized comparisons, the poetic 'I' directs our readerly attention toward a female figure we might otherwise have thought of as merely an ordinary beggar woman.

In fact, this woman *is* 'begging', 'Pouring out sorrows like a sea; / Grief after grief'. And the speaker knows (suspects?) from the first that she is lying: 'Such woes I knew could never be' (*PW*, 2: 223n). But he gives her money anyway, because of her physical appearance: 'And yet a boon I gave her; for the creature / Was beautiful to see'. Soon afterward, this same narrator comes upon two young boys who appear to be related to the beggar woman: 'Two brothers seemed they, eight and ten years old; / And like that Woman's face as gold is like to gold'. These boys are also beggars and are – in the speaker's mind – also liars. The boys approach the speaker with 'a plaintive whine', but he tells them that he has nothing for them, since 'not half an hour ago / Your Mother has had alms of mine'. Then, in a reversed echo of 'We Are Seven', the two boys tell the speaker that he must be mistaken since their mother 'is dead ... She has been dead, Sir, many a day'. The speaker, however, will not doubt the authority of his own perceptual observation of the similarity in external appearance; he insists, 'Sweet Boys, you're telling me a lie; / It was your Mother, as I say!' When they hear his refusal again, the boys turn 'without more ado', apparently unconcerned, and dash off 'to some other play'. Who knows the final truth of this complex rhetorical situation? How might the speaker of the poem know? How might we?

Our sense of the meaning of 'Beggars' is complicated by the interplay between speech and lying (or error) throughout the text. The speaker cannot be sure if this woman is a hopeless beggar or an heroic figure of strength. He gives her alms not because she deserves them, but because he finds her beautiful. His refusal to respond to the boys' begging is complicated by the fact that he calls them 'sweet' even as he doubts their story. The speaker is the one who tells these children who their mother is ('as I say'), and we are never clear why this 'I' cannot respond to the potentially legitimate pleas of both the mother and her children (the family is poor; they obviously need as much money as they can get). Of course, the poem also raises the less likely possibility that the boys are not lying at all. Their mother may be dead, and the speaker may have wrongly assumed that a physical similarity guarantees that these boys (how, likewise, does he claim to know their precise ages?) are this woman's children.

When asked about the meaning of 'Beggars', Wordsworth replied that the lines were 'a poetical exhibition of the power of physical beauty and the charm of health and vigour in childhood even in a state of the greatest moral depravity'.[9] Dorothy's *Journals*, however, shed important light on the evolution of the Wordsworthian voice that claims first-person authority for such a poetic message. Wordsworth began a poem about a begging woman on 13 March 1802. Dorothy says that he based this beggar woman on 'a Woman whom I had seen in May – (now nearly 2 years ago) when John and he were at Gallow Hill' (*Journals*, p. 100). Dorothy's original account of this family of beggars is worth quoting in full for the light it sheds on the first-person speaker in William's lyric two years later:

> On Tuesday, May 27th [1800], a very tall woman, tall much beyond the measure of tall women, called at the door. She had on a very long brown cloak, and a very white cap without Bonnet – her face was excessively brown, but it had plainly once been fair. She led a little bare-footed child about 2 years old by the hand and said her husband who was a tinker was gone before with the other children. I gave her a piece of Bread. Afterwards on my road to Ambleside, besides the Bridge at Rydale, I saw her husband sitting by the roadside, his two asses feeding beside him and the two young children at play upon the grass. The man did not beg. I passed on and about 1/4 of a mile further I saw two boys before me, one about 10 the other about 8 years old at play chasing a butterfly ... They continued at play until I drew very near and then addressed me with the Beggars' cant and the whining voice of sorrow. I said I served your mother this morning. (The Boys were so like the woman who had called at the door that I could not be mistaken.) O! says the elder you could not serve my mother for she's dead and my father's on at the next town – he's a potter. I persisted in my assertion and that I would give them nothing. Says the elder Come, let's away, and away they flew like lightning ... On my return through Ambleside I met in the street the mother driving her asses; in the two Panniers of one of which were the two little children whom she was chiding and threatening with a wand which she used to drive on her asses, while the little things hung in wantonness over the Pannier's edge.
>
> *(Journals*, p. 26: 10 June 1800)

Dorothy read this entry to her brother while he was at work on his poem about 'the Beggar woman', and her reading had a very strange effect: 'After tea I read to William that account of the little Boys belonging to the tall woman and an unlucky thing it was for he could not escape from those very words, and so he could not write the poem. He left it unfinished and went tired to bed' (*Journals*, p. 101: 13 March 1802).

'He *could not escape* from *those very words*, and so he *could not write the poem*' (my emphasis). Although Dorothy does not tell us what the 'very words' were from which William could not escape, her observation points up one way that the words of others complicate the ability to speak as an 'I', even in a work of imaginative literature. Dorothy's words prevent William from finding words of his own. Wordsworth adopts the immediacy and the authenticating veracity of first-person reportage in almost all of his lyrics, as he also does in *The Prelude*. In 'The Beggars' we find him speaking poetically as himself, but also speaking in another sense *as* Dorothy. The narrative details of the poem he appropriates almost directly, as in many other cases, word for word from Dorothy's journal entry ('a very white cap, without Bonnet', 'long brown cloak', 'face excessively brown', 'one about 10 the other about 8 years old', 'so like the woman', 'chasing a butterfly', 'wreathed round with yellow flowers', 'rimless crown', 'whining voice', 'she's dead', 'Come, let's away', 'away they flew'). Of course, he also transforms Dorothy's account in important ways: the father vanishes from the story, as do the animals and the scene of the reunited mother and children.

The 'I' in this case emerges out of Dorothy's first-person journal, mingles with the literary voice of poetic authority that Wordsworth has been developing at least since *Lyrical Ballads*, and declares itself a self-authenticating ('as I say') and self-reflexive ('Said I') narrator who is and is not Dorothy, is and is not William, is and is not a nameless lyrical speaker capable of careful rhymes (day/say, lie/eye, ado/flew), poetic diction (Mantle, Weed, espy, leaves of laurel) and complex allusions (ancient Amazonian files, the twinkling of an eye, ruling Bandit's wife). Indeed, we should notice that the child with the poet's laurel leaves stuck in his hat is presented as another poetic manipulator of language – and also as a liar. Is the first-person speaker of this poem also a poetic liar? Did these events ever happen? Did they happen to 'him' – the poet? In a way, of course, they did (Wordsworth read about them in his sister's journal). In another important way, however, these events are a poetic fabrication designed to get alms (make money once they are published), just as the young boys manipulate language trying to extract a penny or two from their listener. The boys may make up a tale, but so does our poetic narrator. He 'reads' the boys' appearance and then interprets their words, just as we will later 'read' his appearance in the text and interpret his words. This affecting story surely 'looks' true, but in what sense is it true?

We should not leave the rhetorical complexity of the Wordsworthian 'I' without recalling that several of Wordsworth's 'personal' and first-person lyrics were based almost entirely on stories told to him by others. Among this list we can include at least 'The Last of the Flock' (1798 – see his letter of 24 September 1836), 'The Brothers', and 'Hart-Leap Well'. Perhaps the most famous example of Wordsworth's appropriating the story – and even the words – of another person for his own rhetorical purposes occurred in 'The Solitary Reaper' (1805). The poem is a lyrical narrative based on an account Wordsworth had read in the manuscript version of Thomas Wilkinson's *Tours of the British Mountains*, which included the following lines: 'Passed by a Female who was reaping alone: she sung in Erse as she bended over her sickle; the sweetest human Voice I ever heard: her strains were tender and melancholy and felt delicious, long after they were heard no more'.[10] Dorothy, writing in September of 1803, connected the image of local farm laborers with a memory of the Highlands that must have also contributed to William's solitary reaper lyric two years later. Dorothy wrote, 'It was harvest time, and the fields were quietly – might I be allowed to say pensively? – enlivened by small companies of reapers. It is not uncommon in the more lonely parts of the Highlands to see a single person so employed'.[11]

In this case, Wordsworth's use of the Wilkinson/Dorothy image is particularly significant; the solitary reaper provides a prototype of the way meaning emerges in many Wordsworthian poetic texts written between 1798 and 1810: an 'ordinary' experience is rendered remarkable simply by virtue of the powerful emotional effect it has on its first-person speaker. Wordsworth's poetics, particularly in the period 1798–1805, reveal what we might call a 'politics' of point-of-view: first-person narration, with its assumed identification between poet and lyric speaker, becomes a crucial aspect of this characteristically Wordsworthian voice. On these terms, the subject-object relationship in the poem becomes a function, not of any verifiable state of affairs in the physical world, but of the perspective assumed by a flexible and polyvalent first-person speaker. Countless other poets had written in their own voices before; few had ever made their emotional evaluation of the significance of an event into the standard by which the event was to be judged. Implicit in all Wordsworthian lyrics of this sort is a claim about the subject-matter for poetry: an event struck the poet powerfully when it occurred and has remained significant to the poet over time; therefore, that same event is worth recording in verse and making available to others. Such a claim for the value of Wordsworth's own emotional responses is at the center of what Keats will rightly call the Wordsworthian, or egotistical, sublime. Rather than being a weakness, however, this form of expression – 'what seemed important to me is what I will write about for others to read' – becomes a standard for countless subsequent lyrics. From John Clare, Felicia Hemans, Percy Shelley, and Emily Brontë to Adrienne Rich, Seamus Heaney, Derek Walcott, and Louise Gluck, lyric poems have recorded the poet's desire to transform personal experiences into literary texts that may be useful or pleasing to others.

II

The politics of Wordsworth's first-person presentations emerge out of various and multifarious voices that contribute to his sense of himself as an authoritative speaker. To use the term 'politics' in this sense is to fuse, perhaps to con-fuse, two aspects of the meaning of the term. On the one hand, the texts that become *The Prelude* represent the use of 'strategy in obtaining a position of power or control' (*Random House*). That is, Wordsworth uses language to gain control over his experience and to present a self-image, or at least a self-representation: a textual version of the voice he wants to claim as his own. Such a strategic use of 'politics', however, reminds us of the etymological connection between 'politics' and the culture of the city-state, the *polis*. For the *polis* of *The Prelude* (Book VII – 'Residence in London'; Book IX: 'Residence in France'; Book X: 'Residence in France and the French Revolution') is clearly what Wordsworth has to leave behind in order to move to Grasmere and begin 'being himself'. And yet the eighteenth-century model of the polis – a unified, self-governing, self-regulating social structure – has, by 1798 at least, become a model for a new and apparently unified version of personal identity. The city-state parallels the self-state, an internalized and psychologized 'state of mind' with clear connections to the idea of the state as social unit. How the state could govern a diverse nation's people becomes one aspect of another question – how could any individual govern the conflicting voices of plural identity and produce a unified, democratized self? Of course, Wordsworth's problem as an individual parallels France's problem as a nation. Who are the selves that can unify their own identities and form a model for the new state that is emerging? Revolutionary selves need models of order just as revolutionary states do. Romantic selves fashion themselves the same way democratic states do, by establishing apparent forms of agreement among disparate and conflicting voices.

The first-person speaker developed by Wordsworth comes from a model that may be historically as American as it is French. The terror of failed French self-governance by the late 1790s led to a pressing need to find an Americanized *e pluribus unum*. Whose was the one voice, out of many voices, that might arise to assume personal authority over the polis? Such a voice, however personal, would need also to echo the voices of other versions of authority. Was that voice Robespierre?[12] Was it Napoleon? In France's case, the search for that voice led to decades of struggle among conflicting voices and authorities. In the poet's case, the singular voice turns out to be the 'Wordsworth' of the 'poem to Coleridge', a rhetorical 'I' that can unify disparate voices while at the same time representing itself as a powerful vortex of personal, social, and perhaps even 'political' energy. Such a democratic voice would unify the voices of others while also retaining its own integrity. Like Jefferson, Paine, and Franklin, Wordsworth finds a way to speak as himself partly by speaking for others. An author's audience is thus comparable to a politician's electorate. But like any democratized political actor, Wordsworth realizes that his authority lasts only as long as it has the support of a wider audience, electoral or literary.

In this regard, it is revealing that Wordsworth's positive descriptions of revolutionary France are almost always connected to the rural countryside in Book VI of *The Prelude*. Revolutionary France enters the poem with more connections to naturalistic landscapes than to the political activities of urban dwellers. Wordsworth and his Welsh friend Robert Jones arrived in France one day before the first annual celebration of the fall of the Bastille. Among 'sequestered villages' they 'found benevolence and blessedness', and 'saw / Dances of liberty' performed; the 'vine-clad hills of Burgundy', and 'the bosom of the gentle Soane' provide an apt setting for the 'host / Of travellers' that include 'delegates returning / From the great spousals newly solemnized' in Paris (1805, VI, 395–6). But at this early stage in the Revolution the two British travelers do not pause in France. Instead they hurry to Switzerland and the Alps, among other purely naturalized scenes that will set the stage for the poem's sublimely imagined revelation in Gondo Gorge.

Wordsworth also admits that his own time spent living in the heart of the British metropolis was a time during which he was a complete failure in conventional political terms. The 1805 text of Book IX of *The Prelude* says that he lived for a year in London around 1791; he actually spent four months in the city, yet acting by his account as though he were still in Lakeland: 'Free as a colt at pasture on the hills / I ranged at large through the metropolis / Month after month' (IX, 18–20). But this sprightly young equine sensibility knows full well the consequences of his choice; he may be a libertine colt prancing in the *polis*, but he is in no way a political animal: 'Obscurely did I live, / Not courting the society of men' (20–1). In fact, this avowedly nonpolitical – apolitical? – creature admits that under these conditions he became a spectator, not an actor of any kind: 'in the midst of things, it seemed, / Looking as from a distance on the world / That moved about me' (23–5). This point-of-view has one advantage, however. Out of the crush of social life, far away from 'men, / By literature, or elegance, or rank, / Distinguished', the Wordsworthian viewer claims to gain a vantage point from which his 'False preconceptions were corrected', his 'errors of the fancy rectified'. Again it is significant that this apparent autobiographer leaves untold the details of his personal errors in London. When he decides to leave the capital, he departs with only one regret – the loss of the city's bookstalls – and he heads to France, so he says, for a seemingly incidental purpose, 'a personal wish / To speak the language more familiarly' (IX, 36–7). I care deeply for books, the young wanderer – pedlar? vagrant? – says, and I need another language that will make me feel part of a wider family than I do now. Little did the Wordsworth of 1790 suspect how both 'books' and 'familiarity' with the French language (see Annette Vallon's letters) would at once create and help to solve the problems of career and family for the man who was later to become the poet that Coleridge would call 'Wordsworth!'.

Once Wordsworth returned to France (1791), he surrounded himself with scenes of recent political action and 'saw the revolutionary power' (IX, 48) much as he had earlier claimed to 'drink the visionary power' (1799, II, 360). The halls are 'clamorous' however; the National Assembly and the Jacobin Club both represent sites of multivocal conflict, oppositional and radical dialogue. This 'hubbub wild' evokes Milton's hell and is followed by a description of revolutionaries who sound precisely like Miltonic devils engaged in fractious party politics: 'hissing factionists with ardent eyes, / In knots, or pairs, or single, ant-like swarms / Of builders and subverters' (IX, 57–9). Wordsworth admits a split in his own emotions at this point that leads him to erect a false front. He adopts, he says 'the guise / Of an enthusiast' about these revolutionary matters, but he is also willing to record 'affecting more emotion than I felt' (71). Disillusionment (before or after the fact?) will become a central aspect of his developing feelings.[13] In fact, the painter le Brun's portrait of the weeping Magdalene is described as conjuring much more emotion in the young poet than any of the politics around him; the painting provides a better picture of 'the temper' of his mind that any Jacobin speech. Perhaps this portrait is so significant in subsequent recollection because it reminds him of Annette, the one French citizen (and magdalene?) to whom he would be most closely connected during his own revolutionary months.

The appropriateness of theatrical metaphors – a spectator and actor, observing and participating in a drama – to describe Wordsworth's circumstances in France in the early 1790s is confirmed early in Book IX, where the poet describes himself as an innocent member of a fortunate audience; the details of 'ordinary life' – 'speech, / Domestic manners, customs, gestures, looks' – made him feel 'tranquil, and careless', yet these words and gestures 'had abruptly passed / Into a theatre of which the stage / Was busy with an action far advanced' (82–3, 93–5). Every seemingly innocent and neutral detail is actually part of a much larger drama. Wordsworth describes himself as an actor with at least two roles. His attendance at card games, parties, and scenes full of 'punctilios of elegance', gives way – because of 'tedium' – to 'a noisier world', the world of revolutionary action. To this new world the sensitized Wordsworth can only respond by assuming a new role; he must become 'a patriot'. But there are patriots and there are 'patriots'.

In this passage (IX, 96–125), Wordsworth admits the autobiographical need to emphasize those experiences that are important in retrospect, from the vantage point of 1805, rather than those events that seemed important when they occurred, in 1791. Describing his youthful interest in parties and card-games in light of the concurrent events of the revolution he admits: 'I fear / Now in connection with so great a theme / To speak, as I must be compelled to do, / Of one so unimportant' (111–14). I must speak of this unimportant theme (card games, routs) because it was important to me then; but I realize, in retrospect, that the revolutionary action surrounding me – and which I would only fully appreciate later – is actually much more significant. The autobiographer is often plagued by the sense that what has happened to him, and what he has cared about, may not really have been so important after all. Will he tell the tale as it was, or will he shape events to emphasize their subsequent meaning, even while retaining his own image and voice at the center of the narration? Wordsworth compares himself to a 'river' as Book IX opens, suggesting once again the image of many tributaries (voices) contributing to a single, still 'moving', speaker (one voice) in whose voice these verbal streams are all contained in complex, many-currented ways. Every other self is also like a river, never quite the same from one moment to the next.

The French people have been transformed by the circumstances of 1789–91, forced into new roles and, therefore, forced to make utterances they might otherwise never have made:

> 'Twas in truth an hour
> Of universal ferment – mildest men
> Were agitated, and commotions, strife
> Of passion and opinion, filled the walls
> Of peaceful houses with unquiet sounds.

> (IX, 164–8)

In such a time, allegiance itself becomes the result of the roles a person chooses to adopt, and all such roles can change quickly. To choose just one example: thousands of French army officers deserted their troops before 1792, joining emigres at Coblenz and preparing to invade in order to support a return to the *ancien regime*.[14] Loyalties under such conditions, like the personal identities that went with them, often shifted as fast as events could propel them: 'Is Jacques a loyalist? I thought he was'. ' No, not at all; he has changed his mind. He seems to have become a new person overnight'. Wordsworth finds himself in an equally equivocal state of mind, caught up in the revolutionary energy of the moment, but feeling also 'what my soul / Mourned for, or loathed, beholding that the best / Ruled not, and feeling that they ought to rule' (IX, 215–17). Words themselves are suspect and weakened by the level of discord surrounding such events. Describing the numerous and conflicting 'advocates' for radical ideals, Wordsworth says: 'Every word / They

uttered was a dart by counter-winds / Blown back upon themselves'
(261–3). Political identity is not black and white at such a moment;
even a concept like 'the party' cannot stabilize such confusion.

Michel Beaupuy is important to the Wordsworth of 1792
precisely because his image and his voice combine the intellectual-
ism of a noble aristocrat with the democratic emotionalism of a
revolutionary republican. Beaupuy, more than any other figure,
teaches Wordsworth how to assume the role of participant in the
revolution, even if that participation is limited to verbal dialogue:
'Oft in solitude / With him did I discourse about the end / Of civil
government, and its wisest forms, / Of ancient prejudice and char-
tered rights' (IX, 328–31). Beaupuy, who was to die on the eastern
front in 1796, is presented by Wordsworth as a martial figure of
mental balance and emotional restraint: 'For he, an upright man
and tolerant, / Balanced these contemplations in his mind, / And I
... had a sounder judgement / Than afterwards' (IX, 337–41). In
retrospect, of course, Wordsworth is casting his mind forward to
his own much different mood of 1793–5, anticipating The Terror
and the personal disillusionment that would then accompany
rapidly declining prospects for any lasting revolutionary reform.

Wordsworth notes that he and Beaupuy discussed 'How quickly
mighty nations have been formed / From least beginnings' (384–5),
reminding us that nation-builders, like certain selves, can 'build up
greatest things / From least suggestions' (1805, XIII, 98–9). The
secret to this process, whether nation-building or self-creation, is
like the secret of mingling many voices (tributaries) into one verbal
stream: 'together locked / By new opinions, scattered tribes have
made / One body' (IX, 385–7). No less can scattered voices in
dialogue become one voice of apparent poetic authority – an 'I' or
a 'we'. It is, in fact, the 'earnest dialogues' (446) that Beaupuy and
Wordsworth share which will constitute another part of the sensi-
bility that Wordsworth will claim as his own. He admits that this
process of amalgamation is never simple or direct, particularly in
circumstances where 'emotions' are 'wrought / Within our minds
by the ever-varying wind / Of record and report which day by day
/ Swept over us' (547–50). How does one know what to say when
every day brings a new sense of what would constitute an appro-
priate response to events – verbal or violent? Today's anxiously
scripted or spoken revolutionary words may be tomorrow's
treason.

Book X opens with a theatrical account of the 'scenes' through which Wordsworth makes his way as he leaves the Loire Valley, along with a description of the 'body and the venerable name' (X, 30) which the state has assumed (a new 'role' for the image of nationhood) in order to proclaim itself a republic. Lying on his bed in the Paris night, the young Wordsworthian 'patriot' (his word choice) recalls the September massacres and pens dramatized lines of dialogue, lines which he speaks to himself in the text of the poem:

> 'The horse is taught his manege, and the wind
> Of heaven wheels round and treads in his own steps;
> Year follows year, the tide returns again,
> Day follows day, all things have second birth;
> The earthquake is not satisfied at once' –
> And in such way I wrought upon myself,
> Until I seemed to hear a voice that cried
> To the whole city, 'Sleep no more!'

(X, 70–7)

In this remarkable intertext, the poet of 1804 writes lines recalling a Paris bed in 1792, evoking himself as a speaking character in the drama of revolution, then quoting another dramatic speaker (Macbeth) who had murdered a king. The next morning Wordsworth, once again describing himself as narrator, hears a loud crowd in the street, 'Bawling, *Denunciation of the crimes* / *Of Maximilian Robespierre*' (X, 87–8). The poet of 1804 can imagine lines for himself, can quote other voices, and can transform the details of his own experience in order to create a seamless narrative web out of events that had occurred more than a decade earlier. Once again, many voices – a remembered voice in the mind, the voice of Macbeth, French voices in the street, and the present-tense voice of the poet – unite to produce 'Wordsworth', the speaking voice of the 1805 poem. These disparate voices, however, are unified only in a text. The writer that pens poetic lines in 1804 is, literally and figuratively, a different person than the young 'revolutionary' of 1792.

Louvet's 'Je t'accuse' becomes, in Wordsworth's account, another example of dramatic speech that is also a form of revolutionary action. Louvet's accusation had been part of a verbal attack on Robespierre for assuming the role of dictator (29 October 1792). In an earlier debate, Danton had been indicted (told by others what 'role' he had already performed) in the preceding month's massacres. Robespierre responded to Louvet's accusations with words designed to resituate his role in these unfolding events. He then rose to a position of supreme power in 1793, having first scripted and then acted a part that allowed him to achieve temporary ascendancy in the drama of the National Convention.[15] The discourse of revolutionary action, at least in the political realm, is often a discourse of scripted roles and dramatized action. The specific speaker is no longer merely a soldier, merchant, diplomat, or professor. Instead, the speaker *becomes* the role he speaks or the role that is spoken for him: Louvet *is* an accuser, Danton *is* a guilty murderer, Robespierre *is* a supreme leader (at least during this act of the drama). Wordsworth *is* what? That is what the speaker of the autobiographical poem wants to know. But any answer to such a question is only a temporary answer.

Wordsworth describes his own authorial role as recorder of these great revolutionary events in a conflicted way: 'An insignificant stranger and obscure, / Mean as I was, and little graced with powers / Of eloquence even in my native speech, / And all unfit for tumult and intrigue' (X, 130–3). Yet however self-deprecatory he may be, the poet also presents himself as an enthusiast: 'Yet would I willingly have taken up / A service at this time for cause so great, / However dangerous' (134–6). He would have, but he didn't – for at least one significant reason. He leaves France, leaves the Revolution, and leaves Annette (although he doesn't say so) for only one reason – at least by his own account – money: 'In this frame of mind [confused] / Reluctantly to England I returned, / Compelled by nothing less than absolute want / Of funds for my support' (X, 188–91). The budding revolutionary is broke. In this penurious condition he reaches one of the low points of identity formation in his entire autobiographical text. With some financial support, he suggests, 'I doubtless should have made a common cause / With some who perished, haply perished too' (194–5). With a little bit of money he might have died for this noble revolution. As it was, the penniless poet was 'well assured / That I both was and must be of small worth, / No better than an alien in the land'. In fact, the 35-year-old poet looks back on the 22-year-old would-be poet as a financial, professional, and emotional failure: 'With all my resolutions, all my hopes, / A poet only to myself, to men / Useless, and even, belovèd friend [Coleridge], a soul / To thee unknown' (X, 198–201).

Wordsworth returns to England in the autumn of 1792 and begins the long period of disillusionment that culminates in his reunion with Dorothy and his friendship with Coleridge by 1795. In 1794, the words *'Robespierre was dead'* (1805, X, 535, Wordsworth's emphasis) fall on Wordsworth's ears with a force comparable to *'that we had crossed the Alps'* (1850, VI, 591, Wordsworth's emphasis in 1850 edition). Once back in England, Wordsworth worries that the government of Pitt may derive some of its authoritarian control from the model of Robespierre, but the poet restrains himself from writing a political response to English injustice, hinting at a complex self-censorship that masquerades as rhetorical control:

> To a strain
> More animated I might here give way,
> And tell, since juvenile errors are my theme,
> What in those days through Britain was performed
> To turn *all* judgements out of their right course;
> But this is passion over near ourselves,
> Reality too close and too intense,
> And mingled up with something, in my mind,
> Of scorn and condemnation personal
> That would profane the sanctity of verse.

> (X, 636–44)

Once again, we see tensions at work in the production of the Wordsworthian 'I'. Some passions are too 'overnear' the speaker to warrant their telling (passion for Annette? a passionate reaction to Pitt's government?). Some 'reality' is 'too close' to bear repetition in the text. Likewise, scorn and personal condemnation must be kept out of sanctified verse, unless that scorn is heaped on a now distant political enemy – the French.

We should recall that this is the same Wordsworth who claimed, 'Bliss was it in that dawn to be alive, / But to be young was very heaven' (X, 692–3), and the poetic reformer who acknowledged that his moments of political optimism during the 1790s led to a belief that change should come about 'Not in Utopia … But in the very world which is the world / Of all of us, the place in which, in the end, / We find our happiness, or not at all' (X, 723–7). Wordsworth is saying, in effect: I *might* say this, I *need to* say this, I *should* say this, I *can* say this. He is being 'politic' with himself and about himself. In all of these instances, what is said by Wordsworth (or what *can* be said) creates gulfs within the speaker as well as gulfs between the speaker and his imagined or actual audience (himself, Coleridge, Dorothy, partisans, the French, British government officials, subsequent readers). A speaker, even a poet, can speak for as many reasons as his listeners can listen.

Wordsworth admits that his flirtation with Godwinian rationalism was also a role adopted in part to deal with contradictions inherent in the revolutionary position: power had to come from the weakest members of society; violence was directed at bringing about peace; some individuals had to be deprived of their rights in order to assure rights for all. Indeed, the revolution lifts a 'veil', making it harder to continue to 'deceive ourselves' (X, 855–6). The rationalistic 'errors into which' Wordsworth 'was betrayed' (882) are like dramatic voices that should have been ignored. Indeed, Wordsworth employs another theatrical metaphor to describe the dramatized ascendancy of Napoleon in December of 1804. A naturalistic and organic Napoleonic sun, that had arisen 'in splendor, was alive, and moved in exultation among living clouds' (X, 936–7), has now 'turned into a gewgaw, a machine, / Sets like an opera phantom' (939–40). Napoleon's sun-like radiance has become a stage set. The sites of revolution become dramatized versions of stagy words and actions as Wordsworth's belief in revolutionary ideals fades. But revolutionary actors, like poetic voices, are still playing roles, whether those roles are sincere and heroic or hyperbolic and melodramatic.

The theatrical model of revolutionary discourse requires participants who are willing to do more than act, actors who are willing to sacrifice life, liberty, and property. Wordsworth's family, for example, understands and fears his willingness to sacrifice property for his ideals; they express constant worries about his financial and material prospects from the mid-1790s onward. The young Wordsworth had, in fact, gone to France at least partly to 'avoid family discussion of his career, centering at the time on "a paltry curacy" in Harwich' (*Prelude*, p. 314; *EY*, p. 59). Liberty, however, does not seem as likely to be sacrificed by the young Wordsworth; in fact, personal and poetic liberty can be seen as the issues always at the center of Wordsworth's autobiographical and rhetorical decision-making. In the minds of those around him, the decision to go to France in the 1790s, the decision to delay marriage to Mary Hutchinson until 1802, the decision to move to Grasmere, and the decision to avoid commitment to any career other than poet, all look like ways of preserving forms of liberty that are beneficial or suspect, depending on one's point of view. Similarly, the 'Preface' to *Lyrical Ballads* sets forth an argument about the value (and the problems attendant upon) certain forms of poetic liberty: the poet should use the language really used by men; poets create the taste by which they are to be enjoyed; there is no difference between the language of poetry and the language of prose. Whether Wordsworth ever saw himself as willing to sacrifice his life for his principles – political or poetic – is unclear. He never chooses to describe himself as having been in any physical danger in France. His self-authored 'revolution' was presented only as personal and poetic, never once described as militarily or politically engaged.

In May of 1792, Wordsworth writes to Mathews from Blois, claiming that he plans 'to take orders in the approaching winter or spring' in the hopes of achieving – as his friend Jones will? – 'a snug little Welsh living'(*EY*, pp. 76, 77). He adds that Mathews should not expect revolutionary news from him since, 'in London you have perhaps a better opportunity of being informed of the general concerns of France, than in a petty provincial town in the heart of the kingd[om] itself' (p. 77). By February of 1794, however, he writes to Mathews again, noting that 'What is to become of me I know not: I cannot bow down my mind to take orders' (*EY*, p. 112). By May, he commits his politics to paper: 'in no writings of mine will I ever admit of any sentiment which can have the least tendency to induce my readers to suppose that the doctrines which are now enforced by banishment, imprisonment, &c, &c, are other than pregnant with every species of misery. You know perhaps already that I am of that odious class of men called democrats, and of that class I shall for ever continue' (*EY*, p. 119). By June he claims to 'recoil from the bare idea of a revolution [in England]; yet, if our conduct with reference both to foreign and domestic policy contin-ues such as it has been for the last two years how is that dreadful event to be averted?' (p. 124). He is 'a determined enemy to every species of violence' and he deplores 'the miserable situation of the French' (p. 124). Robespierre, lest we forget, was executed two months after Wordsworth wrote this letter.

Wordsworth's self-dramatization in the revolutionary books of *The Prelude* derives partly from his need to cast himself in a role that will be useful to himself and to others, and partly out of his rejec-tion of his own earlier models of self-presentation. He needs to be a Miltonic poet who is also 'just plain folks' (the language really used by men, rustic speakers). He also needs to be a disillusioned revolutionary who has found a way to reinvigorate his life with social (political?) meaning in the wake of various forms of error and terror ('not from terror free' as the poet will remind us elsewhere). Dramatic self-projection is perhaps most likely to occur at just such conflicted moments in the lives of individuals and cultures. Individuals, like societies, remake themselves when stresses on existing structures force them into new forms of action or newly socialized structures of meaning. I particularly need to be a new person if I am going to try and make my way successfully in a new world.

The anthropologist Victor Turner sheds light on this process by noting how many social actions and interactions are forms of dramatized, Turner would even say 'theatrical', presentation. Priests perform their rituals complete with costumes and scripts, *mardi gras* revelers abandon their identities and assume temporary roles for carnivalesque purposes, and mourners speak and act out varying forms of grief at the grave side.[16] This is not to diminish the significance of such social performances, but to remind us that many of the details of social life represent a performance: how would a priest act; how should someone performing as a mother treat her children; how does a poet, prophet, or revolutionary set forth valid ideas in socially legitimate and lasting ways? This is also not to say that such performances are inauthentic or insincere. Mothers performing the roles of mother, poets performing as poets, politicians acting for the good of their constituents, religious leaders donning robes, masks, and music for the sake of their followers: in all such cases we see potentially authentic actions serving important functions for the individuals who are performing these roles and also for other individuals who are members of their audiences. This is no less true for the poet, for whom the performance is often private and textual, than for the more public priest or politician.

Wordsworth's accounts of his time in France, like his descriptions of the French revolution, are complicated by his use of a plastic and polyvocal version of his own identity as a first-person speaker. Dangerous political times always produce the need for secrecy, illusion, false representation, and confusing attribution. We do not have to 'lie' in order to survive such times, but we do need to control our representations of the truth. In Wordsworth's case by

1798, however, the problem is not political so much as it is personal and literary. He is not so worried about being sent to prison or accused of treason as he is about satisfying Coleridge and the new audience for poetry that the two of them have imagined. He also needs to write words that will provide financial support for himself and his sister. What can the poet 'Wordsworth!' say for the good of Coleridge and Coleridge's image of the 'philosophical' William Wordsworth? What can the poet of 'Michael' say that will express his debt to Dorothy while also helping them to pay their literal debts? How can Wordsworth satisfy the expectations not only of his family, but also of the London literary establishment, the wider audience for poetry, his political and revolutionary friends in England and France, and perhaps even his most 'interested' French reader – Annette Vallon? The 1805 text of *The Prelude* emerges as a complex textual response to just such questions.

Assuming roles is the oldest game in the world, but to call role-playing a game is not to detract from its seriousness. Donning masks is a crucial rhetorical strategy in imaginative literature long before and ever since the time of Wordsworth. Wordsworth's own attempt to produce an authentic and authenticating 'I' is more important to the history of such persona formation than has hitherto been acknowledged. The lyrical 'I' of *The Prelude*, particularly its earliest version (1798–9), is not unlike the voice in a dramatic monologue. To analyze the earliest draft of 'the poem to Coleridge' as a dramatic monologue will help us to consider poetic audiences, and their connections to speakers, in our wider assessment of Wordsworth's autobiographical practices. A careful reading of the two-part *Prelude* of 1799 will now reveal that the 'Wordsworth' who has had such a powerful influence on subsequent poetry is a dramatized rhetorical speaker as much as he is an accurate account of a unified 'self'.

3

Sounds into Speech:
the Two-Part *Prelude* of 1799
as Dialogic Dramatic Monologue

Wordsworth's two-part *Prelude* of 1799 is a poem about sounds and voices, about what sounds echo the voice of authority, and about how a number of voices contribute to the poetic making of a self-reflexive speaker who writes primarily for the sake of other people. The fact that the poem had its desired effect by 1805 – Coleridge wrote back to the author of the 'poem to Coleridge' with a poem entitled 'To William Wordsworth' – suggests that voices in dialogue are essential to our understanding of this earliest 'complete' version of Wordsworth's poem on his own life. Bakhtin claims that the 'fragments' of a life can mingle dialogically with the 'stories told by others' to produce an aesthetic object in which 'the hero of a life may become the narrator of it'.[1] In Wordsworth's case, this process is complicated by the fact that the stories contributing to the unified 'I-for-myself' narrative (the phrase is also Bakhtin's) do not always originate in human language, but in a series of human and non-human voices that create a dialogue within which the poet speaks by responding to other sounds and voices. A regularly sequential pattern (silence – sound – voice – speaker – poet speaking) provides a recurring model for the way this poetic voice claims to have gained the authority necessary for speech. The two-part *Prelude* of 1799 reveals how an apparently single-voiced point-of-view can emerge out of conflicting voices that vie for authority when any 'I' begins to speak.

Such an argument develops Paul Privateer's claim that 'Wordsworth's dominant voice – the 'I' authoring itself as a history and a text – can be distinguished from the various resources enabling Wordsworth to author himself'; the interplay of sounds and voices in the earliest narrative drafts of *The Prelude* reveal 'that a self can be materialized in or through language and several dialogic elements like echoes, reflections, imitations, multiple narrators, and different internal forms'.[2] In this sense, Wordsworth's voice is not a voice of personal authority so much as it is the echo of a matrix of forces – ideological, political, poetic, familial – impossible to fully recover or disentangle, but all contributing to an apparently 'unified' poetic speaker. This seemingly integrated voice, however, has important connections to the genre of the dramatic monologue. Wordsworth is speaking from an implicit – if internal – dramatic situation (how do I explain the growth of my mind?) to an unnamed auditor (you, thou, my friend, Coleridge) for a precise purpose (justifying my preparedness to write a great 'philosophical' poem that will be of use to Coleridge and others).

The status of the speaker's voice in this earliest version of the 'poem to Coleridge' has posed continuing problems for interpretation. Johnston and Magnuson, for example, both claim that the origins of *The Prelude*, like the resulting texts, represent an ongoing conversation with Coleridge.[3] Hartman, however, points out that Romantic writers generally see a danger in reducing 'imagination to conversation', in 'a dismantling of hierarchy' for the sake of 'a recovery of vernacular or conversational relationships', and Thomas Weiskel claims that 'to describe *The Prelude* as any kind of conversation seems perverse. Its apparent form is closer to monolithic monologue'.[4] Weiskel, of course, is discounting suppressed or hidden voices in the text, voices that are the source of the very energy that dialogic criticism reveals. If we read the two-part text of 1799 as a specialized form of dramatic monologue, these tensions in the Wordsworthian voice can be seen as part of a dynamic, if also destabilizing, equilibrium. The dramatic monologue, even though spoken by a single person, is often characterized by such an inherent instability in the voice that is speaking – even when that voice represents itself as absolute or authoritative.[5]

Wordsworth's autobiographical 'I' has good reasons for seeing itself as a conflicted voice seeking at least a textual version of authority. The 1799 version of William's life emerges out of epistolary lyric fragments (nutting, skating, boat stealing, snare robbing, owl-hooting boy) some of which are included in the longer self-as-author narrative, some of which disappear and reemerge as self-contained lyrics. The voice in these fragments modulates across a wide range of tones and postures: confident thief, terrified child, sensitive naturalist, thoughtless destroyer, social game-player, somber solitary. The text at once presents and suppresses a variety of conflicting anxieties about past, present, and future. Why did these things happen to Wordsworth? Was there value in these experiences then? Is there a value in them now? Has he been uselessly employed? If not, why not? Does it matter what his audience (single auditor or wider public) thinks of him, or are his own memorable experiences self-sustaining and self-justifying? Can his experiences be of any use to other people? What went wrong in his earlier life that he has now found a way of putting right? What went right in his earlier life that he is now in danger of losing? Is he creating his past, perceiving his past, or both? How is the act of explaining himself to his listener related to his desire to make his life into something useful to himself and to others? Wordsworth is like the speaker in many dramatic monologues because he is trying to *accomplish something* by way of his utterance; he is choosing to speak in precise ways for specific reasons. Like Browning's duke or Porphyria's lover, Tennyson's Ulysses or Tithonus, however, he hints that the 'I' in this poem is not in complete control of its own first-person narration or this particular interpretation of events.

Kristeva's claim, derived in part from Bakhtin, that 'any text is an absorption and transformation of another' is developed in dramatic monologues by the suggestion that every apparent monologue is already a response to other language.[6] More generally, every utterance – literary or otherwise – can be said to absorb and transform those utterances with which it stands in dialogic relationship; in Wordsworth's case such utterances (in dialogue) would include at least the words (or texts) of Coleridge, Dorothy, Milton (and other poetic predecessors), as well as Wordsworth's own earlier poems (ballads, Georgic loco-descriptive, ventriloquizing, meditative). The dramatic monologue and its related forms – dramatic lyric, mask lyric, monodrama – are paradigms for the way meaning emerges in all literary works. Texts reveal themselves, and their meanings, not as isolated signifiers, but as parts of a complex web of verbal codes and conventions that surround their precise rhetorical and historical situation. Why is the author speaking or writing at all, and to whom? How will these words be accepted, received, or understood by someone else? To whom is the author already responding? For what purpose?

In Wordsworth's case the achievement of a 'stable' – and autobiographical – speaking voice is connected directly with his own conversational and poetic exchanges. By 1798, Coleridge wants a philosophical poem that will graft unifying (philosophical) principles onto blank-verse Miltonics and powerful self-ventriloquizing.

Dorothy wants her gifted brother to transform his experience, and their shared experiences, into lasting works of art – the kinds of poems she says that she is unable to write. Other family members want their talented relative to prove his abilities in some socially acceptable and financially lucrative way. William wants to put revolutionary and personal despair behind him, earn a living, find a home, and write a work that 'might' live. All of these conflicting pressures remind us that literary language is always situated in a human context that gives such language less autonomous authority than it claims. Bakhtin's 'dialogics' and Kristeva's 'intertextuality' return criticism from a narrow focus on 'the poetic' to a context within wider social and linguistic systems.[7] Language is more context-dependent than the structural properties of literature often suggest. The concept of dialogism is important to our understanding of all texts because it weakens the independent power of authorial voices, monological speakers, and monoglossial utterances.

In this regard, the autobiographical 'I' in the early texts of *The Prelude* can be compared with Wittgenstein's critique of all verbal meaning. Wordsworth renovates his understanding of experience in ways comparable to Wittgenstein's renovation of our understanding of language as a transmitter of meaning. They both conceive of their task as a form of problem solving, and their methods critique earlier ways of evaluating experience and language, respectively. Philosophical problems, according to Wittgenstein, 'are solved, not by giving new information, but by arranging what we have already known. Philosophy is a battle against the bewitchment of our intelligence by means of language'.[8] Like Wittgenstein's critique of verbal meaning, Wordsworth's autobiographical practice employs what we might call a commonsense approach to autobiographical meaning. The powerful way that certain events affected Wordsworth (drowned man, ice skating, owl hooting, woman in wind, waiting for horses, crossing Alps, climbing Snowdon) is more important than any restrictive 'meaning' we (or he) might ascribe to those events. While Coleridge is seeking intellectual principles that could provide coherence for a vision of the 'One Life' within us and abroad, Wordsworth is simply saying: this is what happened; this is how it affected me. If I can connect with similar feelings again, memory can combine with my ability to make the past new and produce well-being during subsequent periods of crisis or confusion.

For Wittgenstein the path out of philosophical confusion lies in a clear account of the way language works, the way words are actually used: 'A main source of our failure to understand is that we do not *command a clear view* of the use of our words. – Our grammar is lacking in this sort of perspicuity. A perspicuous representation produces just that understanding which consists in "seeing connexions". Hence the importance of finding and inventing *intermediate cases*' (*Investigations*, I, 122). By 'intermediate cases' Wittgenstein means missing links, expressions that show us how words came to be used in different ways, cases where one language-use shades over into another. Wordsworth sets out to accomplish a similar goal in the 1799 account of his earlier life. He finds or invents – it little matters which – examples of significant experience that help him to see connections between his present sense of himself and that 'other being' from the past who employed other rules, another system, and a different 'grammar' for understanding experience.

For Wittgenstein, the meaning of a word is determined by its uses within a larger linguistic system; but meanings and uses can always change over time. The 'meaning' of Wordsworth's experience is likewise a function of the way he *uses* certain experiences in the poetic narrative of his life. We understand the re-imagined events of Wordsworth's life as part of a series of rhetorical relationships that are rendered artistically in order to accomplish specific literary goals. Likewise, Wordsworth's use of the first-person pronoun is connected to Wittgenstein's claim that '"I" is not the name of a person' (*Investigations*, I, 410). The 'I' that speaks *The Prelude* is only another word that gains meaning as a function of the way it is used. In Wordsworth's case, this first-person pronoun is a complex literal and figurative expression designed to accomplish a wide variety of poetic, rhetorical, and biographical tasks. Wordsworth invokes *The Prelude*'s 'I' in order to connect many earlier voices with a singular, apparently unified, voice of authority. In saying that the text of the two-part *Prelude* can be read as a dramatic monologue, I do not mean that this 'I' is not a version of William Wordsworth, but only that it is precisely that, a *version* of personal and poetic identity produced under precise conditions in order to accomplish specific goals.

Wordsworth's verse autobiography begins with a voice already in interrogative dialogue – 'Was it for this?' – and also with a natural voice; or is it just a sound? – 'one, the fairest of all rivers, loved / To blend his murmurs with my nurse's song' (1799, I, 1–2). A nonhuman murmur mixes with a human sound and sets forth the pattern from which the voice described as 'Wordsworth' will eventually emerge. The river's murmur is immediately described as 'a voice / That flowed along my dreams', a natural sound that makes a 'ceaseless music'. The effect of this nonhuman voice on the infant is described as remarkable. The river's sound

> with its steady cadence tempering
> Our human waywardness, composed my thoughts
> To more than infant softness, giving me
> Among the fretful dwellings of mankind
> A knowledge, a dim earnest, of the calm
> Which Nature breathes among the fields and groves.

(I, 10–15)

A sound that makes no rational sense is nevertheless able to compose thoughts, provide knowledge, and evoke calm. The tranquility which, according to the 'Preface' to *Lyrical Ballads*, is required before composition can begin is here connected with the precise recollection Wordsworth chooses – or creates – in order to begin the tale of his developing mind. Like any dramatic speaker, this 'I' asks questions that cannot be answered ('Was it for this?') and refers to extratextual events that only make sense within the dramatic context created by his words: 'Thou, my friend, wast reared / In the great city' (II, 497–8).

Again and again in the 1799 version of the poem on his own life, Wordsworth describes nonhuman sounds that parallel human voices and have an immediate and powerful effect on his growing awareness. The childish 'heart / Panted', the 'bosom beat / With expectation' until the thief of others' traps hears 'among the solitary hills / Low breathings' (I, 39–40, 41–2, 46–7). Hanging high among the ravens' nests, the child hears a 'strange utterance' in the 'loud dry wind' (I, 64), not a language he can understand, but a sound that betokens an apparently supernatural force. Wordsworth attributes these voices to 'spirits'; but, just as spirits are synonymous with 'breath' (*spiritus*), so these sounds are connected to the breath of the child (panting heart) and to the organic breath of nature (loud wind). The stolen boat likewise moves on 'Not without the voice / Of mountain echoes', a sound that gives way to an image of aestheticized unity; the boat is surrounded by echoes as it passes through rippling 'Small circles glittering idly in the moon, / Until they melted all into one track / Of sparkling light' (1799, I, 94–6). From a sound, to a sight, to a voice describing a sight that follows a sound: this progression establishes a pattern that will be repeated often in these narratives until an emerging Wordsworthian 'I' claims authority over its own perceptions.

The ice-skating scene is likewise filled with natural sounds that seem like voices. The skaters hiss, 'imitative of the chace / And woodland pleasures, the resounding horn, / The pack loud bellowing' (I, 158–60). These role-playing pursuers race 'through the darkness and the cold ... And not a voice was idle'. All of these sounds then combine into one sound that prepares the way for another Wordsworthian moment of visual tranquility:

> With the din,
> Meanwhile, the precipices rang aloud;
> The leafless trees and every icy crag
> Tinkled like iron; while the distant hills
> Into the tumult sent an alien sound
> Of melancholy, not unnoticed; while the stars,
> Eastward, were sparkling clear, and in the west
> The orange sky of evening died away.

> (I, 162–9)

The Wordsworthian child skates away from the social scene to achieve an even more powerful evocation of sound that gives way to another aestheticized visual moment. His spinning produces the often-discussed alteration of perceptions – 'the solitary cliffs / Wheeled by me, even as if the earth had rolled / With visible motion her diurnal round'; as his dizziness faded, he 'stood and watched / Till all was tranquil as a summer sea' (I, 180–2, 184–5). But the passage reminds us that such a speaker, describing such events, emerges out of the need to explain perceptions that seem unusual: low breathings, wind in the ears, a rising mountain, destabilizing dizziness. A visual scene or sound gives way to a voice, the voice of a speaker who is becoming a poet. In each case, silence leads to sound, and sound is then transformed into the voice of a poet who is trying to describe an experience. This new voice, however, is often the only sound amid unnerving silence.

'I would record with no reluctant voice' (I, 206), Wordsworth says, reminding us that any voice *might* be reluctant to say what it claims to know or feel. Potentially reluctant to speak for many reasons, literary voices nevertheless work to establish varying degrees of authority. Whether we see the voice of the 1799 *Prelude* as reluctant or not, the possibility reminds us that monologue is always conditioned by dialogue, created out of dialogue, and dependent upon dialogue. Speakers have reasons for speaking forcefully, reasons for remaining silent, and reasons for speaking with hesitation. Speakers' words are not just the words they want to speak; speakers may use words they are forced to speak, words they think they ought to speak, or words they know they should not speak, but speak nonetheless. Autobiographical utterances are particularly complex in this regard because they come into being for so many different reasons. We might say that autobiographers often speak too much because they have so little they can say with real confidence, or that they have nothing at all to say until they overcome their reluctance to speak.

The biographical and historical pressures that led up to the production of Wordsworth's two-part *Prelude* in 1798–9 provide a useful gloss on the rise of autobiography in the nineteenth century. As Bakhtin notes of the novel, such a genre arises at that moment in world history when a monoglossial world of isolated nation-states is giving rise to a polyglossial and multicultural world of nationalized spheres of influence. As a result, 'one of the basic internal themes of the novel', unlike the epic, is 'precisely the hero's inadequacy to his fate or situation'.[9] No single hero is up to the task of unifying the diversity of modern, post Enlightenment, life. Likewise, autobiography results from a need on the part of individuals to account for their emerging roles in complex new social structures and revised cultural expectations. For most of Western history, the need to justify one's place in the world was superseded by a sense that one's 'place' was absolute and determinate, socially irrevocable and theologically inviolate. By 1800, however, many individuals' 'places' become aspects of personal self-definition. Rousseau tells his life-story not only to locate himself in a complex social structure, but in order to explain how a uniquely valuable individual came into existence. And the concept of a unique individual only makes sense if each person is asked to account for his or her own existence in new ways. In Cartesian terms, I must account for myself; therefore, there must be a 'self' for whom I can account.

'Nor with less willing heart would I rehearse' (I, 234)

Wordsworth adds at an important transitional moment, suggesting
a link between his own authorial willingness and his ability to
describe the past. The past does not come back by itself; or, if it
does, its sources are liable to be hidden and mysterious. This claim
precedes a veiled reference to the lyric 'Nutting' – 'The woods of
autumn, and their hidden bowers / With milk-white clusters hung'
(235–6) – but the complete nutting poem has already disappeared
from the narrative text of *The Prelude* by 1799. These combined lines
remind us how much of any text is a matter of authorial willing-
ness; the autobiographer can insert or delete any details that serve
immediate rhetorical purposes. In addition, the autobiographer's
ability to revise, invent, or appropriate material from other texts
produces an author-as-subject who must also account for the
author-as-object. Wordsworth's phrase ('would I rehearse') invokes
a less-often discussed aspect of the self-life writing process. If the
production of a textual identity can be seen as a rhetorical perfor-
mance, then staged *rehearsal* of the details of that role becomes an
appropriate   metaphor   for   the   autobiographer.   Wordsworth
rehearses the details of one version of his past as a way of making
textual sense of his perceived role in the present. Drafts of such a
text are thus practice versions – tryouts, rehearsals – of a performed
textual self.

Bakhtin also reminds us that we must never confuse 'the *repre-
sented* world with the world outside the text (naive realism); nor
must we confuse the author-creator of the work with the author as
a human being (naive biographism)' (*Dialogic Imagination,* p. 253).
This is one of the problems with reading *The Prelude* as a spiritual
autobiography, particularly in its early stages. Wordsworth is not
charting his own spiritual struggles so much as he is providing a
textual paradigm that reveals how such a struggle occurs. Susan
Wolfson develops a Bakhtinian claim by arguing that *The Prelude*
'reads less like a "spiritual autobiography" and more like the
dramatic monologue of a poet struggling to compose his life in
such terms'; she sees Wordsworth's self-narrative as 'a poem of not
one but several plots, advanced by an interplay of voices rather
than by secure and steady government by any one voice, or *the*
voice'.[10] Wolfson's use of the term 'government' is particularly
revealing. Who governs the speech of any individual is as central
a question for Wordsworth by the year 1798 as the question of who
governs a nation, or a family. A democracy of conflicting voices
raises as many problems for the self-state of personal identity as a

democracy of citizens raises for the nation-state. The growth of any poet's voice is, in part, a story of how he came to authorize one version of himself, and of events, over another. Wordsworth hints at this selective process throughout the two-part version of his poem: 'I may not think' (I, 189), 'I might pursue this theme through every change' (I, 199), 'Nor with less willing heart would I rehearse' (I, 234), 'All these, and more, with rival claims demand / Grateful acknowledgment' (I, 247–8), 'Nor, sedulous as I have been to trace' (I, 375), 'may I well forget' (I, 379), 'Nor should this, perchance, / Pass unrecorded' (II, 426–7). In each such instance, the voice of autobiographical authority reminds readers that an author ('I') decides what to include and exclude, while other hidden forces – intertextual? subconscious? cultural? – are directing those same rhetorical decisions without necessarily leaving obvious traces in the text. 'I' describe the world in ways that makes sense to me, but I may not understand all of those forces that make me say what I say, that make me say what 'I' am.

Early on, Wordsworth admits that he must manipulate and evaluate the past in new ways if he is going to create a complex unity out of the conflicting – dare we say accidental? – sources of the powers he now wants to claim as his own. The details of his life, the poet says,

> were a song
> Venial, and such as – if I rightly judge –
> I might protract unblamed, but I perceive
> That much is overlooked, and we should ill
> Attain our object if, from delicate fears
> Of breaking in upon the unity
> Of this my argument, I should omit
> To speak of such effects as cannot here
> Be regularly classed, yet tend no less
> To the same point, the growth of mental power
> And love of Nature's works.

> (I, 248–58)

In order to narrate the growth of his powers, and the reasons that he now loves a vision of the world beyond his mind, he must break out of literary and generic expectations about epic unity in order to include details that would not traditionally have fit into such a story. In order not to overlook important aspects of his narrative, he must revise his sense of heroic argument and define a new kind of hero who is not composed of traditional aspects of greatness. This new 'hero' will be fashioned out of episodes and responses that do not fit into a 'regular class'. With this declaration in place, Wordsworth goes on to describe three events that help him to define a new view of the voice of personal authority: the drowned man of Esthwaite, the woman carrying the pitcher near Penrith, and the stormy hillside above Hawkshead. These 'spots of time' are significant, in part, because they do not 'explain' the precise sources of their power or their specific value to the poet's mind. They are important, but for unexpected reasons.

'I need a voice that can take advantage of the voices I have heard', Wordsworth seems to be saying, 'and of the things I have seen. These memorable events occurred; they affected me power-fully at the time. When I think of those same events now they achieve an even greater power, partly because they link me with my past, and partly because they remind me of – and help me to recreate – powerful feelings I had years before. Don't ask me what the drowned man means; don't inquire as to what I learned from the visionary dreariness surrounding that woman on that windy day. Don't seek to know why the single sheep, blasted tree, bleak music, and noise of wind and water bring workings of my spirit to me in later years. I don't know; nor do I claim to know. I do know, however, that these recollections were important enough to have affected me when they first occurred and significant enough to have stayed in my mind for decades'. A great deal of modern liter-ature arises out of just such a contention; the author (poet, short-story writer, novelist) records specific events that are hard to explain (in terms of their 'meaning') but impossible to forget (in terms of their powerful emotional effect).

For Wordsworth, this is the problem posed by the events of his own past. What is the significance of the 'loud dry wind' that blows through his childish ears high up on the crag? What is the 'meaning' of the drowned schoolteacher? Why should an unknown woman with 'a pitcher on her head' produce a memory now more valuable to him than any memory he records of his parents or his siblings? What is the significance of the objects that surrounded him while he waited for the horses that would take him home one adolescent Christmas time? The 1799 text of *The Prelude* provides little evidence to answer such questions beyond basic psychological associationism. The wind is important because it sounds like a voice and contributes to a memorable scene. The drowned man reminds the poet how many rural 'accidents' produce a wide range of feelings and mental images that seem to be permanent. The storm-tossed woman is significant because she participates in a memory so powerful that Wordsworth cannot find 'colours' or 'words' with which to describe it. The sheep, tree, and wall of the horse-waiting scene are memorable because they are connected with a guilty memory of his father's death (like Jungian synchronicity), and yet they are subsequently able to produce beneficent emotions. Even Wordsworth's attempt to unify such disparate experiences by way of a definition – 'spots of time' – only claims that feelings from the past come 'in aid' of feelings in the present if we allow memory to extend beyond the sensory to include the emotional. Is this any more than a common-sense insight? He remembers not merely what he saw or heard; he remembers how he felt. These feelings give him strength in the present, not merely because they can be recalled, but because the passage of time transforms them into 'far other feelings'. On these terms, 'spectacles and sounds' from the past combine with positive emotions in the present to nourish the mind and restore the 'spirit'.

We need little additional evidence to establish the dramatic aspects of this first-person monologue 'speaker'. The 1799 text is 'spoken' (actually written, then revised and read to Coleridge) in order to calm a generalized fear, to correct a possible mis-perception, to assure a listener, and to stabilize the speaker's sense of himself. 'I began / My story early', says the Wordsworthian voice, 'feeling, as I fear, / The weakness of a human love for days / Disowned by memory' (I, 443–5). My fear, as I began, was that the past might not be available to me in the ways I had hoped. Nevertheless, I planted 'my snowdrops upon winter snows' and you, the listener, 'my friend', will sympathize with my efforts even if 'I have lengthened out / With fond and feeble tongue a tedious tale' (I, 448–9). But my purpose has also been negative: 'my hope has been that I might fetch / Reproaches from my former years'. Why do I need to be reproached? I need a 'power' that 'May spur me on, in manhood now mature, / To honourable toil' (451–3). I need to do good work; this tale may help me do it; or, ironically, this tale may become the best work I can do. I still may fail, however: 'Yet should it be / That this is but an impotent desire'. I may not 'by such inquiry' be 'taught / To understand myself'

(455–6). Likewise, I may fail in my goal for you, my listener (Coleridge), who may not, even after these words, 'know / With better knowledge how the heart was framed / Of him thou lovest' (456-8). But even if I fail in these respects, my tale has another purpose, to bring back 'recollected hours that have the charm of visionary things'. In this task I must necessarily succeed, since it is my words themselves that recall and can produce 'lovely forms and sweet sensations'. My voice is finally the only power that can 'throw back our life / And make our infancy a visible scene / On which the sun is shining' (I, 462–4).

The Prelude's speaker declares his right to speak as a unified voice at the same moment that he records his dedication to a life of textual memorializing.[11] The young Wordsworth describes a specific day when he had been with a group on a fishing trip and then dined on a picnic supper near Coniston Hall. At this crucial moment in the narrative, the 'I' for the first time connects his adolescent emotions with feelings like those of an adult:

> It was a joy
> Worthy the heart of one who is full grown
> To rest beneath those horizontal boughs
> And mark the radiance of the setting sun,
> Himself unseen, reposing on the top
> Of the high eastern hills.

> (II, 156–61)

The emotional capacity of the adult is here described as superior to that of the child in a way uncharacteristic of Wordsworth. Why is 'worthiness' associated with a 'full grown' heart? Is William worried about his immaturity then (1784) or now (1799) while he is writing this account of the past? The recognition of the possibility of feeling like an adult gives way to a dedicatory moment that has important consequences for all subsequent Wordsworthian first-person writing. The conscious decision to *make* a memory gives birth to autobiography:

> And there I said,
> That beauteous sight before me, there I said
> (Then first beginning in my thoughts to mark
> That sense of dim similitude which links

Our moral feelings with external forms)
That in whatever region I should close
My mortal life I would remember you,
Fair scenes – that dying I would think on you,
My soul would send a longing look to you,
Even as that setting sun, while all the vale
Could nowhere catch one faint memorial gleam,
Yet with the last remains of his last light
Still lingered, and a farewell lustre threw
On the dear mountain-tops where first he rose.
'Twas then my fourteenth summer, and these words
Were uttered in a casual access
Of sentiment, a momentary trance
That far outran the habit of my mind.

(II, 161–78)

This passage has received relatively little comment from inter-
preters of *The Prelude*, in part because it disappears after the 1805
version and is only incompletely restored by 1850. But this dedica-
tory praise of a sunset represents the point at which the earlier
voices in the text are unified into a newly singular and apparently
integrated speaker, a confidently autobiographical 'I'.

The adolescent here claims that he is able, for the first time, to
self-consciously link his feelings with objects beyond his own iden-
tity. The ability to plan a future memory from within the present
moment ('I would remember you'), and the ability to imagine his
own death ('that dying I would think on you'), suggest that the
'soul' is now able to see itself as a unified entity. This new 'I' is
compared to the sun; it is a singular power, similar to the natural
light that illuminates the entire valley, filling the sky with a
'farewell lustre'. Words uttered casually at this moment become
crucial for a future benediction; what is now just a momentary
trance will go on to become a habit of mind. A second self –
'conscious of myself / And of some other being' (II, 30–1) – is becom-
ing the self of adulthood, a new voice that can record the passage
from that earlier voice ('some other being') to a new kind of
speaker. For the first time this 'I' can say: I will remember where I
came from; I will be able to recall events from my past. However far
I travel, however long I live, I will be able to return to this time and
this place in my mind, even at my dying moment. Such a realization

provides a new framework for the apparently unified voice of the Wordsworthian adult. This momentary trance at the age of 14 fore-shadows the mind of the emerging adult, just as the faint memorial gleam of the sun evokes memorials of a past that can now be enshrined for future 'renovation'.

The scene immediately following this dedicatory moment in the 1799 text fuses the by then vanished Boy of Winander episode, which was first published only as an independent lyric (1800), with another account of a powerful sound that echoes over a still silent lake. In this case Wordsworth describes an energetic and social group of young Lakelanders hard at play on the 'eastern shore of Windermere': 'And there through half an afternoon we played / On the smooth platform, and the shouts we sent / Made all the mountains ring' (II, 202–4). All good afternoons must come to an end, yet when these children row back across the 'dusky lake', they inex-plicably leave one of their number on a small island, blowing 'his flute / Alone upon the rock'. The effect of this scene on the auto-biographical speaker is as powerful as it is nonspecific:

> oh, then the calm
> And dead still water lay upon my mind
> Even with a weight of pleasure, and the sky,
> Never before so beautiful sank down
> Into my heart and held me like a dream.

> (II, 210–14)

The heart of the sensitive young mind is here paralleled with the bosom of the steady lake in the now-excised Boy of Winander lines. The 'heaven' that was received into the mirroring lake when those Winander owls fell silent is now like the sky, received into the heart of the observer. This adolescent hears a sound that causes him to pay close attention to the scene in front of him; at that moment we recall the maternal waters of the lake in both passages. The sound of the animate owls, like the sound of this human flute, reminds the human speaker that silence and dead stillness are the obvious alter-natives to a sound or a voice. But the sound we hear now has become the voice of a speaking poet, the 'Wordsworth' who stops hanging in silence at precisely that moment when he tells us – his readers – a story of hooting at owls or of his music-making friend.

Asking where this poetic self – this 'I' – begins is like asking to see the origin of a river: it 'hath no beginning' (II, 266). But the fact that a speaking voice has countless tributaries, eddies, pools, shallows, and depths does not mean that such a voice cannot, like a river, represent itself as moving in a precise – if general – direction. It is a mistake, according to Wordsworth, to try and 'parcel out' the 'intellect by geometric rules'. We cannot disentangle the individual currents of a thought any more than we can 'point as with a wand, and say / "This portion of the river of my mind / Came from yon fountain"' (II, 247–9). Likewise, the literary voice that now speaks as this particular poet represents a complex fusion of 'general habits and desires' with 'obvious and particular' thoughts that lack a traceable beginning. If there is unity in such a voice, it is like the unity of currents in a single river, or the countless fibers of a single rope. Wordsworth's voice is *his* voice, but it also contains the voices of others: Coleridge, Dorothy, Milton, the books he has read, the people to whom he has listened, the wind, those hooting Winander owls, and untold other voices and sounds.

After saying that this unified voice of authority has no beginning, Wordsworth then makes a series of claims that become the structural principles of his theory of mental development: 'I held mute dialogues with my mother's heart' (II, 314), 'I deem not profitless these fleeting moods / Of shadowy exultation', (II, 361–2) 'A plastic power / Abode with me, a forming hand, at times / Rebellious' (II, 411–13), 'To inorganic natures I transferred / My own enjoyments' (II, 440–1). The growth of the poet's mind is based partly on this shift from multiple voices outside the self to a unified voice that can call itself 'I'. In fact, the two-part division of the 1798–9 version of *The Prelude* may result from modulations in precisely the voices I have been describing. The voice of Part I recalls numerous auditory and visual events from the past; this voice can even offer a definition of 'spots of time' that articulates a value for such moments in later life. But we await the dramatized voice of Part II for an apparently stabilized 'I' that provides the developmental model of mental growth on which the entire poem depends.

'I held mute dialogues with my mother's heart': the blessed Wordsworthian babe learns to speak only as he learns to feel, receiving words 'nor so / Is satisfied, but largely gives again'. The words he gives back to others will eventually supersede the mute dialogues with the mother's heart, replacing the solitude of 'the quiet heavens' with 'whate'er there is of power in sound / To breathe an elevated mood, by form / Or image unprofaned' (II, 354–6). A voice is a specifically human sound that aspires to the condition of music so that restrictive aspects of form and image can yield to a form of communication that is more abstract, more direct, and perhaps less limiting. But such maternal communication cannot last forever. The literally motherless Wordsworthian speaker will stand 'Beneath some rock, listening to sounds that are / The ghostly language of the ancient earth, / Or make their dim abode in distant winds' (II, 357–9). There are silent human voices (mute), speaking human voices (dialogues), and even voices that have nothing to do with human beings. There are voices flung abroad in the sounds on Salisbury Plain: 'A voice as from a tomb in hollow accents cried' (81).[12] Or are those 'natural' voices from the earth merely sounds echoing in the poet's noisy head? Every nonhuman sound can at least 'sound like' a voice in the ear of a sensitive listener. Likewise, every sound can become part of a language as soon as consciousness transforms it into part of a distinctive first-person voice.

'I deem not profitless these fleeting moods / Of shadowy exaltation' (II, 361–2). Exalting is like exhaling. When the careful listener drinks in, by way of sound, 'a visionary power', the result is always an 'obscure sense / Of possible sublimity': obscure because the language can always be misinterpreted, potentially sublime because our highest moments are often composed of emotional feelings, not perceptual sensations or intellectual understanding. The traditional soul is redefined as the modern self in just such 'fleeting' moods. Such a state of mind produces a new internal spirit: 'Remembering how she felt, but what she felt / Remembering not' (II, 365–6). Here is the Wordsworthian story in a nutshell. My moods, *The Prelude* autobiographer says, are more important for having occurred than for any 'message' they contained: I have feelings; therefore, I am. On these terms, the speaker is always plural and incomplete; he is composed of fragmentary utterances of an identity 'feeling still / That whatsoever point they gain they still / Have something to pursue' (II, 369–71).

'A plastic power / Abode with me, a forming hand, at times / Rebellious'. This creative power is an actor ('acting in a devious mood') but also a version of the 'auxiliar light' projected out of Wordsworth's mind onto the world: 'which on the setting sun / Bestowed new splendour' (I, 318–19). The sunset that leads to Wordsworth's moment of dedication ('the sky never before so beautiful') was memorable because he *made* it memorable: 'Hence my obeisance, my devotion hence, / And *hence* my transport' (II,

423–5): my, my, *my* – the autobiographical speaker here acknowl-
edges that his own creative powers may be the source of all that he
finds valuable. The daffodils are memorable if he says they are. The
leech-gatherer is important if the poet claims him to be.
Wordsworth can make his spots of time important to you or to me
by describing the way they were important to him; such descrip-
tions, however, are not the same as saying what these moments
meant. On the contrary, the midnight storm that 'Grew darker in
the presence of my eye' is important precisely because it grew
darker in the presence of 'my' eye. If we hear in such lines Keats's
Wordsworthian – or egotistical – sublime, so be it. We are also
hearing the principle out of which most subsequent imaginative
literature in English descends: from Wordsworth to Derek Walcott,
from Keats to Seamus Heaney, from Tennyson to Toni Morrison; in
this regard, see also Brontë, Hardy, Hopkins, Woolf, Joyce,
Lawrence, Pynchon, Alice Walker, Achebe, Solzhenitsyn, and
Salman Rushdie. The postromantic literary creator takes moments
of personal emotional significance and seeks to transform them
into words with wider cultural value: that is what modern litera-
ture is; that is what it does.

'To inorganic natures I transferred / My own enjoyments' (II,
440–1): Wordsworth's cat is now out of the bag. The poet voices his
own enjoyments, and then he hears them echoing – like the
Winander owls – across the lake of his own experience. Is it any
wonder at this point that Wordsworth should see 'blessings spread
around me like a sea' (II, 444). The countless – infinite? – voices
(sounds) of nature can be imagined as a single voice if and when
the plastic power of 'my' voice says that they can:

> Wonder not
> If such my transports were, for in all things
> I saw one life, and felt that it was joy;
> One song they sang and it was audible –
> Most audible then when the fleshly ear,
> O'ercome by grosser prelude of that strain,
> Forgot its functions and slept undisturbed.

> (II, 458–64)

If all such voices can be imaginatively unified into a single
voice, then so can the numerous voices that contribute to an

autobiographical 'I'. I will not fail, our dramatic monologue speaker says, 'with grateful voice / To speak of you, ye mountains, and ye lakes / And sounding cataracts, ye mists and winds' (II, 469–71). Your sounds once spoke to me, the adult can say, and I will now speak back to you in a voice that is not uniquely my own, but is not quite anyone else's either.

The Wordsworthian autobiographical text of 1799 ends with a complex image of the human voice as a dangerous thing. The speaker of this dramatic monologue now turns to his silent auditor ('Thou, my friend'), reminding the listener why they are both hearing this poem:

> I speak unapprehensive of contempt,
> The insinuated scoff of coward tongues,
> And all that silent language which so oft
> In conversation betwixt man and man
> Blots from the human countenance all trace
> Of beauty and of love.

> (II, 500–5)

As Bakhtin and Kristeva, among others, have reminded us, there are untold amounts of 'silent' language in the midst of all the language that can be heard.[13] There are words felt but not spoken, words hinted at but never articulated. There are readings between the lines that can blot out possibilities apparently promised by other (nonverbal) forms of human communication. You say what you want me to hear. I say what I think you are thinking. I hear you say what I want to hear you say. Wordsworth's voice, however, is unafraid of such suppressed voices by the time he has finished this poem to his 'beloved' friend. He will speak to his listener, in this case Coleridge, in an effort to produce in him 'Health and the quiet of a healthful mind' (II, 510). The poet's voice stops speaking at this point in order to lead to a new form of silence, not the silence of death, but the peaceful quiet of a hoped-for personal and social health between friends.

We can conclude this account of the 1799 *Prelude* as a dramatic monologue by looking at two fragments of Wordsworth's Goslar writings which were later excluded from the two-part text. According to Jonathan Wordsworth, these fragments 'probably reflect failure to begin work on Part II, and may conceivably represent an early attempt to write an introductory section for 1799'.[14] The fragments are significant for the way they use a meditation on speech in order to justify a certain kind of poetic practice. Both passages also suggest – in terms of autobiographical writing – that speech (a voice that stops being silent) becomes one important means of stabilizing an otherwise unstable self. Why write any poem at all, much less an autobiographical one? The first of Wordsworth's fragments provides one answer:

> nor had my voice
> Been silent – oftentimes had I burst forth
> In verse which with a strong and random light
> Touching an object in its prominent parts
> Created a memorial which to me
> Was all sufficient, and, to my own mind
> Recalling the whole picture, seemed to speak
> An universal language. Scattering thus
> In passion many a desultory sound,
> I deemed that I had adequately cloathed
> Meanings at which I hardly hinted, thoughts
> And forms of which I scarcely had produced
> A monument and arbitrary sign.

(*Prelude*, p. 495)

The tensions revealed in this passage derive from a purely pragmatic theory of language use. My verse is like a ray from the setting sun, Wordsworth says; it sets up a memorial gleam by singling out a significant detail which then becomes, to my mind, a sufficient trigger for recalling an entire picture. But what looks like a universal language is in fact the isolated speech of a single individual, a 'random' point of view that may seem incomplete and arbitrary to others. My view of the poetically described object records its importance to me and reminds me of a 'whole picture', the majority of which remains undescribed. My 'voice', at the same time, creates the illusion of a language that will be understood by others. A more accurate account of this process acknowledges that my poetic bursting forth from silence produces not a sufficient memorial in a universal language, but the passionate scattering of many a desultory – incomplete, partial – sound. I thought I had used words adequately to clothe meanings at which, in fact, I had hardly hinted, Wordsworth implies. I thought I had produced a universal monument when I had barely created an 'arbitrary' sign. This important fragment should be considered not only by all readers of Wordsworth, but also by all readers and writers of autobiography. The passage not only reveals a poet doubting the efficacy of poetic language; it records an autobiographer acknowledging the difficulty of ever speaking in his own voice.

Wordsworth's second fragment describes the poet's work in terms of an ideal goal, while also hinting at the limits of monological speech. We want our language to be more than merely the voice of one person. We want our language to speak for more voices than merely our own. In what kind of work is the autobiographical poet engaged?

> In that considerate and laborious work,
> That patience which, admitting no neglect,
> [?By] slow creation doth impart to speach
> Outline and substance, even till it has given
> A function kindred to organic power –
> The vital spirit of a perfect form ...

(Prelude, p. 495)

'And I would give a substance and a life to what I feel' – 'To inorganic natures I transferred / My own enjoyments' (II, 440–1). The human voice represents an essential difference between the organic and the inorganic. The Wordsworthian speaker longs to give voice not only to the entire organic world (flowers, birds, trees, thorns) – but to the inorganic world as well – ('the loud dry wind', 'voices of the ancient earth'). Words take on an outline only when they are preserved; speech gains a substance only when its vital spirit achieves a 'perfect form' in marks on paper or lines of verse. We need to know who is speaking so that we can know how to respond. That is why Wordsworth is always listening so carefully. But however hard we listen, most of our words are wasted. The dissipating aspects of verbal selfhood – words that vanish into the air, sounds that disappear into silence – can only be restored when the voice that speaks becomes a voice that writes. To write a self is to become a self. To write a self is also to save that self.

What looks like the achievement of a secure voice in the first complete draft of Wordsworthian blank-verse autobiography is, in fact, the creation and discovery – 'creator and receiver both' – of a remarkably complex dramatic character: part voice in the wind, part Milton, part natural echo, part Dorothy, part 'howl along the Bothnic main', part Coleridge, part silent mother, part William Wordsworth. This new voice – this dramatic 'I' – echoes sounds of earlier dead and buried selves – the Winander boy, Lucy, Matthew, the Danish boy – for which the new voice serves in part as an epitaph. The epitaphic 'I', however, seeks to shed its social and historical specificity in order to achieve a more universal authority. The authorized voice of the 1799 self – 'Wordsworth' – wants to account for his turn away from the spirit of violent revolution, to thank Dorothy for her role in converting a paralyzed moral agent into the agent of a greater mind, and to offer his sick friend Coleridge a means of restoring the past for purposes of future benediction. It is to these other voices and tasks that we shall now turn.

4

Coleridge as Catalyst to Autobiography:
the Wordsworthian Self as Therapeutic Gift, 1804–5

In Malta in December of 1804, while Wordsworth was working on the extended version of 'the poem to Coleridge', Coleridge imagined himself to himself in his *Notebooks* as follows:

$$W + D + MW + SH + HDSC = STC$$

In this curious entry Coleridge equates his own identity with the seven human beings to whom he longs to be closest: William, Dorothy, and Mary Wordsworth; Sara Hutchinson; Hartley, Derwent, and Sara Coleridge (his children).[1] This notebook entry also suggests just how complete was the identification between these two poets in Coleridge's mind by the time he left England. But the 1805 text of Wordsworth's autobiographical poem points toward a similar preoccupation with a poetic identity conceived of in terms of another person. The expansion of Wordsworth's autobiographical work in 1804–5 reveals the important role played by the absent Coleridge in the production of an autobiographical epic which is a therapeutic gift from a speaker who is seen by himself and others as healthy, to a listener who is seen by himself and others as unwell.

Amid much recent emphasis on history, suppressed history and transformed history in the silences and the speaking voice of the Wordsworthian autobiographer, *The Prelude* texts remind readers that, while this may be a poem about 'Wordsworth' (whether we see 'Wordsworth' as singular or multiple, biographical or textual), it is also a poem addressed to Coleridge (however unstable 'Coleridge' may be) for purposes that can only be described as therapeutic.[2] Of course therapeutic elements of the poem may apply to both the author of this gift and its recipient, but the text of 1805 claims that the healing properties of these poetic words are directed solely toward Coleridge, the absent party whose presence is figured forth unceasingly throughout each of Wordsworth's attempts to narrate his own life. My purpose is not to restate dialogic elements of *The Prelude* that have been explored by much recent criticism, but rather to stress ways in which Coleridge's 'illness' becomes a powerful force behind the expansion of the two-part text of 1799 into the five-book poem (1804), and later, the autobiographical epic of 1805.[3] In this sense, the 'Wordsworth' of the 1805 version creates himself out of the need to be something useful to Coleridge. This 'Wordsworth' is an autobiographer, but he is also a potential healing force for his sick friend. At the same time, Wordsworth strengthens his own position – and gains a form of rhetorical authority – by setting himself apart from Coleridge. If Coleridge is as sick as he says he is by 1804–5, then perhaps a poem by a healthy poet can help to cure him.

'The poem to Coleridge' is a poem *for* Coleridge, a present designed to help return its recipient to health. But it is also a poem designed to show why a particular view of 'Wordsworth' is essential to a precise kind of psychic healing. As one version of this healing is said to have occurred in the life of the poem's author, a similar 'cure' may also occur in the life of his friend, if the poem's message can be properly received. Considering the text of 1805 as a therapeutic gift reminds us that the textual figure 'Wordsworth' sees himself throughout the poem in relation to an absent Coleridge. In addition, the figure of an unhealthy Coleridge provides powerful motivation for telling this extended autobiographical story in a specifically useful way. The generic complexity evident in the textual history of the poem – unconnected lyric fragments, two-part version of 1799, five-book poem of 1804, thirteen-book unpublished epic of 1805, authorized posthumous version of 1850 – is itself an indication of the need to consider Wordsworth's autobiographical texts beyond the narrow confines of traditional generic categories. Likewise, a poem about its author's identity that is also a gift to another person for purposes of healing (these are words that literally seek to make someone else well) forces us to consider some of the limitations of our ordinary conceptions of genre.[4]

Gift-exchange theory provides a useful model for thinking about the genre of 'the poem to Coleridge' on such terms. Marcel Mauss notes that the giving of a gift is often 'expressed and conceived as a sort of spiritual bond'.[5] In many societies, the giving of gifts creates further obligations on the parts of both parties, but the gift is also designed to bring benefit to the giver and to the recipient. Many gifts appear to be 'disinterested and spontaneous, but are in fact obligatory and interested' (p. 1), a description that helps to explain how a poem 'to' Coleridge could be, at the same time, a poem that enables Wordsworth to get on with a major literary project and to produce a self-definition that becomes useful to him in the future. Coleridge stands to benefit from receiving this gift, just as Wordsworth stands to benefit in different ways from giving it.

Lewis Hyde notes the extent to which all artistic products are gifts of a sort: 'works of art exist simultaneously in two "economies", a market economy and a gift economy. Only one of these is essential, however: a work of art can survive without the market, but where there is no gift there is no art'.[6] Hyde's point is that works of art enter their cultures as 'gifts' from the 'gifted', contributions to a wider society by those who claim to have something special to offer. Most often such gifts are given without immediate concern for financial reward. In this regard, it is 'the exception, not the rule, to be paid for writing of literary merit, and the fees are rarely in accord with the amount of labor' (p. 77). So the issue of artistic gifts arises at that point where writers, painters, composers, and the like, are willing to expend more effort on their productions than may be rewarded by the marketplace. In the case of Wordsworth's autobiography, as in many other poetic examples throughout literary history – 'To a Young Lady', 'To ____ ,' *In Memoriam A. H. H.*, 'To Marguerite ... Continued' – the sense of giving a gift to the culture, or to the already existing body of poetry, coexists with the fact that the poetic gift is addressed to a specific individual, often for very precise and personal purposes.

The poem as gift gains complexity in the genre of the classical elegy, where the poem is given to a person who is no longer in a position to benefit as an actual recipient. Milton's poem to Edward King, Shelley's to John Keats, and Tennyson's to Arthur Hallam, all employ the specific rhetoric of gift-giving, but in these cases the gift is offered as much to the suffering living as it is to the honored dead. In such examples of 'pure' elegy, the ritual aspect of the gift takes precedence over any utilitarian function; or rather, such a poem is useful to its author and its living auditors rather than to its ostensible (dead) recipient. In this way, the poetic elegy is similar to

flowers thrown on a grave, wake tributes, and other forms of ritu-
alized gifts offered to the dead in various cultures. In the case of
Wordsworth's extended autobiographical offering to Coleridge, we
find powerful connections to such elegiac presents. *The Prelude*, as
details of my reading will suggest, can be seen both as a gift to the
'dead' self that was the younger Wordsworth and also to an heroic
younger Coleridge: a figure who, by 1804, has been lost to illness
and the unalterable passage of time. By 1804, the youthful
Wordsworthian self and the healthy Coleridgean self are, literally
and figuratively, 'dead' to the world.

An additional complication arises for any living recipient of a
personally dedicated artistic gift. As Mauss says of many traditional
presents, 'the gift not yet repaid debases the man who accepted it,
particularly if he did so without thought of return' (p. 63). Of
course, Coleridge will 'return' Wordsworth's gift with his own
poetic tribute, 'To William Wordsworth' in 1807. But this return
poem will begin 'Friend of the wise! and Teacher of the Good!', and
go on to claim that Wordsworth's gift is 'divine', its speaker (*The
Prelude* had been read aloud by Wordsworth to Coleridge) a subject
worthy of prayer. Coleridge's 'To William Wordsworth', suggests
that the sense of obligation in this exchange was perceived by the
recipient as completely one-sided. Coleridge claims to have
received much more from Wordsworth's poetic gift than he will
ever be able to return. However reciprocal the exchanges between
Wordsworth and Coleridge may have been between 1798 and 1807,
the relationship was never described in terms of an equality of
concern. Wordsworth seems to have worried constantly about
Coleridge's physical and psychic well-being, while only Coleridge
worried that he could never repay William's gifts to him.

Wordsworth apparently had sufficient reason to be concerned
about Coleridge's health during these years. Apart from two
centuries of biographical speculation about Coleridge's state of
mind and body, Coleridge's own letters provide a useful rhetorical
tool for assessing his needy condition.[7] Between 1800 and 1805
Coleridge complains constantly in his letters about his health. Even
a brief and compressed abstract of these complaints is revealing:
7 January 1801 – 'I have been confined for almost the whole of the
last three weeks with a Rheumatic Fever ... my left testicle has
swoln to more than three times its natural size ... swoln Eyelids,
Boils behind my ears' (To Poole); 23 January 1801 – '5 weeks
confined to my bed ... I am weary of writing of this I – I – I – I – so

bepatched & bescented with Sal Ammoniac & Diaculum, Pain & Infirmity. My own Moans are grown stupid to my own ears' (To Thelwall); 26 March 1801 – Wordsworth pays off a £30 debt for him, and Coleridge writes to Longman, 'My Sickness has left me in a state of mind, which it is scarcely possible for me to explain to you'. By April he is contemplating death from 'a bed of pain' and complaining of 'irregular' gout. September 1801 brings 'Cholera morbus, or bilious colic', as well as 'scrofulous Boils and Indurations in the Neck'. To Godwin in November he is 'miserably uncomfortable'. He tells Southey that he dined with Davy on Christmas day, but returned 'very unwell' and in an 'utter dejection of spirits'. Throughout all of these letters he tends to connect his physical complaints and symptoms with equally unhealthy states of mind.

Early 1802 brings descriptions of improved health amid complaints about 'weak eyes' and 'weak Bowels'. By April he drafts the first version of 'Dejection' in a letter to Sara Hutchinson and the complaints shift in emphasis from the physical to the emotional. He has 'sunk low indeed' (7 May 1802 to Poole) wondering if he shall be alive in a year. In July he fears appearing '*irresolute & capricious*' to Sotheby and is 'better ... tho' by no means strong or well' in a letter to Estlin (26 July). On 1 October he complains to Sotheby again of 'low Fever' and 'deranged' bowels, both of which have left him 'very weak'. By the end of 1802 he describes his health as 'far, very far from what it ought to be'; to Southey on Christmas day of 1802 he has 'indifferent' health, a 'deeply ingrained, tho' mild Scrofula'. He is now imagining Tenerife in the Canary Islands as the only cure for his condition. He also begins to worry more intensely about finding a precise diagnosis for his numerous ills.

The year 1803, of course, is the year in which Coleridge's ailments become complicated by the specter of opium use and abuse. On 8 January he says 'O Southey! I am not the Coleridge, which you knew me. S.T.C.' By February he is discussing his need for red 'Sulfat' and 'Compound Acid', and telling Wedgwood that they should make a 'fair Trial' of 'hemp (*Bang*)', as well as 'opium, Hensbane, & Nepenthe' (17 February). By April and May the complaints include influenza and rheumatic fever treated with 'a grain of opium' and the making of his will. In a long letter of 14 August to Southey he is worried about 'frightful Dreams, & Hypochondriacal Delusions', 'atonic Gout', '*breezes* of Terror blowing from the Stomach up thro' the Brain', and 'paralytic

Feelings'. The first version of the poem that would become 'The Pains of Sleep' appears in a letter of 10 September; within three weeks Coleridge is using his gout medicine as a substitute for ink in a letter to the Beaumonts. By 3 October he is describing his ailments as 'atonic stomach Gout' and 'Mesenteric Scrofula', noting that on that year's tour of Scotland he was forced to part company with the Wordsworths because he was a 'burthen on them' and claiming that 'Wordsworth, himself a brooder over his painful hypochondriacal Sensations, was not my fittest companion'. Early 1804 only produces a litany of complaints that culminate with his departure for Malta in April: 'I have indeed been very, very ill ... the *primary* Seat of the Disease is the Skin' (15 January); 'I am more and more convinced that it is not Gout' (24 January); he is one 'of the sickly &c, who are long sickly' (30 January), 'harrassed in Mind & body for the last 8 or 9 days' (12 March), 'I have been seriously, alarmingly ill' (20 March), 'I have again been miserably ill ... but I am literally *sick* of thinking, talking, & writing about my own miserable Carcase' (26 March: all citations *CL*, 2).

As he leaves England for a healthier clime, Coleridge writes a letter to the Wordsworths confessing the complex relationship between his health and the Grasmere circle, most especially William. The letter is worth quoting at length for its revealing comments on the link between physical and psychic health:

O dearest & most revered William! I seem to grow weaker & weaker in my moral feelings and every thing, that forcibly awakes me to Person & Contingency, strikes fear into me, sinkings and misgivings, alienation from the Spirit of Hope, obscure withdrawings out of Life, and something that you have given to Mortimer, I believe in your Tragedy, a wish to retire into stoniness & to stir not, or to be diffused upon the winds & have no individual Existence. But all will become better once I can sit down, & work: when my Time is my own, I shall be myself again. These Hauntings and Self-desertions are, no doubt, connected with the irritable state of my Bowels & the feebleness of my Stomach; but both they & these, their bodily causes, are exasperated by the rapid Changes, I have undergone ... in the abrupt & violent Transitions from Grasmere and dear you to Liverpool, to London, to Drinkings & Discussings ... O dear dear Friends! I love you, even to anguish love you: & I know no difference, I feel no difference, between my Love of little Sara, & dear little John.

Being equally with me, I could not but love them equally: how could I – the child of the man, for whom I must find another name than Friend, if I call any others but him by the name of Friend – Mary & Dorothy's own Darling – the first *free* Hope of you all!

(CL 2: 1115–18: 4 April 1804)

In this remarkable outburst Coleridge connects his depressed emotional state not only with physical illnesses but with the 'anguish' produced by his love for the Wordsworth family, particularly William, the 'Hope' of them all, a person for whom Coleridge now needs a stronger word than 'Friend'. He is even willing to suggest that love for William and Dorothy – comparable to his love for his children – is part of what produces 'anguish' in him.

I recount this litany of complaints not to enter into an unresolvable debate about the precise nature of Coleridge's illnesses (nor their hypochondriacal or psychosomatic elements), but rather to suggest how consistently his welfare was an issue for the Grasmere circle leading up to the spring of 1804. On these terms, Coleridge's need for health is an often underemphasized factor in the growth of Wordsworth's poem 'on his own life' from a series of loosely connected reflections on the importance of memory (1798–9) into a five-book poem (spring 1804) and then a thirteen-book autobiography of epic proportions (1805). Coleridge complains unceasingly about ill health and its effect on his state of mind for over five years. During those same years, Wordsworth is struggling with the idea of the major philosophical poem that Coleridge has encouraged him to write, revising the 1799 version of the poem on his own life, and eventually expanding the autobiographical poem into a 9,000 line poem to Coleridge. Wordsworth may have written about himself as a way of encouraging himself to write a major work. His autobiographical long poem may be an antechapel to *The Recluse*; it may also in some sense *be* the poem on 'Man, Nature and Society', written by a poet 'living in retirement'.[8] But these autobiographical writings have another very practical purpose; they are produced, and even described by Wordsworth, as a sustained curative 'love' offering to a sick friend.

Wordsworth family letters suggest the extent of their concern for Coleridge by the time of his departure from England in 1804. Dorothy writes to Catherine Clarkson on 9 October 1803 that Coleridge 'is often dreadfully ill' (*EY*, p. 405). In January of 1804 she adds that she has not written to Mrs Clarkson because of the 'uncertainty in which we were respecting [Coleridge]'. William expresses particular anxiety about Coleridge's health in March of 1804 while finishing the five-book version of *The Prelude*. In a letter of that month, William connects completion of *The Recluse* with Coleridge's literal existence: 'I am very anxious to have your notes for the Recluse. I cannot say how much importance I attach to this, if it should please God that I survive you, I should reproach myself forever in writing the work if I had neglected to procure this help' (*EY*, p. 452). Within three weeks he reiterates his wish in a note that is, for William Wordsworth, uncharacteristically emotional:

> Your last letter but one informing us of your late attack was the severest shock to me, I think, I have ever received ... I will not speak of other thoughts that passed through me; but I cannot help saying that I would gladly have given 3 fourths of my possessions for your letter on The Recluse at that time. I cannot say what a load it would be to me, should I survive you and you die without this memorial left behind. Do, for heaven's sake, put this out of the reach of accident immediately ... Heaven bless you forever and ever. No words can express what I feel at this moment. Farewell farewell farewell ... We entreat you to write for ever and ever ... We shall be so distressingly anxious.
>
> (29 March 1804: *EY*, pp. 464–5)

In this same letter, Dorothy tells Coleridge that 'William has begun another Part of the Poem addressed to you. He has written some very affecting Lines, which I wish you could have taken with you'. She is referring to the extended meditation on Coleridge in Book VI of the 1805 version, lines she seems to feel would be helpful for Coleridge to have in his possession as he departs, because they are so 'affecting' and because he is in such need of improved health: 'Our hearts are full of you. May God preserve you and restore you to us in health of Body and peace of mind!' (*EY*, p. 462). The five-book version of the poem (1804) is clearly the text most directly connected to these concerns about Coleridge's physical and psychic health.

Wordsworth echoes Dorothy's request at the close of Book XIII of the 1805 version, when he cites 'a hope, / One of the dearest which this life can give':

> that thou art near, and wilt be soon
> Restored to us in renovated health –
> When, after the first mingling of our tears,
> 'Mong other consolations, we may find
> Some pleasure from this offering of my love.

(423–7)

Wordsworth's love offering to his sick friend is designed to present an account of the mind that is preparing to write *The Recluse*. Wordsworth claims that he can write the narrative of his own life without the aid of Coleridge; in fact, he had dedicated the autobiographical poem *to* Coleridge as early as October 1799.[9] But he claims to need Coleridge in order to write *The Recluse*, or at least to need Coleridge's comments on the apparently overwhelming philosophical project.

As Jonathan Wordsworth and Duncan Wu have noted, it is clear that Wordsworth's plan to expand the short poem into its five-book version was fostered by Coleridge's decision – around Christmas of 1803 – to go abroad for his health, and that Wordsworth's subsequent decision to expand the five-book poem once again occurs just as Coleridge is leaving England in a state approaching mental collapse. But Wordsworth claims to need Coleridge – or at least Coleridge's words (notes, thoughts) in order to write the ostensibly non-autobiographical *Recluse*. These important notes on *The Recluse* by Coleridge were sent to Wordsworth from Malta, but they were given to a Major Adye who died and whose papers were 'burnt as plague-papers'; Coleridge wrote this account to the Wordsworths on 19 January 1805; the lost letter was quoted by Dorothy in a letter to Lady Beaumont of 28 March 1805, six weeks after the news of John Wordsworth's death had reached Grasmere.[10] Wordsworth never received the desired comments from Coleridge, and he never wrote *The Recluse*. By late 1804, however, Wordsworth did have a very sick friend, and he wrote a long poem designed – at least in part – to help cure him.

A reading of *The Prelude* as a therapeutic gift to Coleridge can begin in the powerfully dialogic conclusion to the 1805 text. Wordsworth invokes Coleridge directly at this significant moment in the poem, noting the contrast between past time (1798) 'wherein we first / Together wandered in wild poesy' (XIII, 413–14) and subsequent years of 'much sorrow' and 'private grief'. Then, in the closing lines of the thirteen-book poem, Wordsworth speaks not of himself but of Coleridge's end, 'yet a few short years of useful life, / And all will be complete – thy race be run, / Thy monument of glory will be raised' (428–30). He also describes the collective wisdom the two poets have gained: 'we shall still / Find solace in the knowledge which we have' (435–6). In fact, the two poets are presented only in plural terms as the autobiographical epic ends. The story of Wordsworth's life is in part the story of what he and Coleridge have been to each other.

These closing lines describe Wordsworth and Coleridge as creators and arbiters of a millennial revolution in human understanding and sensibility:

> Blessed with true happiness if we may be
> United helpers forward of a day
> Of firmer trust, joint labourers in the work –
> Should Providence such grace to us vouchsafe –
> Of [humanity's] redemption, surely yet to come.
> Prophets of Nature, we to them will speak
> A lasting inspiration, sanctified
> By reason and by truth; what we have loved
> Others will love, and we may teach them how:
> Instruct them how the mind of man becomes
> A thousand times more beautiful than the earth
> On which he dwells ...

> (XIII, 437–48)

Such collective and plural wishes, however, are contingent on an earlier and essential hope that Coleridge 'wilt be soon / Restored to us in renovated health' (423–4). 'Restored' and 'renovated' – two of the most significant words in the poem on Wordsworth's 'own' life – are here linked directly to the well-being of Coleridge, the person for whom Wordsworth is imagining this version of himself and constructing this identity in a poetic text. My present understanding of my connection to the past, Wordsworth says, has helped to restore and renovate me in times of distress. In a similar way, this version of the growth of my mind records forms of self-awareness that can be a help to your ailing mind and body. What has been good for the healthy ventriloquist, Wordsworth, may be good for the sick philosopher, Coleridge.

'Restored' is, significantly, the same word used to describe Dorothy's return to Wordsworth's life in 1787 after a nine-year separation: 'after separation desolate / Restored to me' (VI, 216–17). This passage praising Dorothy, which leads up to another powerful tribute to Coleridge, performs some very strange rhetorical manipulations of the past. 'O friend, we had not seen thee at that time', Wordsworth says to Coleridge, recalling times when he and Dorothy and Mary shared pleasant walks together: 'And yet a power is on me and a strong / Confusion, and I seem to plant thee there' (VI, 246–7). His present feelings for Coleridge are strong enough to place a ghostly shadow figure amid memories of a time before the two poets had ever met. But why? The subsequent turn clarifies the need for this imaginatively implanted spirit:

> Far art thou wandered now in search of health,
> And milder breezes – melancholy lot –
> But thou art with us, with us in the past,
> The present, with us in the times to come.

> (VI, 249–52)

In an almost biblical cadence, Wordsworth describes Coleridge as being with them now as he was in the past, will be in the future, and as he seems to have been even before they knew each other. What is this powerful, magical force that can heal separations of time, space, and circumstance:

> There is no grief, no sorrow, no despair,
> No languor, no dejection, no dismay,
> No absence scarcely can there be, for those
> Who love as we do.

> (VI, 253–6)

Love may keep us together; but, Wordsworth's hope at this point is certainly wish fulfillment rather than a record of experience, particularly when we consider the amount of sorrow, despair, dejection, and dismay recorded in letters and poetic texts written by those in and around the Grasmere circle during the time of the poets' closest proximity: 1800–4. As for the stated 'absence', in Coleridge's case, it has been occasioned by illnesses of body and mind that prevent even such a loving group as the Wordsworth circle from remaining together:

> Speed thee well! divide
> Thy pleasure with us; thy returning strength,
> Receive it daily as a joy of ours;
> Share with us thy fresh spirits, whether gift
> Of gales Etesian or of loving thoughts.

> (VI, 256–60)

Our loving thoughts to you, Wordsworth claims, are gifts comparable to healing breezes. But these words as a verbal gift must be wish-fulfilling therapy rather than an accurate account of events; when Wordsworth wrote these lines in 1804 he had no reason to believe that Coleridge possessed either 'pleasure', or 'returning strength', or 'fresh spirits'. On the contrary, Wordsworth now claims that Coleridge's health is so damaged that death may soon be the result. The poem reiterates concerns voiced in William's and Dorothy's letters to Coleridge, as if to say: 'we care about you so much that we can imagine you here with us even when you are gone. We remember you so forcefully that you seem to inhabit memories of a time before we had even met. This poem William has long-since dedicated to you is a written embodiment of our loving thoughts that will restore your spirits and health'. But all this is a hope, not a guarantee.

'I would enshrine the spirit of the past / For future restoration' (XI, 341–2) Wordsworth says of himself in describing 'spots of time', and earlier: 'There are in our existence spots of time, / Which with distinct preeminence retain / A renovating virtue' (XI, 257–9). Spots of time are restored to us and then have a renovating virtue (the term 'renovating' replaced 'fructifying' and 'vivifying' in earlier drafts). Likewise Coleridge, in 1804, is beseeched to be restored to the Wordsworth circle in renovated health, a hope that does not seem at all realistic when seen in light of William's and Dorothy's fears for their friend's health (and even his life) during the time when the 'poem to Coleridge' was growing into a book-length account of Wordsworth's own life. Of course, the title to Books XI and XII of 1805, the most precisely therapeutic section of the poem, also suggests a significant link between renovation and restoration: 'Imagination, How Impaired

and Restored'. Imagination is impaired by a maturing tyranny of
the rationalistic senses and by a loss of the ability to connect frag-
mented parts of experience into meaningful wholes. Imagination
is restored by a renovating power that can link memory with
strong emotions. A sensitive mind can connect us to moments of
emotional power from the past; that power can then sustain and
nourish us in the present. At least so William Wordsworth says in
this poem on his own life.

We should also note the precise way in which Wordsworth imag-
ines his relationship to Coleridge in Book VI of the poem:

> How different is the fate of different men,
> Though twins almost in genius and in mind.
> Unknown unto each other, yea, and breathing
> As if in different elements, we were framed
> To bend at last to the same discipline,
> Predestined, if two beings ever were,
> To seek the same delights, and have one health,
> One happiness.

> (262–9)

But as these lines are penned, Coleridge possesses neither the
health nor the happiness that Wordsworth claims for himself. In
fact, during all of the years when Wordsworth is expanding the
two-part poem of 1799 into a five-book and then thirteen-book
text, he is striving in his own life to resolve precisely those personal
'anxieties' that continue to plague Coleridge: marriage, career,
offspring, physical health, emotional tranquility. Wordsworth
becomes, at least according to his own account, resolute and inde-
pendent during the years between 1798 and 1805. Even the death
of his brother John brings about a form of psychic maturation he
is able to describe as healthy. Coleridge, by contrast during this
same period, sinks deeper and deeper into a state of dis-ease and
disintegration from which Wordsworth's poem seeks to rescue
him:

> Throughout this narrative,
> Else sooner ended, I have known full well
> For whom I thus record the birth and growth
> Of gentleness, simplicity, and truth,

And joyous loves that hallow innocent days
Of peace and self-command.

(VI, 269–74)

By 1804, peace and self command are precisely those personal characteristics most lacking in Coleridge. If Wordsworth can *give* Coleridge the Wordsworthian past (or at least a textual version of it), Coleridge may be able to benefit from it – or from an equivalent version of his own past – in the same ways that Wordsworth claims to have benefitted. The healing record of such beneficent influences, of course, appears not only in the 'poem to Coleridge', but also in numerous other lyrics written during these years: 'Resolution and Independence', 'The Immortality Ode' and 'I wandered lonely as a cloud'. In many of these lyrics, Wordsworth offers autobiographically based strategies for dealing with the precise problems which – however much they may have plagued Wordsworth – seem much more threatening and long-lasting in Coleridge's case: despondency, melancholy, distress, despair, sadness, sorrow, isolation, solipsism, dejection.

Throughout the 1805 *Prelude*, Wordsworth refers to Coleridge's weaknesses and strengths in figurative images that are as conflicting as they are complex. At times Wordsworth seems to draw strength directly from Coleridge's powers of intellect; more often, he presents Coleridge's personal limitations in ways that produce rhetorical authority for the Wordsworthian 'I'. The stronger partner offers advice and counsel to the person who is described as the weaker partner in the pair. The figure of 'Wordsworth' gains power in light of Coleridge's weakness. In Wordsworth's long 'tribute' passage in Book VI, Coleridge is presented as a great intellect who now has legitimate reasons for an unhealthy state of mind. In revealing ways, the terms of this description – down to specific words and phrases – are dialogically related to the early epistolary drafts of Coleridge's own 'Dejection: An Ode'.

The young Coleridge, according to both Wordsworth's and Coleridge's accounts, often found himself stranded on the leaded roof of Christ's Hospital in London. From there, he had to close his eyes in order to bring back the world of his childhood, since only the vault of the sky could serve as a natural image in this starkly urban setting. According to *The Prelude*, Coleridge's London 'exile' gave way to a 'stormy course', the thought of which produces a 'pang' in Wordsworth. Coleridge suffered through a 'world of pain' and had 'ten thousand hopes' that are now (1804) 'For ever withered'. Coleridge may possess 'learning, gorgeous eloquence' and 'the strength and plumage' of youth, but the result of his endless 'subtle speculations' produces no benefit to either of these two poets of a new age:

> toils abstruse
> Among the schoolmen, and Platonic forms
> Of wild ideal pageantry, shaped out
> From things well-matched, or ill, and words for things –
> The self-created sustenance of a mind
> Debarred from Nature's living images,
> Compelled to be a life unto itself ...

> (VI, 308–14)

This passage is eerily reminiscent of Wordsworth's description of his own mind at an earlier, and less mature, stage of life: 'Mighty is the charm / Of those abstractions to a mind beset / With images, and haunted by itself' (VI, 178–80). The result of such a mental condition is that Coleridge is 'unrelentingly possessed by thirst / Of greatness, love, and beauty'; but Wordsworth's diction then goes on to claim that such a thirst is unlikely ever to be quenched.

In fact, the tribute to Coleridge ends by noting the pronounced absence of someone like Wordsworth earlier in Coleridge's life, someone with 'maturer age', 'temperature less willing to be moved', 'calmer habits', and 'more steady voice', who could have 'soothed / Or chased away the airy wretchedness / That battened on thy youth' (VI, 324–6). Coleridge's wretched condition has, according to this image, grown gluttonously fat on the withered hopes of a painful youth; but, a personality like the one Wordsworth ascribes to himself might have prevented such corruption from occurring. This is indeed a very strange way to announce that your best friend has 'trod, / A march of glory' that puts 'to shame / These vain regrets' (327–8). Wordsworth concludes the passage by noting that 'health suffers' in Coleridge, otherwise 'Such grief for thee would be the weakest thought / That ever harboured in the breast of man' (330–1). What is this weak health, however, if not the condition brought on by exactly the personal circumstances and constitution Wordsworth has just finished describing. What a curious form of praise for your beloved friend's strengths: if Coleridge were not so sick, the sort of grief Wordsworth feels for him would be ignoble. Under the circumstances, however, Wordsworth's description of Coleridge's weakness is completely justified. In addition, he has written a poem that may help cure this condition, a poem based on the therapeutic model of his own life.

A careful examination of the poem that Coleridge wrote in response to first hearing Wordsworth's autobiography reminds us of the extent to which 'the poem to Coleridge' was perceived as a therapeutic gift by its recipient. Coleridge first heard the complete poem read aloud in January 1807. The result was the poem 'To William Wordsworth: Composed on the Night After His Recitation of a Poem on the Growth of an Individual Mind'. The title may not indicate the precise status of this poem as a gift, but the published text of 1817 makes the relationship between giver and recipient very clear. Coleridge says, 'Into my heart have I received that Lay / More than historic, that prophetic Lay' (2–3). The 'Friend' and 'Teacher' of the poem's opening line becomes Coleridge's curative 'comforter and guide! / Strong in thyself, and powerful to give strength!' (102–3) by the poem's close. Coleridge also refers to the words of Wordsworth's poem as an 'Orphic song indeed, / A song divine of high and passionate thoughts'. Likewise, Wordsworth as autobiographical speaker is a 'great Bard', a voice among the pantheon of the 'truly great' who 'Shed influence' from 'one visible space' that contains a singular and unified 'choir / Of ever-enduring men' (*CPW*, pp. 403–8).

Even more revealing in this poem of tribute to Wordsworth, however, are Coleridge's comments on his own unstable condition at the time. Reflecting on Wordsworth's greatness produces, in Coleridge, a series of powerfully conflicted reactions:

> Ah! as I listened with a heart forlorn,
> The pulses of my being beat anew:
> And even as Life returns upon the drowned,
> Life's joy rekindling roused a throng of pains ——

> (61–4)

Wordsworth's therapeutic text produces a purgative catharsis; Coleridge feels 'pangs of Love', 'fears self-willed', and a strange

form of 'Hope': 'Hope that scarce would know itself from Fear'
(68). As he listens to Wordsworth's recitation of the uniquely
Wordsworthian childhood and maturation, Coleridge claims a
'Sense of past Youth', but of 'Manhood come in vain', a feeling of
'Genius given', but of 'Knowledge won in vain'. Youth and genius
may have existed in Coleridge, but they now seem to have existed
only 'in vain'. And even all the good he has received in 'wood-
walks wild', 'patient toil', and 'commune' with Wordsworth, now
feels like nothing 'but flowers / Strewed on my corse, and borne
upon my bier / In the same coffin, for the self-same grave!' (73–5).
In these lines, the poem 'To Wordsworth' – written on the occasion
of the first reading of 'the poem to Coleridge' – becomes, for a
moment, a perverse elegy on the dead-feeling Coleridgean self.

A praise-poem to Wordsworth, however, is not the place for such
pitiful self-loathing, as Coleridge recognizes in the next passage,
where he connects his own ill health with a psyche unfit to glorify
his friend's greatness:

> That way no more! and ill beseems it me,
> Who came a welcomer in herald's guise,
> Singing of Glory, and Futurity,
> To wander back on such unhealthful road,
> Plucking the poisons of self-harm! And ill
> Such intertwine beseems triumphal wreaths
> Strew'd before thy advancing!
>
> (76–82)

'Ill', 'unhealthful', 'ill': Coleridge describes his mind as barely able
to be cured, even by such a prophetic poem as Wordsworth's auto-
biography. You have felt 'pity' and 'grief' for me 'too long',
Coleridge says to Wordsworth. You had 'communion with my
nobler mind' before 'the howl of more than wintry storms'. And
now I want to assure you that the overall result of hearing your gift
to me has been beneficial: 'for Peace is nigh / Where Wisdom's
voice has found a listening heart' (87–8). Coleridge hears a voice –
as Wordsworth's Winander boy had once heard hooting owls – and
the result, according to Coleridge, is similar: 'In silence listening,
like a devout child, / My soul lay passive' (95–6).

Childlike passivity gives way to confusion, and to a momentary
'hanging' that once again recalls the Boy of Winander.

Wordsworth's 'deep voice had ceased' when Coleridge describes himself: 'my being blended in one thought / (Thought was it? or aspiration? or resolve?) / Absorbed, yet hanging still upon the sound' (109–11). Coleridge doesn't know whether Wordsworth's poem has made him think a thought, aspire to some goal, or resolve to take some action: he is left 'hanging'. This hanging – though it does lead to prayer – seems like another version of Coleridgean irresolution, and also like a poised Wordsworthian moment of psychic potential, not a moment of any actual fulfillment.

Even more revealing of Coleridge's attitude toward Wordsworth's autobiographical gift is an earlier draft of 'To Wordsworth', which was sent to Sir George Beaumont by Coleridge and first published by E. H. Coleridge in 1912. In this first version of the returned gift to Wordsworth (laboriously titled 'To W. Wordsworth. Lines Composed, for the greater part on the Night, on which he finished the recitation of his Poem [in thirteen Books] concerning the growth and history of his own Mind, Jan. 7, 1807, Cole-orton, near Ashby de la Zouch'), Coleridge begins with lines that connect the notion of a gift to divine spirituality: 'O Friend! O Teacher! God's great Gift to me! / Into my heart have I receiv'd that Lay, / More than historic, that prophetic Lay' (*CPW*, p. 579). Coleridge here joins the image of Wordsworth as God's gift to him with the image of the poem that he has 'receiv'd' into his heart. The 'lay' is prophetic rather than historic, we might suppose, because history is merely recorded while prophecy is more strictly 'given'. Prophecy, like poetry, is a gift that can be made use of by those to whom it is directed.

This earlier version of the poem to Wordsworth, like early versions of 'Dejection', included personal details from Coleridge's life that were excised before the poem was published. In the case of 'To Wordsworth', these 'private' matters describe Coleridge's anxiety over the fact that Wordsworth is worried about his friend's health. On the nights when Wordsworth read the dedicated poem aloud, Coleridge says he was listening carefully to those sections that were directly addressed to him. You spoke to me, Coleridge says,

> Me, on whom
> Comfort from Thee and utterance of thy Love,
> Came with such heights and depths of Harmony
> Such sense of Wings uplifting, that the Storm

Scatter'd and whirl'd me, till my Thoughts became
A bodily Tumult! and thy faithful Hopes,
Thy Hopes of me, dear Friend! by me unfelt
Were troublous to me, almost as a Voice
Familiar once and more than musical
To one cast forth, whose hope had seem'd to die ...

(*CPW*, pp. 580–1, 55–64)

This passage was dropped from the published version of 'To Wordsworth', perhaps because it links Wordsworth's concern about Coleridge's well-being with Coleridge's troubling sense of his own unworthiness. Coleridge also notes that utterances of Wordsworth's 'Love' produced in him a 'bodily tumult'. It is as though Coleridge does not want to accept the therapeutic aspect of Wordsworth's poem because it reminds him of just how sick he has been, just how much he is still in need of the cure the poem offers. This earlier 'To Wordsworth' clarifies significant lines in the final version: 'O Friend! my comforter and guide! / Strong in thyself, and powerful to give strength!' (102–3). Whatever Coleridge claims in the powerful lines that follow, he does not claim that he has received strength from the bard who may be powerful enough to give it. Coleridge ends 'hanging', then rising 'in prayer', but the conclusion of Wordsworth's therapeutic reading does not necessarily find the patient any healthier than at the recitation's beginning.

The poem to Wordsworth also reminds us of Coleridge's earlier response to another Wordsworthian lyric. As much recent commentary has noted 'Dejection: An Ode' emerged with a complex textual history in response to Wordsworth's 'Immortality Ode'.[11] We should also recall that the 'dejection' lyric appeared first in letters written by Coleridge that confuse not only the subject of address in the poem but also the status of the text as gift. On 4 April 1802 Coleridge sent a poem called only 'A Letter to ———' to Sara Hutchinson, referring to her by name throughout the text. On 19 July, however, Coleridge writes a letter to Sotheby, claiming that the same poem was written first 'to Wordsworth'. Coleridge adds that 'the greater part' of the dejection poem was 'of a private nature' (*CL*, 2: 814–15). In this epistolary version, Wordsworth is addressed by name in lines that connect gift-exchange with a central aspect of Coleridge's emerging philosophy: 'O Wordsworth! we receive but what we give, / And in our Life alone does Nature live: / Our's is her Wedding-garment, our's her Shroud!' The name 'Wordsworth' was changed to 'Edmund' in the version of 'Dejection' that appeared in *The Morning Post* on 4 October 1802, a day significant as the day of Wordsworth's own wedding (in his wedding-garment? his Blakean shroud?) to Mary Hutchinson. Lamb confirms this connection in a Latin letter to Coleridge of 9 October 1802: 'I am wonderfully pleased to have your account of the marriage of Wordsworth (or perhaps I should say of a certain *Edmund* of yours). All blessings rest on thee, Mary! too happy in thy lot ... I wish thee also joy in this new alliance, Dorothy, truly so named, that other *gift of God*'.[12] Lamb here puns on the meaning of Dorothy's name (God's gift), as Coleridge had done earlier. To give may be also to receive, but the giver must have something worthwhile to offer.

Ruoff is certainly right that the 'intertextual mission' of all of the texts connected with 'Dejection: An Ode' is 'largely to differentiate the poetic impulses, strategies, and practices of Coleridge from those of Wordsworth'.[13] But Coleridge sets out to do this at precisely that biographical moment when Wordsworth's poetic practice is surpassing Coleridge's in the minds of the two poets, and in the minds of their growing audience. Wordsworth claims to owe Coleridge a gift in return for what Coleridge had done for him in the past, particularly from around the time of *Lyrical Ballads*. It is in this spirit that he dedicates the poem on his own life to his friend. But poems that Ruoff, Magnuson and other have seen as Wordsworthian responses to Coleridge's texts – 'Immortality Ode' (1802 and 1804), 'Resolution and Independence' (earlier 'The Leech-Gatherer') – are themselves optimistic therapeutic responses to the negativity and pessimism posed by Coleridgean dejection and psychic isolation.

'Dejection' is particularly complex in terms of its status as gift because, as Ruoff notes, it was offered to a public audience much wider than a single addressee: a letter to Sara, read aloud to Wordsworth and Dorothy (21 April), described in lines to Poole on 7 May (*CL*, 2: 801), large chunks of which were sent to Sotheby and described as written 'to Wordsworth', two passages then sent to Southey, others to Thomas Wedgwood. Ruoff's extensive catalogue of these textual complexities proves the difficulty of assigning any specific recipient as the 'person' to whom this poem was 'given'. The combined texts, however, do show that only two people are ever referred to by name in the poem, at identical points in the text:

Sara Hutchinson and William Wordsworth (Edmund). The 'Dejection' texts also initiated a remarkable series of poetic exchanges between Wordsworth and Coleridge between 1802 and the time Coleridge left England.

Thus, by the time Wordsworth sets out to expand the autobiographical writings of 1799 – first to five books, then to 13 – he may need to give Coleridge a gift, but he also needs to help his friend get well. The text of the 1805 *Prelude*, in fact, begins with the image of a gift from nature to a human child, an inspirational 'gentle breeze' that 'seems half conscious' and is described as a 'welcome friend' (I; 1,4,5). This same opening announces a more specific gift – 'As by miraculous gift 'tis shaken off' – that removes the 'burthen of my own unnatural self, / The heavy weight of many a weary day' (I, 23–4). Who better than Coleridge could understand this burden of self, this weight of weary days? – no one. The real gift – as Coleridge already knows – is internal, not the 'wild water', 'green herbs', and 'fresh fruits' provided by nature, but 'a gift that consecrates my joy':

> For I, methought, while the sweet breath of heaven
> Was blowing on my body, felt within
> A corresponding mild creative breeze,
> A vital breeze which travelled gently on ...

(I, 41–4)

The fact that this inspirational breeze is described as a gift links directly to its therapeutic properties. The psychic breeze is also described as a 'power' and a 'storm' that breaks up winter's frost in the self, bringing with it

> vernal promises, the hope
> Of active days, of dignity and thought,
> Of prowess in an honorable field,
> Pure passions, virtue, knowledge, and delight,
> The holy life of music and of verse.

(50–4)

Such a gift, described in such terms, is surely a cure for what ails a sick poet. The 'glad preamble' ends by describing the gift of creativity as one cure for a 'frost' on the soul. The poem then turns to address Coleridge directly for the first time – 'O friend' (I, 55).

Within a hundred lines Wordsworth calls on Coleridge again to remind him of another truth about poets that Coleridge already knows: 'But, O dear friend, / The poet, gentle creature as he is, / Hath like the lover his unruly times' (I, 144–6). In fact, negative details of Wordsworthian self-description throughout Book I bear remarkable similarity to Coleridge's own self-description in his letters and verse. This poet – is it now Wordsworth or Coleridge? – 'had hopes' and longed to 'fix in a visible home, / Some portion of those phantoms of conceit, / That had been floating loose about so long' (I, 129–31). This speaker also has 'many feelings that oppressed my heart', and has 'been discouraged' by gleams of light that flash 'from the east' and 'then disappear'. This same mind longs to create a work that will live, as he longs to create a life that will work. But the flashes 'mock' him, leading his mind into a 'vain' wish – the desire to 'grapple with some noble theme', yet thwarted by 'Impediments from day to day renewed'. This composite Wordsworthian/Coleridgean speaker is 'meditative'; his only distress is 'his own / Unmanageable thoughts' (I, 148–50). And such a poet also has 'fits when he is neither sick nor well'. Are we hearing about Wordsworth or Coleridge here? Or are we hearing about both psychic sufferers?

Whether this figure describes Wordsworth, Coleridge, or a combination of the two, a more uniquely Wordsworthian voice emerges in the subsequent passage. The speaker is now preparing for 'a glorious work', making a 'rigorous inquisition' through himself, and finding that the news is 'often chearing' (I, 157–60). What gives this newly optimistic poet cause for hope? Once again it is a gift. He does not lack 'that first great gift, the vital soul' (161). In addition, this productive poet possesses 'general truths', 'external things, / Forms, images', and a keen sense of 'Time, place, and manners' (169). All of these possessions will help him tell, not a story of Britain's greatness, or a 'Romantic tale by Milton left unsung' (180), but a 'tale from my own heart, more near akin / To my own passions and habitual thoughts, / Some variegated story, in the main / Lofty, with interchange of gentler things' (I, 221–4). And how does one get the 'vital soul' necessary for such a task? How does one disperse the 'phantoms' that have 'oppressed' the heart? How does one cure his ills sufficiently to write poetry? How might Coleridge accomplish these tasks? Wordsworth is about to tell him.

The key to poetic creativity, Wordsworth says, while invoking his own narrative beginnings ('Was it for this'), is likewise connected to an act of selfless giving. He will succeed in his task, he claims at the close of his long introduction (I, 1–271), if he takes seriously the advice proffered in 'Dejection': if he receives but as he gives. If he is like a 'false steward who hath much received', but who 'renders nothing back' (270–1), then all he can hope for is 'indolence from vain perplexity, / Unprofitably travelling toward the grave' (268–9). If the poet wants more, he must give back; and, at precisely this moment Wordsworth does begin to give back, with a gift that is also a text: 'Was it for this / That one, the fairest of all rivers, loved / To blend his murmurs with my nurse's song' (I, 272–4).

Gift-exchange theory thus provides a useful model for clarifying the referent of Wordsworth's opening question, a question that has received much recent critical commentary.[14] 'Was it for this …?' Was it to make him the person he is now that these influences were given to him? Yes. Was it so that he could render something back artistically for all that he has received from 'nature' over the years? Yes. Was it so that he could learn 'the bond of union betwixt life and joy' (585) and be able to convey the advantages of that message to others? Yes. Was it so that he could give thanks to Dorothy for all that she has meant to him during his emerging adulthood? Yes. Was it so that Coleridge could be cured by Wordsworth's example? That is what Wordsworth hopes.

The close of Book I links Wordsworth's poetic task with Coleridge's health in figurative ways that connect the giving of gifts to the curing of ills. You will not see this 'tedious tale' (the first of thirteen books?) as a waste of time, Wordsworth says to his 'friend', because you – of all people – understand my own need to 'fix the wavering balance of my mind' (650). Nor will Coleridge pass 'harsh judgments' on his friend, because he understands the two stated purposes of Wordsworth's poem: I want to 'be taught / To understand myself', Wordsworth says, and I also want you 'to know / With better knowledge how the heart was framed / Of him thou lovest' (654–7). But the singular pronouns ('thee' and 'I') give way to plural pronouns when Wordsworth states the therapeutic effect of his poetic method. He is now 'loth to quit' the process whereby he can produce for himself and his friend

> Those recollected hours that have the charm
> Of visionary things, and lovely forms

And sweet sensations, that throw back our life
And almost make our infancy itself
A visible scene on which the sun is shining ...

(I, 659–63)

This comes at the close of a passage that had been addressed to 'thee, my friend' (645). Wordsworth's verse can poetically give Coleridge a common past they never actually shared; this imagined textual construct may then offer a visionary history and a health-restoring account of personal and poetic identity for the two friends.

'Certain hopes are with me that to thee / This labour will be welcome, honoured friend' (I, 674–5), Wordsworth concludes. A reading of *The Prelude* as a therapeutic gift rests partly on our inter-pretation of these unnamed but 'certain' hopes. Wordsworth hopes that his story will help himself, but he also hopes that his story will help his friend. He cannot, however, confess the full extent of his personal motivations for writing his 'gift' autobiography; to do so would be to admit the seriousness of Coleridge's illness and concurrent need for a cure. By 1804, however, Coleridge does need this text and its message of self-renovation as much, if not more, than Wordsworth ever needed it. The love offering to Coleridge, read aloud in 1807, is never published during either of their life-times. Even its success as a therapeutic gift is dubious: Coleridge never fully achieved the level of physical and psychic health that Wordsworth wished for him. Likewise, the estrangement of the two poets around 1810 was only partially reconciled by the passage of decades.

Nevertheless, the poem we think of as the poem on Wordsworth's 'own' life is just as importantly the poem *for* Coleridge, a textual attempt by Wordsworth to make a sick friend well. Wordsworth describes his own life in such a way as to make his life useful to another, and perhaps to many others. 'Restored to us in renovated health': that's what William and Dorothy say they want for their beloved Coleridge. Out of that same desire, Wordsworth creates the myth of a poetic past that can be restored in times of personal distress by way of renovating lines of autobio-graphical verse. Wordsworth, as John Stuart Mill will later acknowledge, offers a textual version of his own emotional life, a poetic gift that can be of powerful therapeutic value to others.

5

Dialogizing Dorothy:
Voicing the Feminine as Spousal Sister in *The Prelude*

Amid all the discussion of the presence and absence of Coleridge in Wordsworth's autobiographical epic, much less attention has been paid to the role of Dorothy Wordsworth as a suppressed and speaking voice at crucial moments in the texts that become the poem on her brother's life. While *The Prelude* may be a poem to Coleridge, it is also a poem for Dorothy, and the difference between these two prepositions generates important dialogical energy and expressive rhetoric in the palimpsest that forms Wordsworth's verse life-story. Dorothy helps figure forth a whole range of Wordsworthian women imbedded in various drafts of various poems, from lost children to mad mothers, from Julia to the Maid of Buttermere, from abandoned Annette to the spousal Mary. My emphasis suggests, at least in part, that we take seriously the Wordsworth who, in June of 1832, described Coleridge and Dorothy as 'the two Beings to whom my intellect is most indebted' (*LY*, 2: 536). My purpose is neither to offer another appreciation of Dorothy's role in Wordsworth's domestic arrangements, nor to stress a biographically based reading of specific scenes. Rather, I suggest that Wordsworth figures forth the feminine – and produces important rhetorical power in his most self-creating text – out of a conversation with Dorothy's texts and her 'wise' (and surprisingly active) 'passiveness'.

The feminine in Wordsworth's writing has received increased attention, but less often has Dorothy been discussed as a crucial – if often hidden – presence in the *Prelude*. In recent years, Wordsworth's autobiographical epic has most often been seen as a dialogue with Coleridge or through the complexities of self-life writing and revisionary poststructuralist critiques of verbal authority.[1] Dorothy has become a subject of energetic critical discussion, most often in an effort to reread her texts through feminist theory and thereby position her in a tradition of female romanticism designed to correct the last vestiges of logocentric patriarchy in romantic studies.[2] But readings of *The Prelude* must also acknowledge that William's rhetorical and psychological debt to his sister is potentially more complex than previous accounts of their sibling relationship have suggested. Wordsworth finds a way to speak about himself in 1798–9 partly by incorporating a version of his sister into the voice that is speaking for him. By the time he completes the ego-epic version of 1805, he has produced a therapeutic document for Coleridge. But this text also connects the speaker's voice directly with Dorothy. The speaker of the 1805 poem represents himself as a feminized male voice with links to the mother, to a feminized 'Nature', and to a psychic 'cure' that his account of his own mental development embodies in language. Traces of this feminized figure are evident in details of William and Dorothy's life together that would cause him, decades later, to refer to his sister as a primary source of his 'intellect'. We can profitably connect Wordsworthian ideas of the feminine to Dorothy in the multi-voiced, ostensibly first-person, speaker of *The Prelude*.

In referring to Dorothy as a spousal sister, I do not want to stress incestuous implications of this sibling relationship, but to emphasize the etymology of 'espoused': to be pledged, to be spoken for by another, to have mutual claim on one another *(OED)*. This description certainly characterizes William and Dorothy by the winter of 1798–9, when the first fragments of self-conscious autobiography began emerging in jointly composed letters to Coleridge. At times in the Goslar letters it is hard to distinguish the poet who is composing lyrical fragments of a version of his life from the sister who is recording his efforts to do so. Many of the letters are jointly signed. Many of the passages are written as though the plural pronoun is singular. In the epistolary origins of 'the poem to Coleridge' it is difficult to say who is speaking for whom, writing for whom, or providing this account of events for the Wordsworths' absent friend.

In the winter of 1798–9, William claims that he is unable to learn German, that he cannot get his hands on books to read, and so out of 'self-defense' (a very curious choice of words) he begins penning lyrics about simple childhood memories: ice-skating (which Coleridge had also described in an earlier letter from Ratzeburg), boat-stealing, because Coleridge is living by a lake: a lyrical passage which Dorothy says she may detach from 'the mass of what

William has written' (*EY*, p. 240), and nutting – because it describes a scene in the north of England where, Dorothy says, they must all meet again to 'explore together every nook of that romantic country' (*EY*, p. 241).[3] Thus begins an autobiography on which Wordsworth will work for five decades, a text that will come to be identified by many readers as this poet's most important work, a 9,000 line poem that is perhaps the last self-conscious epic in the English language.

The letter in which these first fragments of autobiography appear was written as an undated correspondence of December 1798 or January 1799 and, though all in Dorothy's hand, it includes direct dictation from William. Wordsworth announces the autobiographical passages as part of his explanation of the origins of this letter to Coleridge: 'Dorothy has written the other side of this sheet while I have been out. She has transcribed a few descriptions' (*EY*, p. 236). Early drafts of two Lucy poems and several autobiographical fragments follow, separated by a comment of Dorothy's that includes another clarification in case Coleridge is still confused: 'The next poem is a favorite of mine – i.e. of me, Dorothy' (*EY*, p. 237). This recurrent need to distinguish the siblings' confusing use of pronouns helps to explain Coleridge's first comment about Wordsworth's relationship to the figure of Lucy: 'Most probably, in some gloomier moment he had fancied the moment in which his Sister might die' (*CL*, 1: 479, 6 April 1799). The entire letter from William and Dorothy was written in response to a letter in which Coleridge had exclaimed in hexameters, 'William, my head and my heart! dear William and dear Dorothea! / You have all in each other; but I am lonely, and want you!' (*CL*, 1: 452). Separated by the cold German winter and strained finances, the friends remain in dialogue about their emotional need for one another and their ability to support each other's scholarly and literary projects.

The undated letter from the Wordsworths includes lines that would later become 'Nutting', a fragmentary lyric that never appeared in any version of the long autobiographical poem. The lines begin with a 'quaint' figure who is disguised in 'beggar's weeds' on the advice of a 'frugal dame'. The lyric goes on to present, as many critics have noted, a narrative that is supercharged with a sexualized view of nature and unexpected reversals of gender expectations.[4] The male figure is passively 'led' by 'guardian spirits' and, when he reaches the 'virgin scene', his first response is a 'wise restraint / Voluptuous' with which he eyes 'the banquet'. He sits 'among the flowers' and hears 'the murmur and the murmuring sound / In that sweet mood when pleasure loves to pay / Tribute to ease'. In this same mood, however, the male speaker suddenly rises up and drags 'to earth both branch and bough with crash / And merciless ravage' (*EY*, pp. 241–2). The nut-picker as fell destroyer learns his lesson, however, when he feels a 'sense of pain' while looking at the 'silent trees and the intruding sky', even as he is 'Exulting, rich beyond the wealth of kings' because of his destructiveness.

The gender implications that close this lyric are particularly confusing. The speaker (William?) requests the 'dearest Maiden' (Dorothy?) to 'move along these shades / In gentleness of heart; with gentle hand / Touch, for there is a spirit in the woods'. But such a feminine figure has been associated with gentleness earlier in the poem in the speaker's, as in the reader's, mind. Likewise, the speaker already knows that there is a spirit in the woods, since he claims to have been led to this bower by 'guardian spirits'. The lyric sets forth a strange interaction between male and female, in which the male figure appropriates the lesson of the feminine early in the poem (what clothes to wear) and late (how to move in and how to touch the woods). At the same time, however, the speaker must act as though a purely masculine transgression has conveyed a lesson that he must now teach to a woman. The male seems to have learned what the female already knows. The female figure may already understand what nature has to teach, but the male speaker still claims the authority to remind this silent female to be gentle.

Particularly interesting in this regard is Wordsworth's later distancing of himself from this richly suggestive lyric. Commenting to Isabella Fenwick, he said that the lines on nutting were 'intended as part of a poem on my own life, but struck out as not being wanted there' (*PW*, 2: 504). Why Wordsworth would not see this lyric as appropriate for *The Prelude* remains tantalizingly unclear. Was it the pantheism of these nature spirits? Was it the admission of his own destructive tendencies in the first-person, as 'I'? We cannot know; but 'Nutting' does hint at two important ideas that will be developed later in the book-length poem: female figures already embody many of the lessons that nature seems to be teaching to the male speaker. In addition, to be a good man, or brother, or poet, may require that the male become more like a female or sister, or journal writer.

By the time they were living together in Germany, Dorothy and

William saw themselves as essential to each other's existence. They spoke to one another in letters, poems, and journal entries in consistently loving and intimate terms. They lived together almost continuously from 1795 until the end of William's life. They traveled to Germany in 1798, to France to see Annette and Caroline in 1802, and to Scotland in 1803 without Mary. Wordsworth also claims, in the 1805 version of the poem, that it was *solely* Dorothy who 'Maintained for me a saving intercourse / With my true self' (X, 914–15) at a time when 'I' had 'lost / All feeling of conviction' and 'Sick, wearied out with contrarieties, / Yielded up moral questions in despair' (X, 897–900). Indeed, Wordsworth closes the first book-length account of the growth of his own mind with a tribute to what James Joyce will later call 'the new womanly man', a feminized figure that links an imaginative projection of maternal nourishment with William's experience of his unmarried sister:

> And he whose soul hath risen
> Up to the height of feeling intellect
> Shall want no humbler tenderness, his heart
> Be tender as a nursing mother's heart;
> Of female softness shall his life be full,
> Of little loves and delicate desires,
> Mild interests and gentlest sympathies.

(XIII, 204–10)

However we might critique the ideology of a passage that links softness, littleness, delicacy, mildness, and gentleness with the feminine, we cannot deny the syntactic association of these feminine characteristics with the heroic and poetic mind that is chronicled throughout Wordsworth's autobiographical narrative.

Nor can we deny that Dorothy was one source of the connection between the womanly and this new version of the manly since Wordsworth immediately goes on to say that she is:

> Child of my parents, sister of my soul,
> Elsewhere have strains of gratitude been breathed
> To thee for all the early tenderness
> Which I from thee imbibed.

(XIII, 211–14)

This early tenderness from Dorothy later came to Wordsworth's aid, he says, in order to 'soften down' an 'over-sternness' and a 'countenance severe'. Wordsworth's extended tribute to Dorothy may strike some contemporary readers as a clichéd masculine response to culturally constructed gender expectations. What is more important to my argument is the role of this tenderness in creating Wordsworth's sense of the 'I' that was speaking throughout the poem on his own early life. As the Wordsworthian speaker goes on to say, Dorothy's effect on his soul ('it') was as permanent as it was profound:

> But thou didst plant its crevices with flowers,
> Hang it with shrubs that twinkle in the breeze,
> And teach the little birds to build their nests
> And warble in its chambers.

> (XIII, 233–6)

Dorothy's 'breath', this passage concludes, 'was a kind of gentler spring / That went before my steps' (XIII, 244–6). In this image, the 'egotistical' autobiographer presents Dorothy as a source of psychic nourishment who gave him a more complete awareness of himself and his surroundings than had been offered by his solitary childhood or his maturing male consciousness.

But the male figure that imbibes 'early tenderness' is also evident in other passages that connect the ability to 'drink in' pleasure from natural beauty with the power of a more precisely maternal feminine. 'I held unconscious intercourse / With the eternal beauty, drinking in / A pure organic pleasure from the lines / Of curling mist, or from the level plain' (1805, I, 589–92). The often discussed 'blest the babe / Nursed in his mother's arms' (II, 239–40) passage claims that the imaginative ability to hold disparate sensations together, and thereby to establish relational meaning, derives from a feminine 'virtue which irradiates and exalts / All objects through all intercourse of sense' (II, 259–60).[5] What the child gains in both of these images is the ability to absorb from the maternal figure a form of psychic nourishment that will eventually serve to restore the adult. Such restoration is always identified with emotions, with a 'passion' that creates the ability to link 'feelings' with external forms. The child's mind becomes 'an agent of the one great mind' (II, 272), a mind clearly identified with the maternal presence embodied in 'the first / Poetic spirit of our human life' (II, 275–6). Wordsworth's poetic spirit arises not in solipsistic isolation but from the ability through which 'by intercourse of touch / I held mute dialogues with my mother's heart' (II, 283–4). Likewise, the 'corresponding mild creative breeze / A vital breeze which travelled gently on' (I, 43–4) sustaining the poet's creative powers, echoes the therapeutic gift William claims to have received early from his mother and later from Dorothy.

Discussions of gender in Wordsworth have often emphasized his tendency to first identify the feminine as 'other', then externalize the maternal as 'Nature', and finally seek to appropriate the objectified feminine for purposes of the dominant masculine voice.[6] Wordsworth does distinguish the voice of consciousness from unconscious nature – often identified with voiceless females or nonhuman voices (wind, rain). He also describes his childhood male consciousness as solitary, brooding, and deceitful. But as often as Wordsworth's poetic texts objectify the feminine, they identify the voice of the speaker with forces or voices that are culturally and textually linked to female subjectivity. In this sense, Wordsworth's own 'voice' partakes of and shapes itself out of the feminine to a greater extent than has been fully acknowledged. This process, particularly in *The Prelude* and in poems written during the same period (1798–1805), relies on Wordsworth's dialogue with Dorothy's texts and her voice in complex and significant ways.

In addition, Wordsworth's drafts of *The Prelude* possess characteristics that have recently been ascribed specifically to women's autobiography. Sidonie Smith notes that potential women autobiographers, particularly prior to the twentieth century, find that 'their stories remain private, their storytelling culturally muted, albeit persistent'.[7] This description applies very well to the status of William Wordsworth's own autobiographical texts during the five decades preceding 1850: private by choice, culturally muted by his sense that self-revelation of this kind was indecorous and egotistical, persistent in that the texts were continuously revised and eventually prepared by the author for posthumous publication. Smith also notes that those few women who have moved from private to public autobiographical utterance traditionally approached their 'position as speakers at the margins of discourse' (p. 44). This characterization certainly fits the male Wordsworthian speaker who begins writing about his past during the Goslar winter of 1798–9; but, his discourse is marginalized not by his gender but

by his poverty, his lack of a profession, and the radically experi-
mental poetic practice of *Lyrical Ballads*, a volume criticized as being
on the periphery of dominant literary concerns from the moment it
first appeared. Wordsworth's anxieties about the relation of his
autobiographical project to *The Recluse*, and his unwillingness to
allow publication of 'the poem to Coleridge', also give these poetic
texts a marginal status, at least until their publication in 1850.

Wordsworth's personal epic presents its speaker's subjectivity in
terms that have been linked to specifically feminine forms of
psychic development and identity formation. Nancy Chodorow
notes the importance of relational thinking to 'female self-defini-
tion': 'Because of their mothering by women, girls come to
experience themselves as less separate than boys, as having more
permeable ego boundaries. Girls come to define themselves more in
relation to others' (p. 93); likewise, Carol Gilligan emphasizes that
while male voices typically stress 'the role of separation as it defines
and empowers the self' female voices characteristically stress 'the
ongoing process of attachment that creates and sustains human
community'.[8] But surely Wordsworth's autobiographical epic seeks,
like all epics, to explain the origins not only of a self, but of a human
community – of a circle that includes at least himself, Dorothy,
Coleridge, and Mary.[9] Likewise, however great Wordsworth's
emphasis on the growth of his own mind, the special powers and
abilities of that mind are often defined in primarily relational terms;
the Wordsworthian mind can connect, draw strength from its
surroundings, make contact with external forces, and bestow itself
on other objects and people. In fact, the mind of the speaker in *The
Prelude* is powerful precisely because of its ability to enlarge its
'sympathies' (II, 181), collapse distinctions into a 'unity' (II, 226),
'gather passion' (II, 243), and 'combine' parts of awareness into
unified wholes. All of these powers are directly attributed to female
influence on the developing consciousness of the child.

Why we should imagine the young Wordsworth any less
affected than a female child by eight years of mothering remains
unclear, even given potential differences in male and female
psychic development. Wordsworth's strong, mutually dependent
relationship with Dorothy by 1795 suggests a male–female bond
that needs to be conceived in wider terms than those often
provided by dualistic theories of psychosexual development.
Wordsworth and Dorothy acted against common cultural assump-
tions of their own age and ours when they set up adult

housekeeping together. Their Aunt Rawson found the entire prospect unsettling: 'William and Dorothy have now a scheme of living together in London, and maintaining themselves by their literary talents ... We think it a very bad wild scheme'.[10] It would be useless to speculate on the precise forces driving this decision, but the potential implications of this famous sibling bond are evident. Was this alignment between the siblings a link in their minds to their parents, particularly to the mother they had both lost in 1778? Was Wordsworth's powerful attachment to his sister by 1795 compensatory for his abandonment of Annette and Caroline in France just three years earlier? Did his refusal to marry until 1802 reflect uncertainty about his own role as a male in his family and in the wider society? Such biographical questions can never be answered definitively, but they remind us of the important relationship between gender and the growth of Wordsworth's mind as described in his autobiographical writings.

Derrida connects displacement of the feminized signifier with the origins of all language and culture: 'The natural woman (nature, mother, or if one wishes, sister), is a represented or a signified replaced and supplanted, in desire, that is to say in social passion, beyond need'.[11] Representation, the need to signify one thing as standing for another, arises – on this view – from the prohibition of incest. Since mother ('or if one wishes, sister') comes to occupy a position of psychic separation in infancy, followed by social separation in adolescence, 'nature' (identified with the feminine) likewise comes to be seen, particularly by males, as unavailable, off limits, existing only across a psychic divide. Nature as mother cannot be completely identified with nature as sister in *The Prelude*, but Wordsworth does link Dorothy to those aspects of the natural world with which he needs to be reunited and also with the personal attributes that will allow for that reunion. I am not claiming that Dorothy serves as a mother-figure for Wordsworth, but rather that the implications of the sister/brother relationship may be as important for our understanding of gender in Wordsworth's writings as the more often discussed mother/child bond.

My argument also suggests that we need to rethink emphasis on gender difference in conceptions of identity, since many of Wordsworth's texts point toward shared aspects of male and female self-presentation. When, for example, Susan Wolfson contrasts 'William's egocentric poetics' with 'Dorothy's poetics of community' (p. 162), we may wonder how Wordsworth's poetics of the solipsistic ego can describe itself as seeking 'similitude in dissimilitude' ('Preface' to *Lyrical Ballads*) and 'Unity entire' ('Home at Grasmere'), or striving to reestablish 'dialogues' like those once held with the 'mother's heart' that led to 'intimate communion' with the loved maternal object and later with the natural world and other people ('Love of Nature Leading to Love of Mankind'). Likewise, when Susan Levin opposes the 'primacy of individual selfhood' in Wordsworth with Dorothy's desire to 'serve a community' (pp. 6–7), we are unclear how this distinction relates to William's claim that it was Dorothy who returned him to a communal world of mature adulthood.[12] The adult Wordsworth by 1805 says that he has gone through a period of solipsistic – perhaps Coleridgean – attraction to isolating self-consciousness, but this state is always described as 'a trouble', a dis-ease, an alienating form of masculine thinking with which the speaker of *The Prelude* no longer wants to be identified. If anything, the figure of Dorothy in many of Wordsworth's lyrics serves as the exemplar of certain beneficial human characteristics and as a model for the speaker's view of crucial aspects of his own identity. She is the figure who helps the once androgynous child move from masculinized adolescent to feminized adult male.

We know how often Dorothy's journals served as a spur to Wordsworth's poetic thinking or as source texts for specific images and phrases. Critics and commentators have cited intertextual connections between Dorothy's *Journals* and at least the following poems by her brother: 'I Wandered Lonely as a Cloud', 'Resolution and Independence', 'A Night-Piece', 'A Whirl-blast from Behind the Hill', 'To a Butterfly', 'The Cock is Crowing', 'Composed Upon Westminster Bridge'.[13] We also know that Dorothy and Mary Hutchinson were the two women who formed the center of Wordsworth's domestic life in the years during which *The Prelude* was composed. In fact, the rediscovery of the 1810-12 love letters between Wordsworth and Mary suggests the extent of his wife's role in Wordsworth's mature view of women, confirming that the autobiographical speaker of 1798–1805 is a more feminized figure than is often supposed. As readers we have a difficult time finding the self-possessed voice of masculine authority in lines like the following from William to Mary:

Oh my beloved ... find the evidence of what is passing within me in *thy* heart, in thy mind, in thy steps as they touch the green grass, in thy limbs as they are stretched upon the soft earth; in thy own involuntary sighs & ejaculations, in the trembling of thy hands, in the tottering of thy knees, in the blessings which thy lips pronounce, find it in thy lips themselves, & such kisses as I often give to the empty air, and in the aching of thy bosom, and let a voice speak for me in every thing within thee & without thee.[14]

If male and female sensitivities can be described as an inseparable unity, and if a male voice can speak for William *in* Mary, then surely female voices can be seen as speaking in and through Wordsworth. In his formative years as a poet, Wordsworth draws on images of the 'feminine' to present many of what he claims are the most positive aspects of his own speaking voice.

As early as 1788, Dorothy is the 'young lady' to whom 'An Evening Walk' is addressed and, by extension, the 'dearest friend' with whom the loco-descriptive imagery in the poem tries to reunite him. She is, of course, the only direct addressee in 'Tintern Abbey', the poem of which Wordsworth said years later, 'No poem of mine was composed under circumstances more pleasant for me to remember than this. I began it upon leaving Tintern, after crossing the Wye, and concluded it just as I was entering Bristol in the evening, after a ramble of 4 or 5 days, with my sister' (*PW*, 2: 517). In 'Tintern Abbey' Dorothy serves as an image of the younger Wordsworth, to whom he can teach the lesson he now knows about a new view of nature. But she is also the person for whose sake the objects around him in the Wye Valley become 'more dear', just as the experiences of the infant child are exalted and irradiated by the 'beloved presence' of the mother. We might even argue that the 'superadded soul', the 'prospect' in the mind, and the 'auxiliar light' in Book II of *The Prelude* (347, 371, 387) all describe an internalized – if ghostly – maternal and sororal presence that counters separation-anxiety in the maturing male consciousness.

'Home at Grasmere' (earlier *The Recluse*, Part First, Book First) records William's connection to Dorothy by 1800, linking her experience to his happiness:

> Mine eyes did ne'er
> Fix on a lovely object, nor my mind
> Take pleasure in the midst of happy thoughts,
> But either She whom now I have, who now

Divides with me this loved Abode, was there
Or not far off. Where'er my footsteps turned,
Her Voice was like a hidden Bird that sang,
The thought of her was like a flash of light,
Or an *unseen* companionship ...

(*Gill*, 104–12)

Once again the text joins a revelatory feminine presence with the poet's ability to take pleasure in things; this power is linked to the claim that the male poet must see her 'Voice' as hidden, her companionship 'unseen'. The passage goes on to refer to her as the 'Favorite of all' and the 'most of all', and then to say that even the 'bowers / Of blissful Eden' did not provide the absolute 'boon' and the 'surpassing grace' given the young Wordsworth by the presence of his sister. Equally significant are the lines in which he describes himself and Dorothy as 'Two of a scatter'd brood that could not bear / To live in loneliness' (*Gill*, 175–6), suggesting that an unspoken sense of isolation contributed to Wordsworth's need to reunite with his sister and then begin to find a poetic way of 'reuniting' with the world.

In fact, the importance of this sibling relationship may help to explain six missing lines of the 'Home at Grasmere' manuscript. These missing lines follow a description of the weaknesses of Wordsworth's youth, a youth which 'Strong as it seems and bold' was 'inly weak / And diffident'. Under these conditions, 'the destiny of life / Remained unfixed, and therefore we were still ...' (*Gill*, 182–4); but here the line breaks off, never providing a referent for what 'we' were. This 'we' refers to William and Dorothy, since it reappears in the passage immediately following the missing lines: 'We will be free' (192). This declaration of the freedom that he and Emma (Dorothy) now share, is connected with another image of the mind as female. Their resolve was made, he claims, 'Not in mistrust or ignorance of the mind / And of the power she has within herself / To ennoble all things' (195–7). Just such a power to ennoble the self has been linked with the spousal sister throughout the poem.

'Home at Grasmere' was never published by Wordsworth. It was composed between 1800 and 1806 (perhaps completely as early as 1800), revised as part of the Preface to *The Excursion* in 1814 – where it is described as the 'Prospectus' to *The Recluse* – revised again but not republished until 1888 under the title *The Recluse*. Part of this complicated history may connect with the difficulty Wordsworth had in confronting the public aspect of such an overtly autobiographical work. 'Home at Grasmere' presents a complex rhetorical interaction between details of Wordsworth's domestic life and Coleridge's desire for the philosophical *Recluse*. We should also recall that this is the text in which the 'egocentric' Wordsworth first describes his desire to use his poetic skill to 'sing' of 'joy in widest commonalty spread' (*Gill*, 968). And finally, the poem was written during the time Dorothy's *Journals* began to provide material for poems as 'Wordsworthian' as 'The Leech-Gatherer' and 'A Night-Piece'. The male speaker in all of these poems depends on and emerges out of a dialogue with his sister's voice.

In many of his autobiographical lyrics, particularly those written between 1800 and 1805, Wordsworth gives female – usually sibling – figures forms of power sought by the poem's speaker; often, he identifies feminized aspects of nature directly with Dorothy. In these poems, Wordsworth emphasizes natural objects with traditional links to women: flowers, birds, butterflies. The sister in 'To a Butterfly', for example, who 'feared to brush / The dust from off' the delicate creature's wings is described as the ideal of the adult poet, who beseeches the butterfly, 'Stay near me – do not take thy flight!' (*PW*, 1: 226). The adult male admits that when he was a child he sought the butterfly only as a hunter would; 'with leaps and spring' he rushed 'Upon the prey'. But now he wants this apparently insignificant insect to serve as 'Historian of my Infancy', a barely substantial object that can nevertheless bring 'A solemn image' to the poet's 'heart', the memory of his youth. 'Dead times revive in thee' the speaker says to the butterfly, connecting Dorothean respect for the creature's fragile life with an ability to connect to past time.

Dorothy's comments on the composition of this poem elaborate a link between feminine respect for the natural world and masculine – even political – forms of domination. Dorothy's journal describes her disheveled yet 'inspired' brother William, who seems intent on capturing the 'moral' of their sibling recollection: 'He ate not a morsel, nor put on his stockings but sate with his shirt neck unbuttoned, and his waistcoat open while he did it. The thought first came upon him as we were talking about the pleasure we both always feel at the sight of a Butterfly. I told him I used to chase them a little but that I was afraid of brushing the dust off their wings, and did not catch them – He told me how they used to kill all the white ones when he went to school because they were frenchmen' (*Journals*, p. 101: 14 March 1802). The feminine child views the insect as a sacred object; the young male sees the same delicate creatures as an image of human and historical enemies (dead Frenchmen). The adult poet 'Wordsworth' in the resulting lyric ('To a Butterfly'), as in so many other poems, has much more in common with the womanly view than with the martial (male) perspective.

Of course, this Dorothy (Emmeline) figure also appears in 'The Sparrow's Nest', approaching the bird's nest and its 'five blue eggs' with a powerful combination of emotions: 'She looked as if she feared it; / Still wishing, dreading to be near it: / Such heart was in her'. In this case, however, the benefit brought to the adult poet by his female sibling's emotional response is described in direct and specific terms:

> The Blessing of my later years
> Was with me when a boy;
> She gave me eyes, she gave me ears;
> And humble cares, and delicate fears;
> A heart, the fountain of sweet tears;
> And love, and thought, and joy.

> (*PW*, 1: 227)

Wordsworth's aesthetic ('Few visions have I seen more fair'), as well as his ideology of the ordinary ('Nor many prospects of delight / More pleasing than that simple sight!') are linked in 'The Sparrow's Nest' to gifts of observation, intellect, and emotional response that derive directly from the childhood figure of his sister. This same female is restored to him in 'later years' at least in part to help him find ways to 'restore' the past for 'future renovation'.

'Among all lovely things my Love had been' (also called 'The Glow-worm') records the speaker's willingness to alter his own response to natural objects for the sake of a female companion. He stops his horse in the middle of a storm, gathers up a glow-worm on a leaf, carries it home, blesses it by name, and places it carefully 'beneath a Tree', all because his love 'had never seen / A Glow-worm, never one'. His actions derive from his respect for the feminine recipient. She is the one who has been among lovely things, having 'noted well the stars, all flowers that grew'. In fact, his emotional response in this instance derives more from his sense of her response than from his own reaction to the glow-worm:

> The whole next day, I hoped, and hoped with fear;
> At night the Glow-worm shone beneath the Tree:
> I led my Lucy to the spot, 'Look here!'
> Oh! joy it was for her, and joy for me!

(PW, 2: 466)

What we might now describe as the culturally 'feminine' tendency to take pleasure in the pleasure of others rather than in one's own achievements is here connected with the poet's ability to reproduce a natural scene for another whose subsequent pleasure becomes the source of his own emotional response. Edwin Stein notes that the glow-worm lyric 'echoes both the healing process worked by Dorothy and the spiritual spousal of the siblings'.[15] Likewise, when Wordsworth writes 'To a Sky-Lark', 'To the Cuckoo', 'The Green Linnet', 'To the Daisy', 'To the Same Flower', 'To the Small Celandine', his response to simple natural objects is conditioned by what we might see as culturally 'feminine' emotional links to nature. Wordsworth derives this central aspect of his voice as a poet from the voice of his spousal sister, Dorothy.

II

From the earliest drafts of The Prelude, Wordsworth's autobiography presents links between male and female pronouns in which a traditionally feminine characteristic is identified with the masculine speaker. The river Derwent blends 'his murmurs' with 'my nurse's song'. The result is thoughts of 'more than infant softness'. The child is aware of powers that are connected to spirits recognized by their 'gentle visitation – quiet powers, / Retired, and seldom recognized, yet kind' (1799, I, 73–4). These powers are paralleled to other, more masculine, spirits who use 'Severer intervention, ministry / More palpable'. Throughout the boat-stealing scene, for example, the boat is referred to as female, suggesting that any phallocentric reading of the passage must account for a feminine vessel and the 'cavern of the willow-tree' to which the vessel returns. The scene imagines a young boy who may be afraid of the paternally phallic mountain but who identifies himself with a swan-like 'she', a vessel that holds him securely and returns him to physical, if not psychological, safety.

Likewise, in the 1805 version, Wordsworth refers to his own 'mind' as feminine when describing his early appreciation of 'the life / In common things' (I, 117–18) around Grasmere that led him to 'Composure, and the happiness entire' (122): 'her wish – where'er she turn she finds' (140), 'the mind itself, / The meditative mind, best pleased perhaps / While she as duteous as the mother dove / Sits brooding' (I, 149–52). Nature is described as female – 'when she would frame / A favored being' (363–4), 'and so she dealt with me' (371), 'surely I was led by her' (372) – as are maternal images of home – 'and from my mother's hut / Had run abroad' (302–3), 'Where'er among the mountains and the winds / The mother-bird had built her lodge' (338–9). The earth rolls 'her diurnal round' (486). The sources of youthful pleasure are 'lowly' but 'beautiful' cottages 'among the pleasant fields' (525, 529), 'calm delight' (580), 'tenderness of thought' (600). My purpose in citing these passages is not simply to list Wordsworth's use of feminine pronouns, but to argue that the speaker in these autobiographical texts creates part of his own voice through identification with feminine characteristics and feminized forms of nature.

Wordsworth's descriptions of the mother/child relationship are important in part because they establish a paradigm for his later relationship with Dorothy. The 'habits and desires' of the soul, as well as 'each most obvious and particular thought' are mysterious and elusive because they have 'no beginning' (1805, II, 233, 235–6). Having said this, Wordsworth goes on to argue that the child's initial contact with the mother's body and 'eye' is the generative source of all 'passion', of the ability to perceive the world clearly, and of the sense of connection as an organic being to a living world. The 'beloved presence' of the feminine other is also the source of the 'virtue which irradiates and exalts / All objects through all intercourse of sense' (II, 259–60). She is the direct source of the emotion that prevents the developing child from feeling like an 'outcast', 'bewildered and depressed'. From the mother 'largely he receives, nor so / Is satisfied, but largely gives again' (267–8). Of course, the mother is here identified with 'Nature' as part of Wordsworth's continuing dialogue with Coleridge. Derrida's 'nature, mother, or if one wishes, sister' reminds us of this poetic conversation between

Coleridge and Wordsworth on the subject of gifts and their recipients: as Coleridge puts it in 'Dejection', 'Oh Lady! (earlier addressed directly to 'William') we receive but what we give / And in our life alone does Nature live' (*CPW*, p. 365). Wordsworth's 'first / Poetic spirit of our human life' thus emerges from a feminized figure who teaches the child to participate in an 'ennobling interchange' – 'creator and receiver both' – by which he comes to value himself and his mind's place amid the 'works / Which it beholds'. A reader may want to argue with Wordsworth's pervasive optimism at this point, but his position is very clear, particularly if we see these lines as a tribute to Dorothy designed to help cure their sick friend Coleridge.

Wordsworth goes on to seek the origins of his adult strength in a condensed narrative sequence: gift, loss, restored powers. The 'mute dialogues' with the 'mother's heart', achieved through the 'intercourse of touch', begin the process that leads to adult 'affections'. But the 'infant sensibility, / Great birthright of our being', is threatened by a 'trouble' that comes into the growing mind 'from unknown causes': 'I was left alone / Seeking the visible world, nor knowing why. / The props of my affections were removed' (II, 292–4). These lines remind us that the mother's literal heart, in Wordsworth's case at least, stopped beating when her child was eight years old. They may also suggest that sensitivity to one's surroundings diminishes as the child matures. In Wordsworth's case, however, the weakened structure of the self is supported as if by magic. The 'props' of his affections have been removed, 'And yet the building stood, as if sustained / By its own spirit' (II, 295–6). This spirit has been made by forces – or should we say voices? – outside of the self. Even when these voices disappear, the self retains a sense of 'possible sublimity'. The same pattern helps to explain the power with which Dorothy reappears in Wordsworth's life in 1795; she returns as support for adult affections now weakened by disillusionment with Godwinian rationalism and failed revolutionary hopes.

Dialogues with the mother's heart explain why the developing soul is figured as feminine in one of Wordsworth's clearest descriptions of the secular and psychologized sublime:

> I deem not profitless those fleeting moods
> Of shadowy exultation; not for this,
> That they are kindred to our purer mind
> And intellectual life, but that the soul –

Remembering how she felt, but what she felt
Remembering not – retains an obscure sense
Of possible sublimity, to which
With growing faculties she doth aspire,
With faculties still growing, feeling still
That whatsoever point they gain they still
Have something to pursue.

(1805, II, 331–41)

The soul requires a feminine pronoun, not merely for conventional reasons, but because the 'purer mind' is linked to a specifically female source. Sublimity is only possible – as a goal, not an achievement – because the masculine voice can never see itself as fully feminine, even if the masculine soul can be identified as a 'she'. The male speaker gains power and authority by appealing to female sources of strength. But Wordsworth does not seek to fully absorb the feminine; rather, he describes a power that remains distinct, even as it is appropriated and shared.

Wordsworth calls the force that makes him a poet a 'superadded soul' that implants his mind with 'A virtue not its own' (II, 347–8). This 'over' soul, however much it may derive from his psychological critique of mothering, is also linked to the childhood image of Dorothy – who 'gave' Wordsworth eyes and ears – and the adult Dorothy who saved him from despair by reestablishing 'a saving intercourse / With [his] true self' (1805, X, 914–15). In both cases, Wordsworth is neither setting Dorothy up as a detached muse figure, nor destructively absorbing her voice to gain rhetorical power over the feminine; rather, he is praising characteristics of his own which he attributes to his sister. He claims to have learned from, shared, and then internalized these same traits. Dorothy helped to make William what he is; he pays her back by speaking through her and for her. At the same time that he 'gives' her a voice in his voice, however, he may also be creating the verbal context for her eventual silencing.

Dorothy can even be described as 'a joy / Above all joys' (VI, 211–12), and linked to a divine messenger in *Paradise Lost*. Like Raphael, the archangel who taught Adam all that a human was allowed to know, Dorothy 'seemed another morn / Risen on midnoon' (1805, VI, 212–13). Like Milton's Raphael, Dorothy is here linked to a message of simplicity, of the need to be satisfied with the ordinary. Raphael says to Adam: 'be lowly wise: / Think only what concerns thee and thy being' (*PL*, VIII, 173), and he then emphasizes the importance of restricting human knowledge to 'That which lies before us in daily life' (*PL*, VIII, 193). Raphael brings an important message that the masculine Adam will need about the value of the ordinary. These Miltonic – and feminine? – lines could have been spoken by Dorothy directly to William, particularly when she was 'rescuing' him from despair.

Many moments of power in Wordsworth's autobiographical writings are linked with imagery, natural forces, and psychic structures that have been culturally encoded as feminine. The Boy of Winander sees a visible scene that enters his mind directly, like a heaven 'received / Into the bosom of the steady lake'. When the owls stop speaking, the silent lake 'responds' by way of this powerful reflected image. The mirroring water is presented as an analogue for the physical mother, and also for the nonphysical (spiritual) nourishment received by the nursing child.[16] Maternal images of breast feeding are figuratively troped with the sensory 'consumption' of an external world. Images can pass into the child's mind as did looks from his mother's eyes; in a similar way, the reflection seen in the lake provides 'food' for the growing consciousness. The image passes into the child's awareness silently, just as the mother 'spoke' her feelings to the infant without ever speaking words. An image is a sort of 'voice' if it leaves a trace behind.

The 'spot of time' depicting the woman with the pitcher on her head also figures forth a powerful female 'speaker'. Although this woman speaks no words in the text, her 'voice' is evident in the fortitude ascribed to her actions: 'and seemed with difficult steps to force her way' (XI, 306). Once again, the female figure possesses a characteristic needed by the male child in order to survive the ordeal of the 'lost guide', the 'naked pool', the 'lonely eminence', and the fearful site of execution. This scene is also important to Wordsworth because it can be linked with another moment when, as an adult, he returned to the precise spot with Dorothy and Mary, 'those two dear ones – to my heart so dear' (316). This revisitation with two female companions, much like the 1798 visit to the Wye Valley with Dorothy, produces 'the spirit of pleasure and youth's golden gleam':

> And think ye not with radiance more divine
> From these remembrances, and from the power

They left behind? So feeling comes in aid
Of feeling, and diversity of strength
Attends us, if but once we have been strong.

(XI, 322–7)

The feminine influences on infancy are here linked to the central
tenet of Wordsworthian epitaphic memorializing. The woman
(mother) has left a power behind in the child: the power to feel
deeply. Similarly, another female, the sister, restores that power in
early adulthood when it has been weakened by masculine rational-
izing (Godwinian) and disappointed political hopes for the French
Revolution. Female feeling comes in aid of weakened male feeling,
and the strength of another gender ('diversity of strength') attends
us, if but once we have known feminine emotions powerful
enough to be likened to divinity.

In Wordsworth's case, the maternal feminine is linked to the
sibling feminine – and also to the spousal feminine – in complex
ways. Dorothy is not precisely a mother-substitute or a wife-substi-
tute for her brother, but the intensity of their sibling relationship –
commented on by Aunt Rawson, Hazlitt, Coleridge, and De
Quincey, among others – may derive in part from the absent
mother. William's love for Dorothy may also be connected to his
unwillingness to marry Mary Hutchinson until 1802. Dorothy's
famous journal entry when the marriage finally occurred evokes a
Lucy-like death of all sensation: 'I could stand it no longer and
threw myself on the bed where I lay in stillness, neither hearing or
seeing anything' (*Journals*, p. 154). Wordsworth must have also
been aware of the sentiment that was conveyed by Dorothy in a
letter to Jane Pollard a month earlier: 'I have long loved Mary
Hutchinson as a Sister ... but ... I half dread that concentration of
all tender feelings, past, present, and future, which will come upon
me on the wedding morning' (*EY*, p. 377). Dorothy refers to
William as 'dearest', 'darling', and 'my Beloved' throughout her
journals and letters, and it is hard to distinguish spousal from
maternal elements in some of her comments : 'After dinner we
made a pillow of my shoulder, I read to him and my Beloved slept',
'I was tired to death and went to bed before him – he came down
to me and read the Poem to me in bed' (*Journals*, p. 102–3: 17 March
1802). Her brother likewise describes the female subject of several
of the Lucy poems as 'my love', and the speaker as her 'lover'.

De Quincey commented on the link between Dorothy's domestic servitude and her influence on Wordsworth's personality. Dorothy's name, De Quincey notes – Greek for 'gift of God' – describes 'the relation in which she stood to Wordsworth, the mission with which she was charged – to wait upon him as the tenderest and most faithful of domestics'.[17] But this devotion to her brother's care and feeding lead to the incorporation of her strength into his, according to De Quincey; her delicately 'sexual sense of beauty' is grafted onto Wordsworth's 'masculine austerity' (p. 201). The silenced woman speaks in the presence of her beloved brother, and he may listen and respond. But domestic and rhetorical power are not sufficient guarantees of feminine authority in the early nineteenth century. In fact, Dorothy's journals and her few poems, like her almost total silence (madness?) later in life, comment powerfully on the relationship between dominant male voices and one suppressed female voice in the Wordsworth family after 1800.

Wordsworthian poetic women, likewise, do not always possess a dominant strength. The Maid of Buttermere, like numerous vagrant women and deserted mothers throughout the early lyrics, reveals male sympathy for the plight of unattached women in society. Mary Robinson's tale, in fact, seems to link Dorothy Wordsworth's childhood with Annette Vallon's adulthood. The Maid of Buttermere passage appears in *The Prelude* as another of those instances when Wordsworth substitutes a third-person narrative for details from his own life story: Vaudracour and Julia, the Arab Dream, the Boy of Winander. Mary Robinson – the Maid of Buttermere – was exactly Dorothy Wordsworth's age, and she grew to adulthood in the Lake District. She is described by Wordsworth as analogous to Dorothy in their links to the maternal force of nature. Explaining his reasons for writing a tribute to a woman at the center of a local sexual scandal, the Wordsworthian 'I' says:

> This memorial verse
> Comes from the poet's heart, and is her due;
> For we were nursed – as almost might be said –
> On the same mountains, children at one time,
> Must haply often on the self-same day
> Have from our several dwellings gone abroad
> To gather daffodils on Coker's stream.

> (1805, VII, 340–6)

The childhood of Mary Robinson is here paralleled to Dorothy's youth and to William and Dorothy's adult sight of daffodils on Ullswater. But these images are brought forth to praise specifically feminine characteristics in Mary Robinson: her 'discretion', 'just opinions', 'female modesty', 'patience', 'retiredness of mind'. The Maid of Buttermere is also closely linked to the story of Annette Vallon and Caroline Wordsworth. Mary – like Annette? – is a woman wronged by a 'spoiler', a 'bold bad man', who 'wooed the artless daughter of the hills' (VII, 325). She then bears a child out of wedlock to a man who abandons her. Mary's feminine characteristics, however, provide the peace of mind needed to survive abandonment by her lover. In Wordsworth's account, the illegitimate child dies, but the mother goes on and 'lives in peace / Upon the spot where she was born and reared'. Although she is a victim of the 'crimes / And sorrows of the world' (VII, 363–4), she possesses a womanly 'mien / And carriage, marked by unexampled grace' that let her live 'Without contamination ... In quietness, without anxiety'. This image combines a wish for Annette's adult well-being with praise of a Dorothean childhood that allows such apparently calm feminine resolution and independence to develop.

The prostitute of Book VII similarly receives Wordsworth's rhetorical concern because she has been harmed by a culture that splits 'the race of man / In twain' (426–7). Wordsworth resists blaming men specifically for this woman's plight; instead, he describes her as a victim, not of her own weakness, but of a corrupt social system. The narrative describes a young Wordsworth arriving at Cambridge in the fall of 1787, where he claims to have heard 'for the first time' in his life 'The voice of woman utter blasphemy – / Saw woman as she is to open shame / Abandoned, and the pride of public vice' (VII, 418–20). The speaker's emotional response to this scene, however, is abstract and ambivalent. He 'shuddered', but the pain he felt was 'almost lost, / Absorbed and buried in the immensity / Of the effect'. This is a strange reaction to the sound of a prostitute cursing, unless we relate it to claims made for female strength and authority elsewhere in *The Prelude*.

A 'fallen' woman, who might have been Dorothy if not for the protection of her brother, who might have been Mary Hutchinson if Wordsworth had not married her, who might be Annette left alone in France, throws a 'barrier' into Wordsworth's feelings. This prostitute also evokes the Platonic myth of the androgynous origin of the sexes and Wordsworth's contemporary fears about the 'pride' that can result from 'public vice'. This powerful psychic barrier 'from humanity divorced / The human form, splitting the race of man / In twain, yet leaving the same outward shape' (VII, 425–7). These lines are difficult to decipher but are very suggestive. We are reminded that men and women share a common shape, but also that the corrupted woman is herself split off from the idealized form of womanhood that the young Wordsworth claims to have possessed until this moment. And when he saw 'such spectacles' later, he describes the effect as a 'milder sadness'; he felt 'thought, commiseration, grief, / For the individual and the overthrow / Of her soul's beauty', but 'farther at that time / Than this I was but seldom led; in truth / The sorrow of the passion stopped me here' (431–5). The convoluted diction of this passage is significant. Stopped Wordsworth from what? Seldom led to what? The sorrow of his passion for whom? There may be more suppressed autobiography in this passage on prostitution that Wordsworth is willing or able to admit. Such a woman clearly represents a threat to the sort of female voice he wants to appropriate. As Jacobus suggests, the figure of the prostitute becomes one of the ways that sexual difference is repressed, 'by being cast out' of *The Prelude*.[18]

The Vaudracour and Julia episode is most often discussed as a suppressed autobiographical narrative of Wordsworth's affair with Annette Vallon. In fact, the story is also important for what it reveals about Wordsworth's sense of the power of the feminine over his own voice. The pair of lovers are raised together, 'Friends, playmates, twins in pleasure' (IX, 573), and their out-of-wedlock pregnancy results from Vaudracour's willingness 'to turn aside / From law and custom and entrust himself / To Nature for a happy end of all' (IX, 602–4). Of course, entrusting himself to Nature may be equivalent to imposing himself on Julia; the narrative does not say. Julia's condition throughout the tale is described in terms of silence, imprisonment, and manipulation by male forces (lover, husband, father, father-in-law) that seek to control her. Once she is locked up in a convent, however, the care of the infant falls to Vaudracour. He does 'attend upon the orphan and perform / The office of a nurse to his young child', who 'after a short time, by some mistake / Or indiscretion of the father, died' (IX, 905–9). The child, without the influence of a mother, dies. The father, without his child or the mother of his child, suffers in a telling way: 'From that time forth he never uttered word / To any living' (912–13). Ten verse-lines later he is described again in terms of silence:

Vaudracour 'never uttered word / To living soul' (921–2). The child cut off from its mother cannot live; the man cut off from the feminine cannot speak. In the Vaudracour and Julia episode, feminized nature gives this couple a child that is taken away from them by a masculine society, leaving the woman imprisoned and the male in silence.

Wordsworth elsewhere contrasts the feminized nature he longs to embrace with a masculine society he seeks to shun (VIII, 471–541). When he sets out to describe the interaction between 'Nature' and 'man' in his affections, he presents the opposition in gendered terms that remind us of Milton's opposition between Adam and Eve: 'For contemplation he and valour formed, / For softness she and sweet attractive grace' (*PL*, IV, 297–8). Wordsworth opposes a feminine 'Nature' ('she') to a masculine social man ('he') in a related way. He then claims that such a gendered view of nature and society held sway in his mind until his early twenties:

> a passion, she,
> A rapture often, and immediate joy
> Ever at hand: he distant, but a grace
> Occasional, and accidental thought ...

> (VIII, 486–9)

The development of the 'poetic faculty' is linked with the first ability to feel emotion, as earlier he had only been able to do in the presence of the mother. The 'mute dialogues' with the mother's heart are now transformed into adult personality, 'No longer a mute influence of the soul, / An element of the nature's inner self' (VIII, 513–14). This emotional capacity comes first from the maternal presence, extends gradually to the objects of nature, and comes finally to appreciate the 'still, sad music of humanity'. As part of this developmental process, the poetic consciousness is temporarily drawn away from emotional responsiveness by the masculine need to rationalize, seeking to understand the world through intellectual systems. At this crucial point in Wordsworth's own life Dorothy returned, restoring and reinforcing a new version of the feminine – and familial – passion he had once gathered from his mother's eyes.

The Miltonic opposition between gendered sex roles is finally replaced by Wordsworth with an androgynous ideal. The poet who succeeds as Wordsworth claims to have succeeded, does so under

the feminine influence of 'All that a darling countenance can look /
Or a dear voice utter, to complete the man, / Perfect him, made
imperfect in himself' (XIII, 201–3). This idealized Wordsworthian
male sounds more like Milton's Eve than like the heroic Adam. The
first-person voice of *The Prelude* offers a figure who has balanced
conflicting voices within himself:

> And he whose soul hath risen
> Up to the height of feeling intellect
> Shall want no humbler tenderness, his heart
> Be tender as a nursing mother's heart;
> Of female softness shall his life be full,
> Of little loves and delicate desires,
> Mild interests and gentlest sympathies.

> (XIII, 204–10)

If *The Prelude* is an epic, it is not an epic of the founding of a great
civilization or race of people, but an epic on the origins of human
identity. The cultural codes of female 'feeling' and male 'intellect'
are critiqued by Wordsworth to offer a new view of the gendering
and engendering of human personality. 'Real' dialogues with
Dorothy, like mute dialogues with the mother's heart, have helped
to facilitate the growth of Wordsworth's feminized male mind – at
least so says the 'I' of *The Prelude*.

Even the source of power finally revealed on Snowdon has
important connections to this androgynous vision of a feeling intel-
lect, a tender heart, and gentle sympathies. The secular revelation
that Wordsworth claims to have experienced on a mountain top in
Wales connects in important ways with 'mute dialogues' between
mother and infant and also with the image of a loving feminine
sibling. The power Wordsworth claims to have felt on Snowdon
derives from nature as a 'she': 'That domination which she often-
times / Exerts upon the outward face of things' (XIII, 77–8). But this
is not just a conventional literary reference to the natural world as
feminine. The 'homeless voice of waters' is a feminine voice: it
emerges from a 'dark, deep thoroughfare', it comes from a 'blue
chasm', a 'deep and gloomy' 'fracture in the vapour' in the 'meek
and silent' sea of mist at Wordsworth's feet. This voice is presided
over by a naked moon, and there is a divine 'under-presence' that
creates in the poet's mind an ability to feel this power.

The scene described atop Snowdon provides the most complete description of the process whereby the infant Wordsworth learned passion from his mother's eyes and the adult Wordsworth had his emotional capacity returned to him by his sister. The powerful 'she' felt on Snowdon is not just 'nature'; it is also an analogue for the maternal Ann and the sororal Dorothy Wordsworth:

> That domination which she oftentimes
> Exerts upon the outward face of things,
> So moulds them, and endues, abstracts, combines,
> Or by abrupt and unhabitual influence
> Doth make one object so impress itself
> Upon all others, and pervades them so,
> That even the grossest minds must see and hear,
> And cannot chuse but feel.

(XIII, 77–84)

Wordsworth's 'sense of God' is closely linked to concepts that have been culturally identified for centuries as feminine. The child learns to feel love for the world by feeling love from the mother. In a similar way, Wordsworth claims – whether rhetorically or not – that Dorothy's unconditional love for him helped restore his ability to love objects and people around him. Not incidentally, he describes the greatest 'power' in the sensible world as '*brother* of the glorious faculty / Which higher minds bear with them as their own' (my emphasis, XIII, 89–90). But this brother-power possesses a 'glorious' sister-power – most critics have called it 'Imagination' – by which 'higher minds' can 'build up greatest things / From least suggestions'. The Wordsworthian imagination draws on the ability, first attributed to the mother, to at once create and receive in the process of loving the infant child. Such minds are not 'enthralled' by 'sensible impressions', nor do they need 'extraordinary calls / To rouze them'. They live in 'a world of life', and their powerful responsiveness to the ordinary makes them 'more fit / To hold communion with the invisible world' (XIII, 104–5). There is more female softness in the voice of *The Prelude* than has hitherto been recognized. Likewise, communal and relational forms of thinking help to authorize the Wordsworthian – sometimes called the 'egotistical' – sublime.

By the end of his autobiographical poem, Wordsworth links a

feminine 'other' and a masculine 'I' into an abstract theory about the origins of poetic selfhood. At the same time, however, the argument retains its links to specific women, culminating in a praise of Dorothy that links her to the high 'theme' of this epic of personal identity. We need only substitute 'the Wordsworthian feminine' for 'Nature' in the following passage to appreciate how the poem connects restoration of 'Imagination and Taste' with a sisterly and androgynous ideal:

> From [my feminine aspect] doth emotion come, and moods
> Of calmness equally are [my feminine aspect's] gift:
> This is her glory – these two attributes
> Are sister horns that constitute her strength;
> This twofold influence is the sun and shower
> Of all her bounties, both in origin
> And end alike benignant.

> (XII, 1–7)

On this account, male genius exists only as the result of another 'ennobling interchange' that joins masculinity to a feminine form of power, female friendship, and a gift of womanly energy:

> Hence it is
> That genius, which exists by interchange
> Of peace and excitation, finds in her
> His best and purest friend – from her receives
> That energy by which he seeks the truth,
> Is rouzed, aspires, grasps, struggles, wishes, craves
> From her that happy stillness of the mind
> Which fits him to receive it when unsought.

> (XII, 7–14)

My purpose is not to make the Wordsworthian autobiographer into a proto-feminist, or to argue that he transcends the powerful gender assumptions of his time. I do want to argue, however, that 'Wordsworth's' voice throughout *The Prelude* owes a crucial aspect of its authority to psychic, biographical, and biological images that the poem continually links to ideas of the feminine.

This is why the adult Wordsworth can claim that 'Nature', like

Dorothy, did 'bring again this wiser mood, / More deeply reestab-
lished in my soul' (XII, 45–6). Likewise, it was the rhetorical figure
of Dorothy, in Wordsworth's praise of her throughout the texts of
1798-1805, who came to her brother's aid by reminding him to see
'little worthy or sublime / In what we blazon with the pompous
names / Of power and action' (48–9). Once the traditional mascu-
line domains of 'power and action' have been critiqued from the
point of view of history, we are close to the center of Dorothy's gift
to her brother. The figurative word may be 'Nature', but the subject
is Dorothy, whose gift to her brother was the lesson he sought to
pass on to others. She

> early tutored me
> To look with feelings of fraternal love
> Upon those unassuming things that hold
> A silent station in this beauteous world.

> (XII, 49–52)

These lines refer to Dorothy insofar as they evoke the 'exquisite
regard for common things' (XII, 242) which William attributes to
her presence in his paean of tribute in the poem's final book.

The passage in which Wordsworth finally declares the subject of
his epic, 'Imagination having been our theme, / So also hath that
intellectual love' (XIII, 185–6), closes with praise for an idealized
Wordsworthian poet who has been shaped by a 'dear voice' and a
'darling countenance'. This is the same poet whose soul has linked
'feeling' and 'intellect', who has a heart as 'tender as a nursing
mother's' and a life full of 'female softness', 'little loves and delicate
desires, / Mild interests and gentlest sympathies' (209–10). At the
close of this tribute to this new womanly man, Wordsworth breaks
his verse-paragraph to begin his final celebration of the 'Child of
my parents, sister of my soul'. From Dorothy he says, he 'imbibed'
'early tenderness'. It was this Dorothy who, as a supplement to the
mother's 'sweet influence', was able to 'soften down' the 'over-
sternness' that caused the masculine Wordsworth to esteem a
limited Miltonic version of love and beauty that 'Hath terror in it'.
Dorothy planted 'flowers' in her brother's rock-like personality and
'countenance severe'. She taught the 'little birds to build their nests
/ And warble in' (XIII, 235–6) the chambers of his soul. Dorothy's
'breath' – need we now say her *voice* – was a 'gentler spring' that

helped him reestablish the link between the common face of 'Nature' and a 'more refined humanity'.

In fact, Wordsworth's last reference to his sister in *The Prelude* claims that Dorothy's influence on him has been greater than even his own text indicates. As he prepares to thank Raisley Calvert for the financial support that freed Wordsworth to begin his life as a poet and his life with Dorothy, he describes the time leading up to the permanent Grasmere abode that would receive him

> with that sister of my heart
> Who ought by rights the dearest to have been
> Conspicuous through this biographic verse ——
> Star seldom utterly concealed from view ...

> (XIII, 339–42)

Dorothy is at the center of this 'biographic verse', however concealed she may have been from public view. *The Prelude* recounts Wordsworth's vision of her intellectual and domestic life and of its powerful impact on the growth of her brother's mind. Wordsworth's autobiography is thus also a biography of at least Dorothy and Coleridge, the two people to whom Wordsworth's 'intellect' was 'most indebted'.

The feminized aspect of this 'I' is an important source of Wordsworth's ability to give a 'gift' to Coleridge – as Dorothy had given a gift to her brother – and also of the poet's power to offer a less gender-bound version of personal identity than had been provided by the traditional cultural category of 'the masculine'. Many of Wordsworth's subjects (butterflies, daisies, lesser celandines, daffodils, unpretending little rills, skylarks, sparrows, single women) were startling to his early readers precisely because they crossed generic boundaries traditionally separating male from female readers and writers. These were not 'manly' poems. Wordsworth sometimes speaks as Dorothy in order to speak for 'himself'. Yet he also pays tribute to the psychic support he has received from his remarkable sister. At times he does claim egotistical authority for his 'own' poetic voice, but that voice is neither unitary, nor monologic, nor ever strictly 'masculine'.

The voice in which Wordsworth writes the 1805 'poem to Coleridge' is not the voice of a brother who has killed off his sister (in the Lucy poems) so that he can assume her authority, nor of a patriarchal nature-sage bent on isolating himself in abstruse mental abstractions. Rather, 'Wordsworth' (the 'I' of *The Prelude*) is a poetic speaker who sees a specifically feminine wisdom as having conferred part of the power that helped him to become a writer. The biographical Wordsworth, we should remember, seemed as 'passive' and as marginalized to most of his society as did any woman – at least insofar as the concepts of 'useful' activity and 'important' work were defined in patriarchal, masculine terms. The young adult Wordsworth had no job, made no money, and offered almost no practical service to the wider culture. In 1805, it was no more important to English society for a Lakeland balladeer to sing of a retarded child, describe the sight of daffodils, or tell his own life story, than it was for his sister to fold the laundry, prune the roses, or keep a journal. This may help to explain another reason why Wordsworth hesitated to make his self-life-writing public until after his own death in 1850. Wordsworth's autobiographical texts, like Dorothy's *Journal*, forced readers – then, no less than now – to reevaluate standards of masculine and feminine activity, redefine categories of valuable work, and reconsider the cultural basis of conventionally gendered forms of thinking.

In the process of thanking Dorothy for the valuable gifts she has given him, Wordsworth produces the myth of a self-sustaining identity that can create strong links to the past by emphasizing its emotional powers and relational capacities. Wordsworth's autobiography may give an even more subtle gift to Dorothy than it does to Coleridge; it offers her a textual version of her brother in which she can hear herself speaking. If the voice that narrates *The Prelude* is masculine, that speaker has voiced the feminine as spousal sister in order to explain why he has a story worth telling to men and women.

6

Colonizing Consciousness:
Culture as Identity in Wordsworth's *Prelude* and Walcott's *Another Life*

It may seem strange to end a book about Wordsworth's textual practices with a discussion of a contemporary poet from the Caribbean, but the claims already made in *The Revolutionary 'I'* are finally valuable only if they can carry us beyond Wordsworth into a wider discussion of the genre of autobiographical writing. Literary selves, however we may seek to define or destabilize them, present themselves in complex and richly textured ways. Wordsworth's 'politics' of self-presentation – and the ways he chose to be 'politic' in the process of such self-presentation – bear comparison with numerous subsequent autobiographers, those directly influenced by Wordsworth and those related to him in more elusively intertextual ways. Wordsworth's voice did emerge out of an interplay of voices and forces that we have already explored: his sister Dorothy, his friend Coleridge, his own earlier lyric voices, discourses of the French revolution, Miltonic blank verse. But Wordsworth's poetic voice went on to shape at least as many voices as it was shaped by; we need only consider Wordsworth's reputation from 1850 to the present to appreciate the ongoing power of his textual identity in the voices of others. A comparison to one such voice should allow us to conclude that Wordsworth's autobiographical writings are important not merely for what they say, but for the ways they have continued to have their say over the past two centuries.

Derek Walcott is an ideal candidate for such a comparison – not merely because a great deal of his writing might be described as Wordsworthian – but because his autobiographical writing, which often seems uniquely tied to his own West Indian background, reveals a textual identity that is, in its own way, another version of a revolutionary 'I'. Walcott's autobiographical *Another Life* has become one of the most significant works of contemporary poetry from the Caribbean. Walcott's book-length poem has been praised for its powerful lyricism, its evocative characterizations, and its effective depiction of the colonial and post-colonial situation in the Caribbean basin. Perhaps the most enthusiastic praise the poem has received comes from Kenneth Ramchand, who described the 1973 publication of *Another Life* as the 'literary event of the West Indian year'; Ramchand went on to claim that the poem 'contains more metrical variety and experimentation, and ... is more compressed and less self-indulgent than the only other poem in English that approaches it for stature, but the most convenient way of suggesting its richness and importance is to describe it as Walcott's and the West Indian's *The Prelude'.*[1] Whether or not we agree completely with Ramchand's evaluation, he points to a connection that is significant and suggestive. A discussion of Walcott's *Another Life* in relation to Wordsworth's *Prelude* suggests links between Walcott and the Wordsworthian tradition of verse autobiography. Our understanding of Wordsworthian strategies of self-presentation also benefits in important ways from a comparison to Walcott. Such an analysis is a useful way of concluding a study of Wordsworth's strategies of self-presentation because it links long first-person poems, separated by almost two centuries, with current developments in autobiographical theory. Finally, reading Walcott's poem alongside Wordsworth's affirms the role of culture, and multiple voices, in the development of personal identity, particularly as that process occurs in autobiographical texts.

If it is true that Walcott is a sort of Caribbean Wordsworth, then Wordsworth is an earlier version of a colonized consciousness like the one described in Walcott's poem. Reading Walcott in light of Wordsworth suggests that colonization is always a crucial metaphor for literary accounts of 'coming into consciousness'. Every autobiography records the desire to aesthetically shape one's experience and the concurrent realization that one is, at the same time, being culturally shaped by that experience and by the 'voices' that contribute to it. Identity, in Walcott's and Wordsworth's poems, emerges out of an interaction between culture and an aesthetic posture that seeks to critique all cultural identifications. The resulting autobiographical voice – in both poems – seeks an 'artistic' position free from social limitations, while at the same time revealing the complex forces that prevent such an aesthetically neutral position from ever emerging. The textual self defines itself only in the context of its circumstances. Any literary 'I' is shaped by biology and society – formed into a version of 'itself', perhaps – but always affected by external voices and forces over which it has no final control.

While Ramchand may have been the first to cite the connection between *Another Life* and *The Prelude*, he did not develop the Wordsworthian side of his parallel. Edward Baugh extends Ramchand's comparison in 'The Poem as Autobiographical Novel: Derek Walcott's "Another Life" in relation to Wordsworth's "Prelude" and Joyce's "Portrait"', an essay that is thorough and convincing in its analysis of the structure of *Another Life*, but which likewise never develops the details of the comparison to Wordsworth.[2] Walcott's poem is, in fact, a subtly transformed and modernized version of *The Prelude*. The intertextual relation between these two poems helps us understand the cultural context of those autobiographical writings that employ a poetic or lyrical mode. In addition, Wordsworth's earlier text also reveals the forces of intellectual colonization at work in a Caribbean context like Walcott's. Like Wordsworth, Walcott needs to draw on a variety of voices in order to produce the singular voice that becomes his own. These voices (whether human, natural, imagined, or transcribed), derive from a wide range of sources: literary, social, personal, and psychological. In addition, Walcott's numerous 'voices' also help to further reveal the rhetorical complexity of any autobiographical 'I', whether English Romantic or Caribbean contemporary.

Stylistically, Walcott's poem owes debts to Yeats, Pound, Eliot, and Whitman. But the real source texts for *Another Life* are Walcott's own early autobiographical poem, 'Epitaph for the Young', and Wordsworth's 'poem to Coleridge'.[3] Walcott's 'Poem to St. Omer', as *Another Life* might be called, not only draws on the tradition of the dedicatory verse autobiography. His poem enriches that tradition by describing an artistic sensibility that emerges out of its relationship to a variety of colonizing cultural forces: art and literature of the past and present, the natural environment, the society on the island of St. Lucia, the teacher (Harry Simmons), the first and lost love (Anna/Andreuille), and the fellow artist (Gregorias/Dunstan St. Omer). Like Wordsworth, Walcott synthesizes rhetorical postures of optimism, anxiety, certainty, and despair into a complex voice, an 'I' that resonates a confident poetic authority. But this same 'I' reveals the extent to which it must echo the voice of others in order to speak 'as itself'.

Walcott's cryptic title has most often been explained by referring to the 'divided child' described in book one of the poem. The conflicting worlds of Walcott's ancestral and hereditary past – the white world of the colonizing British and the black world of the St. Lucian slaves – like the racially divided world of his Caribbean present, represent, each to the other, 'another life': 'my white grandfather's face ... my black grandfather's voice' (p. 64).[4] As Lloyd Brown has noted, the poet struggles to incorporate the dual racial and cultural sides of his identity and the result is a kind of tense unity: 'this new integrated consciousness constitutes *another* life, the mature completeness within which the poet accepts the diverse sources of his selfhood' (p. 136). Brown sees this as part of a more characteristically West Indian dilemma: 'the quest for national consciousness and identity is not only a localized cultural act, but it is also a reflection of every individual's need to achieve a sense of complete or creative selfhood; and on this basis the individual or national consciousness of the West Indian is developed in response to a universal need' (pp. 136–7). But Walcott's problem is no less a function of what Philip Lejeune has called 'the multiplicity of authorities implied in the work of autobiographical writing, as in all writing'.[5] Of course, every autobiographer is confronted with a version of the same dilemma: how can a 'complete or creative selfhood', a singular and unified speaker, emerge out of the dialogic diversity of any individual's cultural context? How can Walcott or Wordsworth speak as himself, when so many others would speak as and for him?

Walcott reveals one aspect of such complexity by using Matthew Arnold's 'To Marguerite ... Continued' as the epigraph to 'Part Four' of his own poem. The Arnoldian passage suggests the gulf that separates Walcott as an adult from the earlier sources of his inspiration. Adulthood has produced yet 'another' life in Walcott, a literary and Westernized poet who feels that an 'estranging sea' now divides him from his teacher, his best friend, and his first love, all of whom stood for so much in the earlier sections of the poem. On these terms, the 'other' life in the poem composes memories of childhood than can be regained only fleetingly in adulthood. The mature artist begins to sense that this earlier life is as much a textual creation of the present as it is a re-creation of any literal past. Walcott, like his predecessor Wordsworth, 'makes' his own voice by remaking many voices from his past. These voices then combine to produce an adult 'I' who claims to be able to speak with a new literary authority. This new adult speaker, however, senses the multiplicity of voices that have gone into the construction of his own confident 'I'.

Walcott as adult autobiographer gives the people he remembers from his youth 'a stature / disproportionate to their cramped lives', primarily because he remembers them as they seemed to him then, when he beheld them at 'knee-height'; in those early days, the adults' 'thunderous exchanges / rumbled like gods about another life' (p. 40). Here Walcott adopts an additional ambiguous use of 'another' to suggest the Caribbean adults' sense of worlds beyond what seemed to them to be their limited cultural realm. Years would have to pass before Walcott could see the things he read of in the literature of the 'outside' world: 'an orchestra, / a train, a theatre, the spark-coloured leaves / of autumn' (p. 40). In a Caribbean world without orchestras, trains, theaters, or autumn, how could the young child understand the things he read of, described in books with such 'processional arrogance'. Nor could he understand the cultural forces that produced the 'cramped' lives he would never imagine describing in pejorative terms until much later. Walcott's analysis suggests one way that colonization works in the Caribbean context. Language creates a sense of unknown European modes of experience that come to be identified with a local absence, an apparent cultural shortcoming. Born into this unjustly diminished Caribbean world, of racially mixed ancestry, and far removed from the European world of which he read as he matured, how could he become anything but 'a divided child?' (p. 40). But a divided child may have a great deal to say about the sources of his own sense of selfhood.

Likewise, such a world of personal division is not unique to a culturally-divided consciousness in the contemporary Caribbean. Walcott actually produces a much more typical account of personal identity. He describes the experience of a self-conscious individual in any culture, any person who develops a sense of the gulf that separates aspirations from reality, the world of possibility from the world of actuality. Wordsworth, as we have already seen, recounts just such a self early in *The Prelude*. Thinking of his youth from the uneasy vantage point of adulthood he says: 'I seem / Two consciousnesses – conscious of myself, / And of some other being' (1805, II, 31–3). Wordsworth here describes the 'vacancy' that separates him as an adult from the days of his most vivid childhood memories. Yet the power of these memories is still able to produce 'self-presence' of the earlier identity in the adult poet's mind. No matter how far Wordsworth moves from the experiences of child-hood, these events continue to exert a power that can textually unify an apparently unstable self. Another life – 'some other being' – is drawn from the past in order to help define the present life. Identity is created by combining a pressing personal need in the present moment with a (re)membered version of the past.

The two Wordsworths, 'myself / And some other being', have more in common with the divided child described by Walcott than might at first seem apparent. Wordsworth, the middle-class, rural son of a father who died early in his life, describes a world of natural objects that become particularly valuable to him. His sympathies enlarge as 'the common range of visible things' grows 'dear' (1805, II, 182) to him. Yet he also draws strength from the culture around him: from local legends, fairy tales, and a wide range of significant experiences that eventually lead him to trans-form his thoughts into the raw material for artistic creation. Walcott likewise loses his father at an early age and grows up surrounded by the need to draw his identity from the natural objects and the culture around him. This task is complicated by his mixed race and middle-class ancestry, his provincialism, and his sense of a Caribbean environment which cuts him off from the rest of the world. At the same time, this seeming lack of historical and cultural context gives him a clean slate on which to inscribe a version of himself. Caribbean provincialism, Walcott would later say, was an asset, because it allowed him to have a more complete 'communion with things that the metropolitan writers no longer care about'.[6] These links to a non-urban sense of 'family, earth, and history' are strikingly similar to the feeling Wordsworth describes when he leaves the sophistication of Cambridge and London to return to the Lake District and begin writing his own autobiographical poem. Walcott's realization that he might turn the 'limited' world of his childhood into the subject of significant art reminds us of Wordsworth's claim that he began telling his own life story because he was 'diffident' of his own powers, confident only about the precise details of what he 'had felt and thought' (*EY*, p. 586).

Walcott claims that his first affections for artistic representation were not derived from reality but from art itself. The epigraph from Malraux with which Walcott opens his poem notes that the painter Giotto was 'more deeply moved by the sight of works of art than by that of the things which they portray' (p. 3). Walcott begins his own poem by citing his early attempts to become a painter. He depicts painting as a way of learning to see and thereby coming to love one's surroundings. The pictures painted by his teacher Harry Simmons, and the world of art they represent, are depicted as yet 'another life, / a landscape locked in amber, the rare / gleam' (p. 5). This image reminds us of Wordsworth's claim, in his epiphany of the drowned man, that the childhood sight of a dead body caused him no fear, because he had 'seen' such sights before in stories he had heard or read. Wordsworth describes the dead man, whose body rose up through the water with a 'ghastly face':

> And yet no vulgar fear,
> Young as I was, a child not nine years old,
> Possessed me, for my inner eye had seen
> Such sights before among the shining streams
> Of fairyland, the forests of romance ...

$$(1805, V, 473–7)$$

For Wordsworth, as for Walcott, the world of art helps to stabilize experience by making it more recognizable and permanent. Because the child has imagined death before, his actual confrontation with a corpse produces 'a spirit hallowing what I saw / With decoration and ideal grace'. The result is primarily aesthetic but is also emotional; the image comes to possess a 'dignity, a smoothness, like the words / Of Grecian art and purest poesy' (V, 478–81). For Walcott, no less, aesthetic categories transform the apparent ordinariness of the world of St. Lucia into a landscape notable for its natural beauty and human richness.

The similarities between Walcott's St. Lucia and Wordsworth's Lake District may be obvious, but they are also startling. Natural beauty in both environments contributes to the emerging identity of the literary artist. The human world, although rich and diverse, seems often secondary to the child's sense of his own psychic interactions with his surroundings. Both poets sense, however, that the world of natural objects may actually assume a secondary role in the psyche, derived from the effort that transforms nature into artistic representation. The jutting mountains, deep valleys, and unpopulated landscapes of Walcott's childhood remind us of precise details in Wordsworth's Lake District. In both cases, however, it is the ability of the adult mind to create aesthetic images out of these natural objects that forms the basis for a relationship between formal art and personal identity. Every description needs a describer, a point-of-view that can re-present the world artistically. Once that describer is invoked in the first person, the world can take on whatever power this 'I' may say it possesses.

Walcott introduces his own autobiographical 'I' with the painterly sights of a literary ocean, 'where the pages of the sea / are a book left open' (p. 5). Like Wordsworth, this St. Lucian lyricist connects his own first experience of death with a vision of water. At the funeral of a neighborhood child, Walcott recalls how

> The world
> stopped swaying and settled in its place.
> A black lace glove swallowed his hand.
> The engine of the sea began again.

(p. 9)

Walcott has been waiting for the dead child to rise up, like Wordsworth's drowned man of Esthwaite, as a spirit: 'the live child waited / for the other to escape, a flute / of frail, seraphic mist'. But the only sounds and sights that arrive are associated with voices in shells and the rolling of the sea. Wordsworth, no less significantly, begins the earliest versions of the poem that would become *The Prelude* with the watery sounds of the river Derwent: 'Was it for this / That one, the fairest of all rivers, loved / To blend his murmurs with my nurse's song' (1799, I, 1–3). This water sends a first 'voice' that flows through the child's dreams, making a 'ceaseless music' that gives the young consciousness a knowledge 'of the calm / Which Nature breathes among the fields and groves' (1799, I, 14–15).

Walcott likewise provides one of the climaxes of his own book-length autobiography with another image of water, this time associated with the literary imagination that produces books:

> So, I shall repeat myself,
> prayer, same prayer, towards fire, same fire,
> as the sun repeats itself and the thundering waters
>
> for what else is there
> but books, books and the sea,
> verandahs and the pages of the sea ...

(pp. 139–40)

Walcott cites a series of adult memories which retain a precise value because of their connection to his past. 'Holiest' of all of these images, he claims, is 'the break of the blue sea below the trees' (p. 140). Walcott's lines are subtly reminiscent of Wordsworth's climactic description of the sea in the closing book of *The Prelude*. Having scaled Mount Snowdon, Wordsworth sees at his feet an ocean of mist and beyond that 'the real sea', which renders up a 'roar of waters, torrents, streams / Innumerable, roaring with one voice' (1805, XIII, 49, 58–9). The crack in the mist through which this sound rises becomes an analogue for Wordsworth's own creative imagination. Such an analogy only makes sense, however, from the singular perspective provided by a self-described first-person observer.

Walcott produces another echo of this imagery in the description of his first memorable departure from the island of his birth. He leaves behind the people who have been most important to him – Gregorias and Anna – and, as the plane rises into the sky, he gains a perspective remarkably similar to Wordsworth's atop Snowdon:

> I watched the island narrowing, the fine
> writing of foam around the precipices, then
> the roads as small and casual as twine
> thrown on its mountains, I watched till the plane
> turned to the final north and turned above
> the open channel with the grey sea between
> the fishermen's islets until all that I love
> folded in cloud. I watched the shallow green
> breaking in places where there would be reef ...

(pp. 108–9)

Thus the sight of water, like the sound of water, serves in both Walcott and Wordsworth to unify disparate sense impressions into a textual unity that describes natural and psychological processes. The text, through the voice of an ostensibly authoritative 'I', creates an artistic unity that can surpass any order provided by the physical world.

Many of Walcott's specific details echo Wordsworthian images, or they evoke a Romantic sense of the self emerging into consciousness through its natural and cultural surroundings: 'Across the pebbled back yard, woodsmoke thins, / epiphany of ascension. The

soul, like fire, / abhors what it consumes' (p. 12). Walcott, like
Wordsworth in his preface to *Lyrical Ballads,* is powerfully affected
by the language of ordinary people. In Walcott's case, however, this
language echoes the polyglot sources of St. Lucian voices, including
the 'Jacobean English' of the King James Bible. In Walcott's colo-
nized ears this version of English 'rang, new-minted, / the speech
of simple men, / evangelists, reformers, abolitionists' (p. 23). Of
course, we can easily describe Wordsworth's voice in similar terms.
Milton, the King James Bible, Cambridge academics, Coleridge,
Dorothy, Cumbrian rustics: all become verbal sources of the voice
that Wordsworth would eventually claim as his own. No less does
the patois of Walcott's Caribbean culture combine with the
language of the European culture he is appropriating through
human voices and books to produce a new and powerful voice: his
own.

Like Wordsworth, Walcott records the artistic difficulties atten-
dant on adopting a narrowly dogmatic approach to religion. The
emerging St. Lucian artist finds in the natural world a religion
deeper than any organized faith, a religion that connects him with
his African origins. The 'pragmatic / Methodism' of his infancy
gives way to a sacramental view of the entire world, grounded in
the tribal authority of the wilderness – 'the bush' (pp. 24–5).
Walcott once noted that 'Whether you wanted to accept them or
not, the earth emanated influences which you could either put
down as folk superstition or, as a poet, accept as a possible truth'.[7]
Walcott begins to hear in seashells and in wind-blown water the
same kind of voices Wordsworth heard in mountain rocks and the
wind through dry grass. Wordsworth tells of 'low breathings',
'strange utterances', and 'unknown modes of being' that fill his
increasingly sensitized mind, leading to a 'sense of God, or what-
soe'er is dim / Or vast in its own being' (XIII, 72–3). Walcott's
awareness, derived from the power of these earth-emanated influ-
ences, leads him away from the desire to 'be a preacher' and 'write
great hymns' (p. 24) toward a longing for an aesthetic harmony that
will unite culture and identity into an artistic whole, a poem. In the
case of these two poets, one result of this transmuted religious
longing is the writing of autobiography. To make your own life
meaningful in a text is one way of making the world around you
meaningful. The sublunary mundane in both poetic autobiograph-
ies becomes revelatory in secular and literary terms.

Walcott's assertion that an ordinary sight can become remarkable in the mind of the artist is reminiscent of Wordsworth in the Lucy poems, 'The Solitary Reaper', and 'Resolution and Independence':

> Beside the road,
> a beautiful, brown Indian
> girl in rags. Sheaves
> of brown rice held in brown,
> brittle hands, watching us
> with that earth-deep darkness
> in her gaze. She was
> the new Persephone,
> dazed, ignorant,
> waiting to be named.

(p. 73)

The poet takes the mundane materials of his ordinary world and transforms them into a self-described myth. 'The radiance of sharing extends to the simplest objects' (p. 15), Walcott claims. The 'inventory of accidents' that become significant in our mind causes us, if we can intensify their value artistically, to heighten our emotions and 'weep for dumb things' (p. 15). But Walcott's emotions, like Wordsworth's, may sometimes lie too deep for voices or tears.

Any doubt that Walcott has Wordsworth in mind as he writes *Another Life* is dispelled when he ironically invokes 'intimations of immortality' to describe his first 'immoral' longing for 'Other men's wives' (p. 101). Earlier in the same section of his poem, Walcott describes the desire 'never to leave' his island in precisely Wordsworthian terms:

> to sit and watch the twilight in this harbour
> igniting other lives, watching the herring-gulls rehearse
> with each dusk their cycle of departure,
> to watch the visionary glare
> tarnish to tin.

(p. 100)

In this powerful image, which is also reminiscent of Wallace Stevens's 'The Idea of Order at Key West', we hear the Wordsworth of the 'Immortality Ode': 'Whither is fled the visionary gleam?' As

Wordsworth's gleam fades with adulthood, so Walcott's tarnishes into a diminished but still powerful vision. Both poets declare the need for a voice that can survive over time. Such a voice survives, in part, by drawing on images from the past that can be revivified by literary acts of textual re-collection and poetic re-creation.

The connection between Gregorias (Dunstan St. Omer) and Coleridge forms another important link between *Another Life* and *The Prelude*. Though Walcott's poem is not dedicated to St. Omer, Gregorias appears as the focus of part two of the poem, 'Homage to Gregorias', and remains a powerful influence on the developing consciousness of the narrator. In Walcott's case, the primary source of intellectual influence seems to be a composite figure of St. Omer and Harry Simmons, the art teacher. In Walcott's description of St. Omer/Gregorias, however, we hear direct echoes of the Wordsworth-Coleridge collaboration. Gregorias is the figure of the inspired artist whose soul is dangerously intensified by his own emotional and aesthetic vision. As a painter, Gregorias has 'abandoned apprenticeship / To the errors of his own soul' (p. 56). As Walcott's closest friend, Gregorias comes to embody the unrestrained imaginative and intellectual energy that Wordsworth often ascribed to Coleridge.

The young Walcott, like Wordsworth, claims to be galvanized by a more purely verbal imagination. As a result, he finds himself caught – unlike Gregorias – in the realm of the metaphoric, seeking always the 'paradoxical flash of an instant' which might nevertheless reveal a 'crystal of ambiguities' (p. 56). Walcott envies Gregorias the 'explosion of impulse' that characterizes his work, but realizes that the same explosion is partly responsible for grotesqueness and 'aboriginal force' (p. 57), the destructive qualities that form part of Gregorias's artistic spirit. The potential danger associated with unrestrained imagination has a clear parallel in Wordsworth's view of Coleridge. This dangerous force manifested itself in Coleridge's imaginative and narcotic excesses. In Walcott's poem such creative excess is recorded in the drunken rantings which cause Gregorias's canvas to be 'crucified against a tree' (p. 50).

We might also argue that the Anna of Walcott's poem, based on Andreuille Alcée, has an analogue in one unspoken influence on Wordsworth's *Prelude*. Wordsworth's own first love affair – with Annette Vallon – produced an illegitimate child and a sense of guilt that led the poet to expunge all direct accounts of her from his autobiography. But the details of this relationship find their way into

'Vaudracour and Julia', the fictionalized account of two lovers that appeared in drafts of Book IX of *The Prelude* until 1832, when it was extracted and published as a separate poem. Wordsworth suppresses this story from his 'life' in part so that he can speak with the cultural authority of a 'great' poet. In Walcott's case, the influence of Anna/Andreuille clearly equals that of the best friend and the art teacher. Anna is depicted in the strongest possible terms: 'The disc of the world turned / slowly, she was its centre' (p. 83); 'There have been / other silences, none as deep. There has since / been possession, none as sure' (p. 97). Of Vaudracour's love for Julia, Wordsworth says similarly: 'he beheld / A vision, and he loved the thing he saw ... all paradise / Could by the simple opening of a door / Let itself in upon him' (IX, 582–3, 591–3). A woman, in both cases, is described as helping to shape the poet's sense of himself. For each of these autobiographical speakers, however, the woman's power is intensified by the fact that she is subsequently lost to him.

Walcott's aesthetic identity, like Wordsworth's, takes shape not only through a sensitivity to such powerful human influences, but also through Walcott's version of 'spots of time', epiphanic moments of psychic intensity that fuse thought, feeling, and language into a textual unity. Such a process is particularly important to any poet who is worried about unifying the scattered elements of consciousness or culture into a textually coherent version of the self. If the disparate phenomena of perception can be fused into at least a textual unity, then perhaps the fragmentary contents of memory can be linked with a powerful sense of the present to produce an integrated aesthetic consciousness. Georges Gusdorf, one of the foremost theoreticians of autobiography, sheds light on this process when he claims that all self-life writing 'is a second reading of experience, and it is truer than the first because it adds to experience itself consciousness of it. In the immediate moment, the agitation of things ordinarily surrounds me too much for me to be able to see it in its entirety'.[8] As autobiographers, Walcott and Wordsworth read themselves into history partly by writing a history for themselves. This process results from fusing a sense of communal identity with an equally powerful sense of the poet's uniqueness as revealed in certain powerful and personal moments.

Writing an autobiography in poetry rather than in prose suggests a lyrical, atemporal approach to experience, a textual emphasis on significant moments rather than on a linear and narrative chronology of the self. In *Another Life* and *The Prelude* we find poets living in worlds that may contribute to this lyrical tendency. In Walcott's case, the fragmentation of Caribbean culture – the diversity of its racial, ethnic, and social histories – like the diversity of individual West Indian lives, leads to an emphasis on the solidity of private moments. The discrete individual must search to find a personal place within a multifarious culture. This phenomenon is evident, for example, in Walcott's alphabetical list of the diverse residents of the town of Castries: Ajax, Berthilia, Choiseul, Darnley ... Weekes, Xodus, Zandoli. In Wordsworth's parallel case, revolutionary movements of the late eighteenth and early nineteenth centuries, augmented by fragmentation of religious, scientific, and cultural authority, produce a similar emphasis on the solitary individual seeking unity within a destabilized world. Both poets inhabit worlds where personal integrity is challenged by social and historical diversity. Whose voice is the voice of authority when numerous forces conflict for cultural ascendancy?

As Gusdorf notes, autobiography emerges only when 'at the cost of a cultural revolution humanity must have emerged from the mythic framework of traditional teachings and must have entered into the perilous domain of history'.[9] Both Walcott and Wordsworth inhabit worlds that have left traditional pasts to embark on much less certain futures. The Caribbean author seeks stability in the face of a chaotic society that often seems to lack a history. Waves of forced and unforced migration, like the absorption of the native culture, produce in St. Lucia a disparate, multivocal society. The English Romantic poet likewise seeks a stable order in response to the convulsions of culture brought on by the Enlightenment, European wars, and the rise of industrialism. For the twentieth-century Caribbean poet, no less than for his English Romantic counterpart, epiphanic moments of textual unity, spoken by a unifying 'I', become one way of steadying personal identity on the unstable sea of cultural history.

Perhaps the most Wordsworthian epiphany in *Another Life* occurs at the climax of section one, when the 'divided child' experiences a spot of time that leads to a textual self at once engendered and made meaningful through art. I quote this entire passage because it reflects so well on the interactions among culture, identity, and authorship in Walcott's poem:

> About the August of my fourteenth year
> I lost myself somewhere above a valley

owned by a spinster-farmer, my dead father's friend.
At the hill's edge there was a scarp
with bushes and boulders stuck in its side.
Afternoon light ripened the valley,
rifling smoke climbed from small labourers' houses,
and I dissolved into a trance.

I was seized by a pity more profound
than my young body could bear, I climbed
with the labouring smoke,
I drowned in labouring breakers of bright cloud,
then uncontrollably I began to weep,
inwardly, without tears, with a serene extinction
of all sense; I felt compelled to kneel,
I wept for nothing and for everything,
I wept for the earth of the hill under my knees,
for the grass, the pebbles, for the cooking smoke
above the labourers' houses like a cry,
for unheard avalanches of white cloud,
but 'darker grows the valley, more and more forgetting'.

(pp. 41–2)

This passage derives from a whole series of Romantic texts and assumptions. More importantly, it reflects Walcott's ability to force traditional Romantic images to yield up new and enhanced power. Walcott's dedicatory moment occurs at precisely the age of Wordsworth's own commitment to a life of poetic memorializing in *The Prelude* (1799, I, 450–70). Likewise, Walcott's description of his younger self reminds us of Wordsworth waiting on the 'highest summit' of a 'crag' for the horses that would take him home to learn of his father's death, and also of the 'blasted tree', and 'stone wall' (1805, XI, 349, 355, 377–8), images which remain connected in his memory for a lifetime. Walcott's 'serene extinction / of all sense' echoes Wordsworth's crossing of the Alps in *The Prelude*, where the poet describes a glory in himself evident only 'when the light of sense / Goes out in flashes that have shewn to us / The invisible world' (1805, VI, 534–6). Two poets separated by a century and a half and a wide ocean claim to derive their autobiographical voices from remarkably similar powers.

Walcott's epiphanic trance likewise reminds us of Shelley's

dedicatory epiphany in *Laon and Cythna* (later *The Revolt of Islam*). Shelley records an 'hour' in his youth that burst his 'spirit's sleep': 'a fresh May-dawn it was, / When I walked forth upon the glittering grass, / And wept, I knew not why' (22–4).[10] Shelley's weeping originates in his sudden recognition that he lives in 'a world of woes', a land where the 'strong still tyrannise' and the selfish rule amid 'harsh and grating strife'. He now longs to dedicate himself to a life of artistic creation that will reveal these injustices, but he also longs to speak with personal authority. For Shelley, as for Wordsworth and Walcott, emotional dedication to heroic art is an initial step toward producing the first-person voice of a poet.

Walcott ends his own dedicatory epiphany with a quote from George Meredith's 'Love in the Valley', and with a powerful image of his commitment to an artistic purpose wider than solipsistic self-recognition. A forgetfulness associated with darkness is possible, according to Meredith's poem, only 'if forgetting could be willed' (38).[11] But we cannot forget the sources of our personal strength or the memories that tie us to our past. Walcott concludes his passage with an image that would have been unavailable to the culture that produced Wordsworth, Shelley, or Meredith:

> For their lights still shine through the hovels like litmus,
> the smoking lamp still slowly says its prayer,
> the poor still move behind their tinted scrim,
> the taste of water is still shared everywhere,
> but in that ship of night, locked in together,
> through which, like chains, a little light might leak,
> something still fastens us forever to the poor.

> (p. 42)

Recalling the Middle Passage of his African ancestors, whose only access to the New World came via slave ships, Walcott drops all first person pronouns and evokes a powerful sense of shared community. His uncontrollable weeping on the hillside has reminded him that for all his attempts to seek a European identity, he is part of a world of suffering unknown to the artistic masters he might serve. Walcott achieves one of the fullest realizations of his own poetic voice by embracing the conflicting sides of his cultural identity. His black grandfather and white grandfather merge in this powerful recognition, in an image that links the language of

Wordsworth and Shelley with the memory of slaves chained in the hold of a Middle Passage vessel.

At one other point in *Another Life* Walcott achieves comparable poetic energy by reflecting on his ancestral African past. He imagines himself as a child, putting a seashell to his ear and hearing a sound that betokens another world. The child

> who puts the shell's howl to his ear,
> hears nothing, hears everything
> that the historian cannot hear, the howls
> of all the races that crossed the water,
> the howls of grandfathers drowned
> in that intricately swivelled Babel,
> hears the fellaheen, the Madrasi, the Mandingo, the Ashanti ...

(p. 136)

Walcott goes on to recall countless Chinese and East Indians who were also brought to Caribbean shores against their will. For all of these subjected cultures and races 'the crossing of the water has erased their memories'. Of course, it is now only Walcott who hears these imaginative sounds in a shell. Transformed into poetry, such sounds are able to return the memory of these enslaved souls to the surviving West Indians who descend from them. In the process, Walcott recalls surprisingly Wordsworthian sounds: 'rocks that muttered close upon our ears – / Black drizzling crags that spake by the wayside / As if a voice were in them' (1805, VI, 562–4). The ancestral echoes Walcott hears and records are, perhaps not surprisingly, a reimagined version of Wordsworth's 'workings of one mind, the features / Of the same face'; Walcott finds a way of speaking for himself by speaking for countless others, producing, as a result, a newly-minted Caribbean version of humanized 'types and symbols of eternity' (VI, 568–9, 571).

Just as Wordsworth ends *The Prelude* by turning once again to his best friend Coleridge, so Walcott ends by returning to Gregorias, his own best friend from childhood, the painter whose 'explosion of impulse' helped Walcott form his own personal artistic credo. Like Coleridge, Gregorias sometimes dances 'with that destructive frenzy / that made our years one fire' (p. 144). But in these earlier days the two aspiring artists, even when 'lit' (drunk) felt themselves to be 'the light of the world!' (p. 145). Their aesthetic collaboration fired sparks in both developing minds. This is Walcott's repetition of the modern conceit that reclaims an ancient connection between poets and divinity. It is likewise a final echo of Wordsworth's affirmation of the primacy of self-awareness: 'to my soul I say / "I recognise thy glory"' (VI, 531–2), and later, 'All that took place within me came and went / As in a moment, and I only now / Remember that it was a thing divine' (VIII, 708–10).

The self creates itself by recreating its past. In Walcott's Caribbean world this process is particularly important, since the colonial individual so often claims to lack a viable sense of history. Identity emerges from the interplay among personal memory, the wider culture, and a personalized cultural memory that can perhaps only be imagined in the poet's most supremely creative moments. But this process is no less at work in a poet from a colonizing culture like Wordsworth's England. Wordsworth also feels cut off from a stable, idealized past. He too feels alienated from his fellow human beings and from an increasingly diverse and multi-vocal world. Wordsworth likewise feels colonized by a whole series of forces outside of himself over which he has no control. Otherwise, why would Wordsworth, like his Caribbean counterpart, work so hard to establish a literary version of a secure identity, to establish verbal contact with others by way of autobiography, to shape the voices of numerous others into his 'own' voice.

We write in order to describe who we are, and also in order to say where we have originated. Avrom Fleishman answers a question that applies equally well to Walcott and Wordsworth: 'Where does the language of self writing come from? From the community's narrative discourse, to be sure, especially from those authoritative texts which embody the prevailing schema of a life – whether simply human, heroic, or divine ... Life stories, like lives, are modeled after idols of the tribe and constitute a subgroup sometimes difficult to distinguish from its other narratives of history and fiction'.[12] Poetic autobiographers consistently cross this boundary between the imagined story of their own lives and the recreated history of their tribes. In a voice like Wordsworth's or Walcott's we hear just such an attempt to produce an 'authoritative text' which, by speaking for a powerfully realized literary self, can also speak for the culture that produced it.

What emerges from a parallel reading of *Another Life* and *The Prelude* is not merely a series of direct poetic influences, or a simple tracing of common structures and imagery, but remarkable

similarities between textual identity formation in two vastly differ-
ent worlds. The worlds that characterize this difference – the
English Lake District of the late eighteenth century and the island
of St. Lucia in the twentieth century – yield up, via these texts, two
strikingly similar poetic developments. The adult autobiographer
has been produced and controlled – we might more accurately say
'colonized' – by a whole series of cultural forces: material, social,
economic, emotional. These forces, embodied in childhood and
reimagined by the adult, determine the individual's sense of iden-
tity, but also produce uncertainty about that identity.
Autobiography seeks to situate the voice of a self in a specific
cultural context. At the same time, the voice of any self resists such
situation, seeking always a personal and revitalized version of
culture. The self creates itself in response to – and in dialogue with
– a series of forces and voices that are almost impossible to recon-
struct completely. But textual identity – the 'I' that speaks the
autobiographical poem – is an attempt at just such an act of artistic
reconstruction. The self is made out of the world it inhabits, but it
concurrently makes itself in response to that world. Jerome
McGann oversimplifies modern literature by claiming that 'the idea
that poetry, or even consciousness, can set one free from the ruins
of history and culture is the grand illusion of every Romantic
poet'.[13] Autobiographers like Walcott and Wordsworth do not want
to free themselves completely from either history or culture; rather,
they want to create themselves poetically out of a history – their
own – that can link them to the permanent, yet still dynamic,
cultures that produced them. In Walcott's Caribbean, no less than
in Wordsworth's Cumbria, the reformation of culture is tied to the
formation of poetic voices and personal identities.

Notes

PREFACE

1. *Subjectivities: A History of Self-Representation in Britain, 1832–1920* (Oxford: Oxford University Press, 1991), p. 4. As Michael Riffaterre has it, 'verisimilitude is an artifact, since it is a verbal representation of reality rather than reality itself: verisimilitude itself, therefore, entails fictionality', in *Fictional Truth* (Baltimore: Johns Hopkins University Press, 1990), p. xv. Gagnier concludes her analysis by claiming that 'the study of autobiography is not merely a genteel (or gentile or genital) literary exercise but a gauge of citizens' degrees of social participation and exclusion, consensus and revolt', p. 278.

2. See *The Random House Dictionary of the English Language* (New York: Random House, 1969).

3. *On Autobiography*, trans. Katherine Levy, ed. Paul John Eakin (Minneapolis: University of Minnesota Press, 1989), p. 131. Paul Smith notes that skepticism about the autobiographical subject, or speaker 'is not to say, of course, that the "subject" has no history or real existence (any more than Barthes' famous essay on "The Death of the Author" [1977] denies the existence of real people writing)', in *Discerning the Subject* (Minneapolis: University of Minnesota Press, 1988), p. 111. Paul Jay traces the romantic 'aesthetics of self-creation' to Hegel, in *Being in the Text: Self-Representation from Wordsworth to Roland Barthes* (Ithaca: Cornell University Press, 1984), pp. 42–3.

CHAPTER 1   SILENCING THE (OTHER) SELF: WORDSWORTH AS 'WORDSWORTH!' IN 'THERE WAS A BOY'

1. *Jean-Jacques Rousseau: Transparency and Obstruction*, trans. Arthur Goldhammer (Chicago: University of Chicago Press, 1988 [1971]), p. 125. Starobinski adds that a 'self-portrait is not a more or less faithful copy of a subject called "the self". It is a vital record of a search to discover the self. I *am* that search ... [the writer must] give up looking for a "true self" in an unvarying past and seek instead to create a self through writing', p. 198. Wordsworth's connection to Rousseau's autobiographical assumptions and technique deserves more attention that it has received. See, for example, Huntington Williams, *Rousseau and Romantic Autobiography* (Oxford: Oxford University Press, 1983), who notes that 'Rousseau's autobiography is a textual exchange with his own pre-autobiographical writings ... Rousseau constructs an image of himself, literally invents himself in these pre-autobiographical texts', p. 3. Felicity Nussbaum argues that in 'eighteenth-century England, "identity", "self", "soul", and "person" were dangerous and disputed formations, subject to appropriation

by various interests'; as a result, 'eighteenth-century works of self-biography are less quests toward self-discovery in which the narrator reveals herself or himself than repetitive serial representations of particular moments held together by the narrative "I"', in *The Autobiographical Subject: Gender and Ideology in Eighteenth-Century England* (Baltimore: The Johns Hopkins University Press, 1989), pp. 18, 38.

2. See *The Prelude: 1799, 1805, 1850*, ed. Jonathan Wordsworth, M. H. Abrams, and Stephen Gill (New York: Norton, 1979), p. 492. Citations to the poem, unless otherwise indicated, will be drawn from this edition and will specify version.

3. Stephen Gill, *William Wordsworth: A Life* (Oxford: Clarendon, 1989). Gill's introduction warns of the dangers of a text like *The Prelude* which presents a version of the self to an implied audience while at the same time creating a textual self for the poet to live up to in his own subsequent life. Gill notes that 'poetic evidence' is often the only evidence we have for the 'facts' of Wordsworth's experience, adding that Wordsworth 'did not scruple elsewhere to tamper with the "facts" if they spoiled an imaginative conception', p. 7. See also Gill's '"Affinities Preserved": Poetic Self-Reference in Wordsworth', *SIR* 24 (1985): 531–49, which emphasizes Wordsworth's 'refusal to acknowledge a frontier between poetic fiction and verifiable, experienced fact', p. 532.

4. *Prelude*, 'MS drafts and fragments', p. 485. See also *The Prelude: 1798–9*, ed. Stephen Parrish (Ithaca: Cornell University Press, 1977) for variants of early manuscript materials and photographic reproductions of the texts. The Cornell edition is an indispensable volume for an understanding of the textual origins of the Wordsworthian autobiographer. Few Wordsworthian passages have received more comment in recent years than 'There was a boy'. Paul Magnuson sees the passage connected to Wordsworth's anxieties about completing a major poetic project: *Coleridge and Wordsworth: A Lyrical Dialogue* (Princeton: Princeton University Press, 1988), p. 202 ff. Tilottama Rajan, in *Dark Interpreter: The Discourse of Romanticism* (Ithaca: Cornell University Press, 1980) p. 211, calls the boy a 'revenant' or 'surrogate' speaking for the 'power of imaginary representation, but also for the duplicity of its substitutions'. Alan Bewell links the boy with an anthropological critique, a 'hypothetical history of the process by which the child is ushered into language', in *Wordsworth and the Enlightenment: Nature, Man and Society in the Experimental Poetry* (New Haven: Yale University Press, 1989), p. 209. Other important discussions of 'There was a boy' include: James K. Chandler, *Wordsworth's Second Nature: a Study of the Poetry and Politics* (Chicago: University of Chicago Press, 1984), pp. 109–11; Frances Ferguson, *Wordsworth: Language as Counter Spirit* (New Haven: Yale University Press, 1977), pp. 167–70, 242–9; Stephen Lukits, 'Wordsworth Unawares: The Boy of Winander, the Poet, and the Mariner', *TWC* 19 (1988): 156–60; Robert Rehder, *Wordsworth and the Beginnings of Modern Poetry* (London: Croom Helm, 1981), pp. 81–90;

Charles J. Rzepka, *The Self as Mind: Vision and Identity in Wordsworth, Coleridge, and Keats* (Cambridge, Mass.: Harvard University Press, 1986), Chapter 2; Andrew M. Cooper, *Doubt and Identity in Romantic Poetry* (New Haven: Yale University Press, 1988), p. 187, and Jonathan Wordsworth, *William Wordsworth: The Borders of Vision* (Oxford: Clarendon Press, 1982), pp. 28–31, who also notes that 'to judge from MS JJ, the original first-person drafts of "There was a boy" followed the boat-stealing by a matter of hours, or days at most. It is a warning of the difficulties of generalizing about Wordsworth's mood that lines of such perfect composure should be so close to an incident of "stealth and troubled joy"', p. 48. Geoffrey Hartman's claim, in *Wordsworth's Poetry: 1787–1814* (Cambridge, Mass.: Harvard University Press, 1987 [1971]), that the poet looking at this child's grave is Wordsworth 'mourning the loss of a prior mode of being by replacing the boy with himself' is, in one sense, the starting point for my argument: 'The poet who stands at the child's grave knows that consciousness is always of death, a confrontation of the self with a buried self', pp. 21–2. A series of such dead (and textually buried) selves help us to understand silenced rhetorical voices that eventually modulate into the speaking 'Wordsworth'.

5.   Susan Wolfson, in *The Questioning Presence: Wordsworth, Keats, and the Interrogative Mode in Romantic Poetry* (Ithaca: Cornell University Press, 1986), claims that the major poems of Romanticism are all 'critically implicated in perceptions that provoke inquiry, experiences that elude or thwart stable organizations, events that challenge previous certainties and require new terms of interpretation', p. 18. She notes that 'Wordsworth's autobiography not only embodies his intended or willed self-image, but records other voices of which the author may have been unaware before they were written and which prove disturbingly tenacious in the autobiography once articulated', p. 138. Lucy Newlyn points out that Wordsworth needed to develop a 'language of indeterminacy in which to make his most challenging claims': *Coleridge, Wordsworth, and the Language of Allusion* (Oxford: Clarendon Press, 1986), p. 136. Newlyn adds that his finest poems involve a mixture of temporally distinct manuscript materials, an alteration of past events, and an occasional presentation of claims that are 'palpably untrue' or 'deliberately misleading', pp. 137, 170. This aspect of Romantic fictionalizing has implications even for editorial practice, as evidenced in Jack Stillinger's useful call for 'a more fluid notion of literary authority' (p. 27) than the one required by the current practice of favoring the earliest versions of texts: 'Textual Primitivism in the Editing of Wordsworth', *SIR* 28:1 (1989): 3–28. Stillinger advocates dispensing with the concept of a 'final text', while praising Wolfson's emphasis on 'revision as a continuous process of self-reading, self-reconstructing, and *The Prelude* as a poem constituted by all of its texts at once', p. 28. Such views encourage us to see all textual selves as subject to self-creation, self-revision, and ongoing dialogic revision.

6.   Jean-Jacques Rousseau, *The First and Second Discourses and Essay on the*

Origin of Language, ed. and trans. Victor Gourkevitch (New York: Harper & Row, 1986). In a closely related point, Rousseau parallels speaking to emotion and writing to intellect: 'Writing, which might be expected to fix [or to stabilize] language, is precisely what alters it; it changes not its words but its genius; it substitutes precision for expressiveness. One conveys one's sentiment in speaking, and one's ideas in writing', p. 253. Rousseau anticipates Yeats, arguing that the process of writing autobiographically substitutes a formal textual version of identity for the unstable sensory textures of lived experience.

7. *The Figure of Echo: A Mode of Allusion in Milton and After* (Berkeley: University of California Press, 1981), p. 18.

8. Coleridge hints that all acts of poetic artistry may be forms of self-creation and wish fulfillment, including his own definition of 'Nature' as a category with any intrinsic 'value' to humans: *Coleridge: Poetical Works*, ed. E. H. Coleridge (Oxford: Oxford University Press, 1912 [1969]), p. 429. His own sense of tensions between dramatic and ventriloquistic forms of lyricism emerges throughout the *Biographia Literaria, BL* 1: 34; 2: 43–4, 100, 135.

9. *Byron's Poetry*, ed. Frank McConnell (New York: Norton, 1978), p. 51. All Byron citations are from this edition. Byron is the master of the self-recorded awareness of himself in the process of creating the textual identity that was to become 'Byron' in the minds of the European reading public. See Jerome Christensen, *Lord Byron's Strength* (Baltimore: Johns Hopkins University Pres, 1993), particularly Chapter 1, 'Theorizing Byron's Practice: The Performance of Lordship and the Poet's Career', and Chapter 5, 'The Speculative Stage: *Childe Harold III* and the Formation of Byron'. Christensen's Byron is as much a self-parodist as he is a self-creator.

10. Critiques of this 'dead' boy suggest the problem inherent in two extremes in contemporary Wordsworth criticism. If we see the 'dead' boy as fundamentally rhetorical and textual, as de Man does in 'Time and History in Wordsworth', *Diacritics* 17: 4 (1987): 4–17, then the dissolution of language is merely an analogue for the dissolution of self so often implied in totalizing versions of poststructuralist theory: the self is a tissue of rhetorical postures subject to banishment with the wave of a deconstructive wand. If, on the other hand, we seek to date this fictional boy's death, or work to connect the textual boy with some actual person or event – new historically – we run the risk of providing anecdotal 'solutions' to interpretive problems that may distort resonances in the text. This 'dead' boy *is* a version of Wordsworth's earlier self, he *may be* connected to some actual dead child that Wordsworth had in mind when he penned these lines, and he *is* also a textual creation that functions in certain ways within the rhetorical structure of the poem. For such a middle-ground position see David Haney's suggestive essay on the development of Wordsworth's poetic voice by 1798: 'The Emergence of the Autobiographical Figure in *The Prelude*, Book I', *SIR* 20 (1981): 33–64. Haney cautions that 'the exigencies of poetic autobiography preclude any discussion of an objectively "true" state of affairs which the poet

could be accused of perverting', p. 63. This insight complicates all
new historical attempts to shift readers' attention – in, say, 'Tintern
Abbey' – away from textual cottages and hedgerows to extratextual
smokestacks, paupers, and revolutions. See, for example, Marjorie
Levinson's *Wordsworth's Great Period Poems: Four Essays* (Cambridge:
Cambridge University Press, 1986), pp. 34–7. We might just as appro-
priately focus on the monastic history of the abbey 'a few miles' away
from the scene, the condition of Wordsworth's clothing in 1798,
Dorothy's mental state, or any other anecdotal information we can
link to the text, however tenuously. My argument, like Levinson's,
rests on the premiss that Wordsworth suppresses various voices,
thereby creating a palimpsestic text. My emphasis on the complexi-
ties of the first-person speaker, very much unlike Levinson's
argument, stresses the difficulty of ever knowing precisely what facts
or experiences Wordsworth is repressing.

11. W. B. Yeats, *Essays and Introductions* (New York: Macmillan, 1961), p.
509; Yeats adds: 'A poet writes always of his personal life ... he never
speaks directly as to someone at the breakfast table ... he is never the
bundle of accident and incoherence that sits down to breakfast; he
has been reborn as an idea, something intended, complete'.

12. See letters 266, 267 and 268 in Volume 1, *Collected Letters of Samuel
Taylor Coleridge*, ed. Earl Leslie Griggs, 6 vols (Oxford: Clarendon,
1956–71). Coleridge's identification of this textual voice as
'Wordsworth!' may have contributed to Wordsworth's sudden will-
ingness to continue with the project of recording his own life in
verse. Wordsworth's uncertainty about that same identification may
help to account for his unwillingness to publish this earliest version,
or any other version, of his autobiography during his own lifetime.

13. Magnuson offers the most complete account of connections between
Wordsworth's pluralistic ventriloquism and Bakhtinian dialogics;
describing the 1798–9 texts of *The Prelude*, he says: 'When
[Wordsworth] seems to be the most personal and individual, he
comes close to ventriloquizing Coleridge's voice and appropriating
his texts. When he claims to be turning to childhood for the steady-
ing cadences of nature's calm and the disciplines of fear and terror,
he recalls poetry that has already been composed': *Coleridge and
Wordsworth: A Lyrical Dialogue* (Princeton: Princeton University
Press, 1988), p. 194. More recently, Susan Eilenberg has linked the
'appropriative power of Wordsworth's voice' to Wordsworth's and
Coleridge's 'impressive but not limitless willingness to share literary
property', in *Strange Power of Speech: Wordsworth, Coleridge and
Literary Possession* (Oxford: Oxford University Press, 1992), pp. 4, 15.
Don Bialostosky offers Bakhtinian readings in *Making Tales: The
Poetics of Wordsworth's Narrative Experiments* (Chicago: University of
Chicago Press, 1984) and also in *Wordsworth, Dialogics, and the Practice
of Criticism* (Cambridge: Cambridge University Press, 1992), particu-
larly Chapter 2 'Wordsworth's dialogic art' and Chapter 3, 'Dialogics
of the lyric'. See also Gordon Thomas, 'The *Lyrical Ballads* Ode:
Dialogized Heteroglossia', *TWC* (1989): 102–5. Coleridge was the first

to note this aspect of Wordsworth's voice in his criticisms of the ventriloquistic aspects of Wordsworth's contributions to *Lyrical Ballads*, *BL*, 2: 59, 135, 150. Coleridge was generally hostile to the idea of lyric speakers adopting dramatic postures: 'I am always vexed that the authors do not say what they have to say at once in their own persons ... I have no admiration for the practice of ventriloquizing through another man's mouth', in *Specimens of the Table Talk of the Late Samuel Taylor Coleridge*, ed. H. N. Coleridge (London: John Murray, 1886), p. 174. Contrast, however, Coleridge's view of truth: 'I regard truth as a divine ventriloquist', *BL*, 1: 164. Reeve Parker, in '"Oh could you hear his voice": Wordsworth, Coleridge, and Ventriloquism', in *Romanticism and Language*, ed. Arden Reed (Ithaca: Cornell University Press, 1984), pp. 125–43, notes that the self 'made by the work' is more 'genuine' than the biographical self, p. 125. Jerome McGann's comment about Byron is likewise true of Wordsworth; such a poet, says McGann, 'discovers his voice in a conscious and dialectical act of poetic ventriloquism', in *The Beauty of Inflections* (Oxford: Oxford University Press, 1985), p. 286. In Wordsworth's case, as in Byron's, we might say self-ventriloquism.

14.　'Preface' to *The Excursion*, in *The Poetical Works of William Wordsworth*, ed. Ernest de Selincourt and Helen Darbishire, 5 vols (Oxford: Clarendon Press, 1940–9), 5: 1–2. All subsequent citations, with the exception of *The Prelude*, are to this edition. Note Edward Bostetter's comment that the story of the Solitary in *The Excursion* 'is, in part, a curious jumbling of Wordsworth's own life', in *The Romantic Ventriloquists: Wordsworth, Coleridge, Keats, Shelley, Byron* (Seattle: University of Washington Press, 1975 [1963]), p. 75. Bostetter also comments on the shift from the ventriloquized Pedlar of 'The Ruined Cottage' (1798) to the self-consciously autobiographical Poet of *The Prelude*. My argument claims much more rhetorical control on Wordsworth's part than Bostetter's 'curious jumbling'. See also Kenneth Johnston, *Wordsworth and 'The Recluse'* (New Haven: Yale University Press, 1984), who is persuasive in his discussion of the 'dialectical intertwining between *The Recluse* and *The Prelude*'; noting that the Pedlar and the narrator of 'The Ruined Cottage' are both versions of Wordsworth. Johnston points out one final way in which Wordsworth dialogizes the self to produce an autobiographical voice: 'one version of himself is telling the story to another', p. 27. For Johnston, the resulting confusion is obvious: 'Wordsworth tries to decide [between 1793 and 1798] if he can tell a story or if he must *be* his story', p. 27.

15.　Fenwick comments in Norton *Prelude*, pp. 536–8. Charles J. Rzepka links such uncertainty about self-presentation to a wider crisis of loss and skepticism: 'when the personal trauma of early parental loss coincided with great artistic gifts, the works that resulted gave rise to innumerable echoes in the collective consciousness of English nineteenth-century society, a society whose Great Parent had abandoned it', in *The Self as Mind: Vision and Identity in Wordsworth, Coleridge, and Keats* (Cambridge, Mass.: Harvard University Press, 1986), p. 30.

CHAPTER 2   THE POLITICS OF SELF-PRESENTATION:
WORDSWORTH AS REVOLUTIONARY ACTOR IN A LITERARY
DRAMA

1. Lynn Hunt, *Politics, Culture, and Class in the French Revolution*
(Berkeley: University of California Press, 1984), pp. 12, 24. Hunt
quotes Rousseau on the principle that led the revolution to be
conceived, at least in part, in terms of rhetorical practice. Language
became essential to political change in France when 'government
became an instrument for fashioning a people', p. 2. If we replace
'government' with 'literature' in Hunt's phrase, we produce a very
Wordsworthian claim about the function of the poet. Hunt also notes
that the 'origins of the Revolution are to be found in a crisis of social
mobility and status anxiety within an amalgamated elite made up of
nobles and bourgeois', p. 5. This sentence describes another dilemma
that confronted Wordsworth (and Coleridge) by 1798: how might
two obscure ballad writers fashion literature for an increasingly
democratized citizenry out of the hierarchical and aristocratic poetry
of the past. Alan Liu draws a related connection between poetry and
political action in 'Wordsworth and Subversion 1793–1804: Trying
Cultural Criticism', *Yale Journal of Criticism* 2: 2 (1989): 55–100: 'liter-
ary action may be explored *as* action rather than as representational
displays', p. 63; on these terms, writing poetry *is* a form of political
activity. Hunt notes that revolutionary times produce a 'constant
displacement of political authority' and a subsequent need to substi-
tute a personal 'charisma' that comes to be 'most concretely located
in words, that is, in the ability to speak for the Nation', p. 26.
Wordsworth participates in this process by choosing to speak not so
much for his nation as for humankind, for 'Nature', and even for 'a
motion and a spirit' that 'rolls' (like a voice?) through all things. See
Hunt's more recent elaboration on the extent to which 'politics do
depend on imagination', in *The Family Romance of the French
Revolution* (Berkeley: University of California Press, 1992), p. xv.
2. François Furet, *Interpreting the French Revolution*, trans. Elborg Forster
(Cambridge: Cambridge University Press, 1981), p. 31. Furet points
out the eighteenth-century need for 'responsible spokesmen' for
which the nation increasingly turned 'to the *philosophes* and men of
letters'; literature assumes a politicized role when the function of
authors 'as opinion-makers who wielded no practical power whatso-
ever, was to shape political culture itself', pp. 36, 37. The idealized
function of literature envisioned by Wordsworth in the 'Preface' to
Lyrical Ballads (1800) stands as a paramount example of this historical
shift from the poet as a chronicler of social norms to the poet as a
shaper of a cultural future. Michel de Certeau evokes a similar
connection between literary self-expression and prescriptive social
practice when he claims that the 'problem of the speaker and of his
identity became acute with the breakdown of the world that was
assumed to be spoken and speaking: who speaks when there is no
longer a divine Speaker who founds every particular enunciation?

The question was apparently settled by the system that furnished the subject with a place guaranteed and measured by his scriptural production. In a laissez-faire economy, where isolated and competitive activities are supposed to contribute to a general rationality, the work of writing gives birth to both the product and its author', in *The Practice of Everyday Life*, trans. Steven F. Rendall (Berkeley: University of California Press, 1984), pp. 156–7. Under such conditions, 'a new king comes into being: the individual subject, an imperceptible master', p. 157. In Wordsworth's case, just such a verbal monarch is able to see his self-described mind as 'lord and master, and that outward sense / Is but the obedient servant of her will' (*Prelude*, 1805, XI, 271–2).

3. *Wordsworth and Coleridge: The Radical Years* (Oxford: Clarendon Press, 1988), p. 42. See particularly Chapter 2, '"Pretty Hot in It": Wordsworth and France, 1791–92'. See also Ronald Paulson, *Representations of Revolution (1789–1820)* (New Haven: Yale University Press, 1983), pp. 248–55.

4. *PW*, 1: 245. Recall also Wordsworth's claim in his 'Preface' to the 1814 *Excursion*: 'the first and third parts of "The Recluse" will consist chiefly of meditations in the Author's own person … in the intermediate part ("The Excursion") the intervention of characters speaking is employed, and something of a dramatic form adopted', 5: 2.

5. Quoting from a Fenwick note, *PW*, 2: 477. This is precisely what Coleridge calls ventriloquism: a lyric poem in which 'two are represented as talking, while in truth one man only speaks', *BL*, 2: 135.

6. See Wordsworth's note to 'The Thorn', where he expresses his need to make the thorn as 'permanently an impressive object' to others through language as it had been to him during his own experience, *PW*, 2: 511. This process, of course, connects with his goal of throwing a 'colouring of imagination', over objects so that otherwise 'ordinary things' might appear remarkable in a poem. See 'Preface' to *Lyrical Ballads*, *PW*, 2: 386.

7. Coleridge also links the passion that stimulates the poet to write with the language used to express the feeling: 'as every passion has its proper pulse, so it will likewise have its characteristic modes of expression', *BL*, 2: 71.

8. *Journals of Dorothy Wordsworth*, ed. Mary Moorman (Oxford: Oxford University Press, 1973), p. 92.

9. *The Correspondence of Henry Crabb Robinson with the Wordsworth Circle*, ed. Edith J. Morley, 2 vols. (Oxford: Clarendon, 1927), 1: 53.

10. The Wilkinson lines were not published until 1824, but Wordsworth credited them in an 1807 note. See *PW*, 3: 445. See also Gill's Oxford edition of the poems, p. 717. Whatever its numerous sources, one of Wordsworth's most ostensibly 'personal' poems records an experience that did not happen to him.

11. *PW*, 3: 444. See also 'Recollections of a Tour Made in Scotland', in *Journals of Dorothy Wordsworth*, ed. E. de Selincourt (Oxford: Clarendon, 1941).

12. Roe cites the possibility that both 'Coleridge and Wordsworth

discovered in Robespierre an alarming, distorted version of themselves', *Radical Years*, p. 209. Likewise, David Erdman notes the possibility that Wordsworth's 'feeling of guilt about "regicide"' were grounds for 'the poet's later "moral questions" and "despair"', p. 92, in 'The Man Who was not Napoleon', *TWC* 12: 1 (1981): 92–6. See also Erdman's 'Wordsworth as Heartsworth; or, Was Regicide the Prophetic Ground of Those "Moral Questions"?' in *The Evidence of the Imagination: Studies of Interactions between Life and Art in English Romantic Literature*, ed. Donald H. Reiman et al. (New York: New York University Press, 1978), pp. 12–41.

13. A related discussion of tensions between revolutionary disillusionment and textual self-creation can be found in Andrea Henderson, 'A Tale Told to be Forgotten: Enlightenment, Revolution, and the Poet in "Salisbury Plain"', *SIR* 30 (1991): 71–84. Richard G. Swartz argues that Wordsworth responds to these tensions by developing a 'politics of ambition' throughout *The Prelude*; see 'Wordsworth and the Politics of Ambition', *Nineteenth-Century Contexts* 13: 1 (1989): 91–120.

14. Simon Schama, *Citizens: A Chronicle of the French Revolution* (New York: Knopf, 1989), pp. 586–93, and also Chapter 4, 'The Cultural Construction of a Citizen', pp. 123–82. Hubert C. Johnston claims that revolutionary rhetoric often followed the fortunes of revolutionaries; he notes that, by 1793, 'the radicals were occupied in a futile attack on one another and the rhetoric became confused when former friends called one another "traitors, anarchists, or disorganizers", depending on whether they were pro-Mountain in Paris or Federalist in sentiment. By that time the revolutionary rhetoric, both moderate and radical, was threadbare and ridden with cliches; it mirrored a tired society', in *The Midi in Revolution: A Study of Regional Political Diversity, 1789–1793* (Princeton: Princeton University Press, 1986), p. 81. See also George Armstong Kelly, *Victims, Authority, and Terror: The Parallel Deaths of d'Orleans, Custine, Bailly, and Malesherbes* (Chapel Hill: University of North Carolina Press, 1982).

15. See Nigel Wood's claim that 'on the stage of history Wordsworth feels like an actor that has missed his cue', in *The Prelude*, ed. Nigel Wood (Buckingham: Open University Press, 1993), p. 169. For a related discussion see Mary Jacobus, '"That Great Stage Where Senators Perform": *Macbeth* and the Politics of Romantic Theory', *SIR* 22: 3 (1983): 353–88. Roger Shattuck, in *The Innocent Eye: On Modern Literature & the Arts* (New York: Farrar, Straus, Giroux, 1984), notes that in 'the absence of station and self assigned by mere birth, it is as if playacting offered a means of forging a self and creating a community', p. 118. Shattuck points to the 'theater state' concept, proposed by Clifford Geertz, and the 'social drama' theory of Victor Turner and Richard Sennett as examples of a modern 'tendency to construe the self or character as something virtual and problematic, as an entity capable of coming into being only in performance', p. 118. In the 'Preface' to *The Excursion* Wordsworth notes literary 'performances, either unfinished, or unpublished', which engaged him while preparing this fragment of a 'long and laborious Work', *PW*, 5: 1-2.

16. Victor Turner, 'Liminality and the Performative Genres', in *Rite, Drama, Festival, Spectacle: Rehearsals Toward a Theory of Cultural Performance*, ed. John J. MacAloon (Philadelphia: ISHI, 1984), argues that 'genres of performance' include a wide range of activities – religious rituals, familial activities, artistic practices – and that 'social structure is itself a performance', p. 26. Brian Johnston, in 'Revolution and the Romantic Theater', in *Theater Three* (Spring 1988): 5–20, connects the 'histrionics' of revolutionary activity with a dramatized politics and artful productions staged for political purposes. Michael Gassenmeier notes how many of 'Wordsworth's metaphors are burdened with weighty political connotations': for example, 'domination', 'tyranny', 'usurpation', 'lord', 'master', 'servant', 'slave'; in '"Twas a Transport of the Outward Sense": Wordsworth's Own Account of his Visions and Revisions of the French Revolution', in *Beyond the Suburbs of the Mind: Exploring English Romanticism* (Essen: Die Blaue Eule, 1987), p. 132. Jeffrey Baker sees *The Excursion* as an 'inner debate between opposed aspects of the poet's personality ... The chief protagonists in the poem are not merely two conflicting elements within a divided self; they are, I suggest, two distinct possible selves, between whom, at a crucial point in his life, the poet had to choose', in 'Casualties of the Revolution: Wordsworth and his "Solitary" Self', *Yearbook of English Studies* 19 (1989), p. 95. See also Richard Gravil, '"Some Other Being": Wordsworth in *The Prelude*', *Yearbook of English Studies* 19 (1989), p. 127.

CHAPTER 3   SOUNDS INTO SPEECH: THE TWO-PART *PRELUDE* OF 1799 AS DIALOGIC DRAMATIC MONOLOGUE

1. *Art and Answerability: Early Philosophical Essays by M. M. Bakhtin*, ed. Michael Holquist and Vadim Liapunov, trans. Liapunov (Austin: University of Texas Press, 1990), pp. 154–5.
2. Privateer, *Romantic Voices: Identity and Ideology in British Poetry, 1789–1850* (Athens, Ga.: University of Georgia Press, 1991), p. 12.
3. See Johnston, *Wordsworth and 'The Recluse'*, Chapter 2: 'The First *Prelude*, 1798–1799' and Chapter 4: 'Building Up a Work That Should Endure: The Construction of the 1805 *Prelude*'. Magnuson stresses the multiplicity of dialogues in Wordsworth's texts, noting that 'as the work on *The Prelude* grew through 1805, the dialogue became more a dialogue with his own earlier work and less a dialogue with Coleridge's poetry', *Lyrical Dialogue*, p. 212. Wordsworth thus 'sacrifices' the dialogic younger voice of the radical composite-speaker (Coleridge-Wordsworth) in order to create the self-originating voice of the adult, more 'respectable', Wordsworth.
4. Hartman in '"Was it for this ...?" Wordsworth and the Birth of the Gods', in *Romantic Revolutions: Criticism and Theory*, ed. Kenneth Johnston et al. (Bloomington: Indiana University Press, 1990), p. 19; Weiskel in *The Romantic Sublime: Studies in the Structure and Psychology of Transcendence* (Baltimore: Johns Hopkins, 1976), p. 169.

Weiskel's psychologized version of transcendence tends always monologically to unify disparate poetic voices.
5. See my 'Dialogism in the Dramatic Monologue: Suppressed Voices in Browning', in *Victorians Institute Journal* 18 (1990): 29–51. See also A. Dwight Culler, 'Monodrama and Dramatic Monologue', *PMLA* 90 (1975): 366–85; Ralph W. Rader, 'The Dramatic Monologue and Related Lyric Forms', *Critical Inquiry* 3 (1976): 131–53; and Adena Rosmarin, *The Power of Genre* (Minneapolis: University of Minnesota Press, 1985). Herbert Tucker, in 'Dramatic Monologue and the Overhearing of Lyric' in *Lyric Poetry: Beyond New Criticism*, ed. Chaviva Hosek and Patricia Parker (Ithaca: Cornell University Press, 1985), pp. 226–46, claims that 'dramatic monologue in the Browning tradition is, in a word, anything but monological', p. 231. We can extend Tucker's claim to include romantic proto-dramatic-monologues such as Wordsworth's 'The Thorn', Coleridge's 'The Three Graves', Byron's 'The Prisoner of Chillon', and Shelley's 'Julian and Maddalo'.
6. Julia Kristeva, 'Word, Dialogue, and Novel', in *Desire in Language*, ed. Leon S. Roudiez (New York: Columbia University Press, 1980), p. 66; and see M. M. Bakhtin, *The Dialogical Imagination*, trans. Caryl Emerson and Michael Holquist, ed. Holquist (Austin: University of Texas Press, 1981), pp. 426–8.
7. See Gary Saul Morson and Caryl Emerson, *Mikhail Bakhtin: Creation of a Prosaics* (Stanford: Stanford University Press, 1990), p. 4 and Kristeva, 'The Ruin of a Poetics', in *Russian Formalism*, ed. Stephan Bann and John E. Bowlt (New York: Harper & Row, 1973), pp. 102–19. Such views on intertextuality stress the inseparability of texts and their sources.
8. Wittgenstein, *Philosophical Investigations*, trans. G. E. M. Anscombe (Oxford: Blackwell, 1972), I, 109, p. 47e. Austin Quigley, in 'Wittgenstein's Philosophizing and Literary Theorizing', *NLH* 19: 2 (1988): 209–38, describes Wittgenstein's method in very Wordsworthian terms. Wittgenstein, according to Quigley, uses 'repeated images of journeying, of failing to get under way, of getting lost when under way, and of arriving at the wrong destination', p. 210.
9. Bakhtin, *Dialogical Imagination*, p. 37. Starobinski also describes a process of self-fashioning shared by Rousseau and Wordsworth: 'At one moment my past seems darker, at another brighter, than it really was ... For the essence is not the objective fact but the feelings, and past feelings can be revived, can be called up in one's mind and transformed into present emotions. The sequence of events may not be available to memory, but the sequence of feelings is, and around those feelings forgotten facts can be reconstructed', *Transparency and Obstruction*, pp. 196–7. Rousseau admits this truth about the falsity at the center of the autobiographical act: 'I may omit or transpose facts, or make mistakes in dates; but I *cannot go wrong about what I have felt*, or about what my feelings have led me to do; and these are the chief subjects of my story', *Confessions*, trans. J. M. Cohen (New York:

162 *Notes*

Penguin, 1953), Book 7, pp. 262–3. Wordsworth all but quotes these lines when he tells Beaumont that he had simply written what he had 'felt and thought' so as not to 'be bewildered', *EY*, pp. 586–7.

10. Wolfson, *Questioning Presence*, p. 138. Wolfson quotes Wordsworth's internal dialogism, 'Thus strangely did I war against myself', (1805, XI, 74), arguing that he confronts 'his most troubling questions about autobiography in confronting the enigmas of others' self-narratives', pp. 139, 140. I would add that Coleridge's conversation poems and Dorothy's *Journals* are examples of precisely such enigmatic 'self-narratives' that have the effect of producing 'self-war' within Wordsworth.

11. In the 'Essay on Epitaphs' Wordsworth links poetry with a form of speaking for the dead; epitaphs, he says, 'often personate the deceased, and represent him as speaking from his own tomb-stone ... By this tender fiction, the survivors bind themselves to a sedater sorrow, and employ the intervention of the imagination', *Selected Prose*, ed. John O. Hayden (New York: Viking, 1988), p. 335. D. D. Devlin, *Wordsworth and the Poetry of Epitaphs* (Totowa, NJ: Barnes & Noble, 1981), p. 83, notes Wordsworth's tendency to speak for others' voices that have been silenced by death or overwhelming emotion ('Michael').

12. The genesis of the Salisbury Plain poems suggests 'one of the most turbulent periods of Wordsworth's life', and his 'overwrought imagination' at the time of composition, (*Gill*, p. 685). Just how hard a time Wordsworth was having speaking in his own voice is evident in this chronological history: parts of the poem were apparently begun in 1791–2, the text was substantially composed 1793–4, revised and enlarged as 'Adventures on Salisbury Plain' in 1795, parts extracted and published as 'The Female Vagrant' in 1798, revisions and first publication of the complete poem in 1842 as 'Guilt and Sorrow; or, Incidents upon Salisbury Plain'. This half century of textual history hints at the complexities involved in sorting out the 'author-function', or any stable authority at all, for the speaker in such a work. See also Gill's edition of the poems, *The Salisbury Plain Poems of William Wordsworth* (Ithaca: Cornell University Press, 1975).

13. *The Kristeva Reader*, ed. Toril Moi (New York: Columbia University Press, 1986), pp. 24–74 and Tzvetan Todorov, *Mikhail Bakhtin: The Dialogical Principle*, trans. Wlad Godzich (Minneapolis: University of Minnesota Press, 1984), particularly Chapter 4, 'Theory of the Utterance' and Chapter 5, 'Intertextuality'. Todorov says, 'Bakhtin uses "dialogic" and "dialogism" in a very broad sense that makes even the monologue dialogical (i.e. it has an intertextual dimension)', p. 63.

14. *Prelude*, p. 495. See also Cornell Wordsworth, *The Prelude: 1798–99*, ed. Stephen Parrish, pp. 161–5. These often overlooked fragments express the poetic difficulties attendant on speaking, not only in one's own voice, but in any voice at all. Compare Geraldine Friedman's claim that *The Prelude* 'questions the legitimacy of autobiography as self-representation', in 'History in the Background of Wordsworth's "Blind Beggar"', *ELH* 56: 1 (1989), p. 125.

CHAPTER 4   COLERIDGE AS CATALYST TO AUTOBIOGRAPHY: THE
WORDSWORTHIAN SELF AS THERAPEUTIC GIFT, 1804–5

1. See *The Notebooks of Samuel Taylor Coleridge*, ed. Kathleen Coburn, 3
   vols. (New York: Pantheon, 1961), 2: 2389. Coleridge then equates
   this same list of people with the phrase 'Ego contemplans'. Coburn
   notes that 'Ego contemplans' is a synonym for 'personal identity'
   throughout the *Biographia Literaria*. Coleridge confirmed the extent
   of his self-unification with Wordsworth in a letter of December 1798:
   'I am sure I need not say how you are incorporated into the better
   part of my being', *CL*, 1: 453.
2. Alan Liu claims that he does not want to question Wordsworth's
   'genius'; rather, he wants to 'recover the origin of the given', in
   Wordsworth: The Sense of History (Stanford: Stanford University Press,
   1989), p. 359. Liu sets out to do this by working to 'historicize the
   problem of literary authority', and by claiming that Wordsworth's
   'most sustained theme is the realization of history' while 'his largest
   theme is the denial of history', pp. 39, 359. Liu's volume is a tour-de-
   force, curiously conditioned by his own autobiographical reflections
   which appear as an epilogue. My argument claims that our sense of
   specific voices echoing in Wordsworth's head (both sensory and
   textual) are more valuable to our understanding of the production of
   The Prelude than any ultimately unrecoverable version of the broad
   category Liu calls 'history'. We may never 'know' what Wordsworth
   thought about Napoleon (beyond what he said), but we can offer
   concrete evidence about his concern for Coleridge's health in 1803–4.
   For the sort of history that may be effectively recoverable see Duncan
   Wu, *Wordsworth's Reading 1770–1799* (Cambridge: Cambridge
   University Press, 1993).
3. See Jack Stillinger, *Multiple Authorship and the Myth of Solitary Genius*
   (Oxford: Oxford University Press, 1991), particularly Chapter 4,
   'Mutiple "Consciousnesses" in Wordsworth's *Prelude*', pp. 69–95, and
   Chapter 5, 'Creative Plagiarism: The Case of Coleridge', pp. 96–120.
   Martin Danahay emphasizes a tension throughout *The Prelude*
   between communal voices of multiplicity and the search for a voice of
   autonomous authority: 'the ambition of representing himself as a
   unique, single individual makes it difficult for Wordsworth to assert a
   connection to any wider sense of human community', in *A Community
   of One: Masculine Autobiography and Autonomy in Nineteenth-Century
   Britain* (Albany: State University of New York Press, 1993), p. 51.
   Wayne Koestenbaum sees a powerful psycho-sexual element in the
   Wordsworth-Coleridge collaboration, particularly in Coleridge's
   desire 'to mingle identities with other men', in *Double-Talk: The Erotics
   of Male Literary Collaboration* (New York: Routledge, 1989), p. 71. That
   Wordsworth is useful to interpretive strategies as diverse as queer
   theory and eco-criticism (see Jonathan Bate, *Romantic Ecology:
   Wordsworth and the Environmental Tradition* [London: Routledge, 1991])
   argues powerfully for the continuing utilitarian value of his texts. As
   interpreters, we use his words partly to suit our own purposes.

4. Clifford Siskin, in *The Historicity of Romantic Discourse* (Oxford: Oxford University Press, 1988), emphasizes the general romantic tendency to destabilize traditional genres: 'Ever since Wordsworth began *The Prelude* by confessing a swerve from conventional epic expectations into extended self-revelation, what I call the "lyric turn" has played a central role in creative *and* critical narratives', p. 15. By the 'lyric turn' Siskin means the writer's ostensible need to produce 'a more private' text than conventional generic expectations might allow. See also Adena Rosmarin, who connects Wordsworth's practice of speaking as and for others with Ezra Pound and the 'mask lyric', in *The Power of Genre*, pp. 109–10. Roger Sales politicizes our understanding of Wordsworthian lyricism by linking 'real estate' with textual memorializing, in *English Literature in History: 1780–1830: Pastoral and Politics* (New York: St. Martin's, 1983), pp. 52–69: 'pastoral poets may well have put their own words into the mouths of their jolly shepherds, but isn't neighbor Wordsworth doing exactly the same by refusing to recognize that rustics have an unfortunate habit of speaking in dialect? ... [In "Michael"] Pastoral platitudes about the "sedentary power" of aristocratic estates being the bulwark of poor old Michael's small estate disguised the sharp practices of real estate', p. 69.

5. Mauss is the starting point for all subsequent work on gift-exchange theory; see *The Gift: Forms and Functions of Exchange in Archaic Societies*, trans. Ian Cunnison (Glencoe, Ill.: The Free Press, 1954), p. 11. See also Emerson's essay 'Gifts', in *The Complete Essays and Other Writings of Ralph Waldo Emerson*, ed. Brooks Atkinson (New York: Random House, 1940); Emerson well describes the conflicted mood in which Coleridge seems to have offered his own poetic gift ('To William Wordsworth') in response to hearing Wordsworth's gift to him ('the poem to Coleridge'): 'you cannot give anything to a magnanimous person. After you have served him he at once puts you in debt by his magnanimity', pp. 404–5.

6. Lewis Hyde, *The Gift: Imagination and the Erotic Life of Property* (New York: Random House, 1979), p. xi. Wordsworth fulfills Hyde's definition of the 'modern' artist who, having 'chosen to labor with a gift must sooner or later wonder how he or she is to survive in a society dominated by market exchange'; in such a society 'getting rather than giving is the mark of a substantial person', p. xiii; or, as we might say, 'getting and spending we lay waste our powers'. Hyde describes one additional aspect of exchange that characterizes the poetic texts of the Grasmere Circle: 'when gifts circulate within a group, their commerce leaves a series of interconnected relationships in its wake, and a kind of decentralized cohesiveness emerges', p. xiv. Hyde is perhaps the first critic to 'address the situation of creative artists' in terms of gift-exchange theory. Raimonda Modiano draws on Hyde to describe the model of literary confluence (antithetical to Bloomian anxiety-producing influence) that Coleridge employs at the beginning of *Biographia Literaria*; see 'Coleridge and Wordsworth: The Ethics of Gift Exchange and Literary Ownership',

TWC 20: 2 (1989): 113–20. Modiano argues, perhaps too harshly, that 'Wordsworth borrows from Coleridge the very weapons with which he stages his intellectual victory over his friend', p. 113.

7. Richard Holmes points out that Coleridge's farewell letters of 1804, in which he 'suggested that he expected to die abroad', may have also reflected a metaphoric wish: 'perhaps it was not death he hoped for, but a symbolic death of the old self', in *Coleridge: Early Visions* (New York: Viking, 1990), p. 359. This sense of the need to replace an old self with a new self – a constant attempt at refashioning his identity – helps to explain Coleridge's career chaos, mood swings, failed relationships, and intellectual proteanism. W. J. Bate, in *Coleridge* (Cambridge, Mass.: Harvard University Press, 1987 [1968]), reminds us that it was Coleridge who 'coined the term "psychosomatic" a century before it was generally adopted by the medical world', p. 103. Opium addiction was without doubt one cause of Coleridge's litany of symptoms: swellings, sweats, dizziness, self-loathing, digestive distress. Bate sees Coleridge's illness, no doubt correctly, as a complex combination of somatic and psychosomatic elements, pp. 101–6. Molly Lefebure claims that Coleridge was simply 'a junkie', a 'classical case of nineteenth-century morphine-reliance' whose 'imaginative powers and concentration were literally destroyed by the drug'; she then credits him with remarkable 'courage' and a 'basic integrity' that allowed him to overcome his addiction, in *Samuel Taylor Coleridge: A Bondage of Opium* (London: Gollancz, 1974), pp. 14, 15. For additional discussion of Coleridge's illnesses and their complex relationship to Wordsworth, see also Norman Fruman, *Coleridge: The Damaged Archangel* (New York: Braziller, 1971) and Thomas McFarland, *Romanticism and the Forms of Ruin: Wordsworth, Coleridge, and Modalities of Fragmentation* (Princeton: Princeton University Press, 1981).

8. Kenneth Johnston argues for this connection, claiming that *The Recluse* does exist as a body of texts (never unified by Wordsworth) including at least *The Prelude*, *The Excursion*, 'The Ruined Cottage', and 'Home at Grasmere,' in *Recluse*, pp. xii–xx.

9. The poem is referred to in numerous ways throughout Wordsworth's life. He describes it most often as 'the poem to Coleridge' or 'the poem on my own life'. *The Prelude* is the name only given to the text by Mary Wordsworth upon her husband's death, a title that represses both the connection to Coleridge and the anxiety Wordsworth expressed about having written 9,000 lines based on his own experience (*Prelude*, pp. ix–x). Eugene Stelzig argues that the 'rhetorical mode' of the poem is that of a 'man speaking confidentially and at protracted length to one other man', in 'Coleridge in *The Prelude*: Wordsworth's Fiction of Alterity', *TWC* 18: 1 (1987): 23–7. Stelzig claims that Wordsworth seeks a 'doubling or reduplication, through STC, of his own self' designed to 'disarm, interest, charm and win over his future readers', pp. 26, 27. Wordsworth's relationship to those readers is well described by William H. Galperin, who recounts Harriet Martineau's description of the aging poet laureate. The Wordsworth

described by Martineau is, according to Galperin, 'sufficiently detached from Wordsworth the man to make the act of being "Wordsworth" a performance that, to Martineau's eyes, seems almost a self-reflexive gesture', in *Revision and Authority in Wordsworth: The Interpretation of a Career* (Philadelphia: University of Pennsylvania Press, 1989), p. 244. A thoroughgoing reader-response approach to Wordsworth appears in *Wordsworth's Informed Reader: Structures of Experience in His Poetry*, by Susan Edwards Meisenhelder (Nashville: Vanderbilt University Press, 1988), a reading that may overstate the poet's tendency to 'use his life as an educational tool', p. 2.

10. The fate of Coleridge's missing *Recluse* comments was described in a lost letter from Coleridge to the Wordsworths on 19 January 1805. Dorothy quotes from Coleridge's letter in her own letter to Lady Beaumont on 28 March 1805, in which she also records the news of John Wordsworth's burial (*EY*, pp. 573–4).

11. See Gene W. Ruoff, *Wordsworth and Coleridge: The Making of the Major Lyrics: 1802–1804* (New Brunswick: Rutgers University Press, 1989). Ruoff's critical method, of placing the poems of 1802–4 in direct conversation, sets forth precise details of dialogical interchanges like those that fueled the production of *The Prelude* texts. To cite just one example: 'When Wordsworth responds to [Coleridge's verse letter to Sara Hutchinson] with "The Leech-Gatherer", his major concerns will not be the passages Coleridge rewrites for Sotheby and uses as the basis for the received text of "Dejection" but those suppressed passages of erotic complaint. When Wordsworth risks once more the figures and topics of erotic pastoral, he will do so with a firmer sense of their hidden and treacherous powers', p. 103.

12. This letter was translated by Canon Ainger. See James Dyke Campbell's notes to *The Poetical Works of Samuel Taylor Coleridge* (London: Macmillan, 1893), p. 626.

13. See Ruoff, *Major Lyrics*, p. 86. Note also Stephen Prickett's claim, in *Coleridge and Wordsworth: The Poetry of Growth* (Cambridge: Cambridge University Press, 1970), that unlike Wordsworth, Coleridge 'never looked for *thoughts* in nature', p. 161. Wordsworth sees nature as a source for thought; Coleridge, by contrast, searches his mind for thoughts that will help him unify apparently random details of the natural world.

14. 'Was it for this?' has generated a torrent of criticism in recent years. Geoffrey Hartman, '"Was it for this ...?": Wordsworth and the Birth of the Gods', in *Romantic Revolutions: Criticism and Theory*, ed. Kenneth Johnston et al. (Bloomington: Indiana University Press, 1990), pp. 8–25, notes that the birth of the gods is finally the birth of language, because 'poetic words' can 'endow a silent light with shape, sound, and being', p. 24. John A. Hodgson, in '"Was It for This ...?": Wordsworth's Virgilian Questionings," *TSLL* 33: 2 (1991): 125–36, connects the origins of *The Prelude* with an Aeneas-like 'search for vocation, for orientation, for insights into the working out of his destiny', p. 131. See James K. Chandler, *Wordsworth's Second Nature*, pp. 187–90 and Alan Liu, *The Sense of History*, pp. 399, 521. See

also Robert Young, 'The Eye and Progress of His Song: A Lacanian Reading of *The Prelude*', in *William Wordsworth's The Prelude*, ed. Harold Bloom (New York: Chelsea House, 1986), pp. 125–35. Young's reading leaves the Wordsworthian 'I' floating between encounters 'forever missed', p. 135. For all its indeterminacy, the Wordsworthian speaker is actually more stable – at least more rhetorically stable in its texts – than Young's Lacanian emphasis suggests.

CHAPTER 5   DIALOGIZING DOROTHY: VOICING THE FEMININE AS SPOUSAL SISTER IN *THE PRELUDE*

1.   For *The Prelude* as a dialogue between Coleridge and Wordsworth, see particularly Magnuson, *Coleridge and Wordsworth: A Lyrical Dialogue*; Ruoff, *Wordsworth and Coleridge: The Making of the Major Lyrics*; Susan Eilenberg, *Strange Power of Speech*; and McFarland, *Romanticism and the Forms of Ruin* and 'The Symbiosis of Coleridge and Wordsworth', *SIR* 11 (1972): 263–303. Poststructuralist critiques of *The Prelude* began with de Man's 1967 lecture 'Time and History in Wordsworth', first published in *Diacritics* 17: 4 (1987): 4–17, an issue devoted to 'Wordsworth and the Production of Poetry', that includes essays by Andrzej Warminski, Frances Ferguson, Reeve Parker, Cynthia Chase, and Cathy Caruth. Other important poststructuralist readings of *The Prelude* can be found in Frances Ferguson, *Wordsworth: Language as Counter-Spirit* (New Haven: Yale University Press, 1977) and Arden Reed, ed., *Romanticism and Language* (Ithaca: Cornell University Press, 1984), particularly the essays by Susan Wolfson, Cynthia Chase, Timothy Bahti, and Reeve Parker. See also Bahti's essay 'Figures of Interpretation – The Interpretation of Figures: A Reading Of Wordsworth's "Dream of the Arab"', *SIR* 18: 4 (1979): 601–28, and Ross Woodman, 'Wordsworth's Crazed Bedouin: *The Prelude* and the Fate of Madness', *SIR* 27: 1 (1988): 3–29. A useful corrective to the potential excesses of deconstructive romanticists can be found in W. J. T. Mitchell's 'Influences, Autobiography, and Literary History: Rousseau's *Confessions* and Wordsworth's *The Prelude*', *ELH* 57: 3 (1990): 643–64. Mitchell concludes with a useful reflection on the possibility of a pragmatic criticism: 'can the notion of influence, historicized in the way I have indicated, help us to move from the interpretation of texts to something like historical explantion? Does it offer us a way to explain, not just what a text means, but what it *is* and *does* and why?', p. 661.

2.   Rachel Crawford offers the useful term 'sororal' to describe the intersection of Dorothy and William in Wordsworth's poetic texts, in 'The Structure of the Sororal in Wordsworth's "Nutting"', *SIR* 31 (1992): 197–211. Crawford employs 'the term "sororal" as a deliberate parallel to the term "the feminine" in order to indicate that the figure of the sister goes beyond autobiographical and even specific metaphoric significance. Her active, if concealed, role in the poet's conception of his vocation is textualized in his work', p. 199. Any

reflections on Dorothy's status as sister should perhaps recall Schiller's 1795–6 link between sisterhood and 'nature': 'we see in irrational nature only a happier sister who remained in our mother's house, out of which we impetuously fled abroad in the arrogance of our freedom. With painful nostalgia we yearn to return as soon as we have begun to experience the pressure of civilization and hear in the remote lands of art our mother's tender voice. As long as we were children of nature merely, we enjoyed happiness and perfection; we became free, and lost both', in Friedrich von Schiller, *Naive and Sentimental Poetry*, trans. J. A. Elias (New York: Ungar, 1966), p. 100. For critiques of Dorothy's own texts see Elizabeth A. Fay, *Becoming Wordsworthian* (Amherst: University of Massachusetts Press, 1995); Susan M. Levin, *Dorothy Wordsworth and Romanticism* (New Brunswick: Rutgers University Press, 1987); Margaret Homans, *Woman Writers and Poetic Identity* (Princeton: Princeton University Press, 1980); and *Bearing the Word: Language and Female Experience in Nineteenth-Century Women's Writing* (Chicago: University of Chicago Press, 1986), particularly Chapter 2: 'Building Refuges: Dorothy Wordsworth's Poetics of the Image'. See also Alan Liu, 'On the Autobiographical Present: Dorothy Wordsworth's Grasmere *Journals'*, *Criticism* 26 (1984): 115–37; and Meena Alexander, 'Dorothy Wordsworth: The Grounds of Writing', *Women's Studies* 14 (1987): 195–210 and her *Women in Romanticism: Mary Wollstonecraft, Dorothy Wordsworth, and Mary Shelley* (Savage, Md.: Barnes & Noble, 1989). Kurt Heinzelman has critiqued the economic implications of Dorothy and William's domestic arrangements and the ways that 'the Grasmere writings of both brother and sister attempt to socialize the activity of writing and thus to place it within a larger idea of economy that included not only their own household but also the households of their neighbors and friends'(p. 52), in 'The Cult of Domesticity: Dorothy and William Wordsworth at Grasmere', in *Romanticism and Feminism*, ed. Anne Mellor (Bloomington: Indiana University Press, 1988), pp. 52–78. See, in the same volume, Susan J. Wolfson, 'Individual in Community: Dorothy Wordsworth in Conversation with William', who argues that Dorothy's writings 'reveal efforts to test modes of experience and self-representation different from those privileged, practiced, and promoted by the brother', p. 139. My argument suggests that such Dorothean 'modes' reveal themselves in her brother's voice to a greater extent than has previously been acknowledged.

3. It may be significant that Dorothy's lines immediately preceding her transcription of the masculine excesses of 'Nutting' conclude with her wish for a vocal reunion of the three friends: 'and I would once more follow at your heels, and hear your dear voices again', *EY*, p. 241.

4. Homans claims that the female figures in 'Nutting' 'exist to let the boy make his discovery, and, making it himself, to mature', *Woman Writers*, p. 512; but she also claims, in *Bearing the Word*, that the bower destruction is one of those experiences 'from which

Wordsworth as a brother would protect his sister', thus representing the way the brother wants to mediate between his sister and the sublime, p. 137. Dorothy, on these terms, 'enters the poem not in her own right but in answer to the poet's and the poem's need'; Homans connects this pattern with Dorothy's 'appearance' in 'Tintern Abbey', p. 120. I would argue, by contrast, that the 'lesson' learned by the male speaker in both of these poems is tied to knowledge attributed *to* the feminine figure and later, in *The Prelude*, internalized as a feminine aspect of the masculine voice. Wordsworth does not need to 'protect' the sister-figure from becoming a ravager of natural scenes; as she is represented in both poems she would never do such a thing. Only a male would destroy in this wanton way, a male who needs to learn to be more like a woman. Mary Jacobus, in *Romanticism, Writing, and Sexual Difference* (Oxford: Clarendon, 1989), calls 'Nutting' Wordsworth's 'most obviously sexual and sexualizing approach to nature's gender', a 'Wordsworthian strip-tease of sexualized nature', pp. 254, 256. Marlon Ross argues that 'Nutting' 'effaces the issue of the growth of the female mind' by producing a 'hierarchy of gender' that makes the man always 'the determiner of female knowledge and position', p. 395, in 'Naturalizing Gender: Woman's Place in Wordsworth's Ideological Landscape', *ELH* 53 (1986): 391–410. My point almost reverses this relationship; the poet/speaker in 'Nutting', as in 'Tintern Abbey', learns what the maiden already knows (or has not forgotten) – he learns to be a 'virgin' again, or at least to *want* to be one.

5.   The 'infant babe' passage has received widespread comment, particularly since romanticists have sought to revise Freudian readings by way of Lacanian insights. Jacobus notes that Wordsworth's developmental theory implies that the child may also be 'gathering dangerous passions' in an inverted version of 'maternal seduction'; she sees the boy as subject to growth and division, therefore needing to 'get rid of the mother', in *Romanticism, Writing, and Sexual Difference*, pp. 211, 213. According to Barbara Shapiro, the 'motivating force in [Wordsworth's] poetry is not to recapture the lost mother but to fortify the self in relation to her, to become a power like her', in *The Romantic Mother: Narcissistic Patterns in Romantic Poetry* (Baltimore: Johns Hopkins University Press, 1983), p. 94. Richard Onorato sees this 'imagined' mother (Wordsworth can't *really* remember this nurturing moment) as 'the essential reality of the world', p. 623, at least for the infant; the same mother then becomes one of many 'lost objects of love and wonder' that have to be replaced by language, particularly poetic language that can 'return through imagination to the past', p. 624, in 'The Prelude: Metaphors of Beginning and Where They Lead', in Norton *Prelude*, pp. 613–25, a revision of pp. 100–15 of Onorato's influential *The Character of the Poet: Wordsworth in 'The Prelude'* (Princeton: Princeton University Press, 1971). Andrzej Warminski says – analyzing the rhetoric of the 'blessèd babe' passage – that 'Wordsworth's mother died so that the Wordsworth Baby could become an "I" and the Boy Wordsworth could become a poet',

in 'Facing Language: Wordsworth's First Poetic Spirits', *Diacritics* 17:4 (1987): 24. Warminski relates this textual form of dying to other deaths in Wordsworth's texts: a young Lucy, the Danish boy, the drowned schoolmaster. Others die into texts, we might say, so that 'Wordsworth' can be born into them.

6. Homans argues that 'when nature is Mother Nature for Wordsworth, she is valued because she is what the poet is not', but that this same 'Mother' 'is no more than what he allows her to be', p. 13; likewise, 'each Wordsworthian landscape contains the buried presence of a maternal or feminine figure, whether she is a figurative maternal quality diffused through nature, or a more literal figure who once lived', *Woman Writers*, p. 25. See also Alan Richardson, who claims that Wordsworth's 'incorporation of feminine qualities approaches a metaphoric heart transplant': 'Romanticism and the Colonization of the Feminine', in *Romanticism and Feminism*, p. 16. Marlon Ross notes that the general 'Romantic desire to articulate visions that can speak for the whole, in the end, is betrayed by the poet's need to adopt a masculine position in order to fulfill that desire', *Romanticism and Feminism*, p. 49. Sandra M. Gilbert and Susan Gubar call Wordsworth a 'masculinist', in *The Madwoman in the Attic: The Woman Writer and the Nineteenth-Century Literary Imagination* (New Haven: Yale University Press, 1979), p. 211, and link his epic pretensions to Milton. Too often, however, feminist criticisms tends to avoid the complexities of gender in the Wordsworthian voice, or in male voices generally. Wordsworth's texts indicate more awareness of the 'politics of gender' than Ross claims, and his 'masculine posture' ('masculinism') is much less stable – or monologic – than either traditional humanists or dualistic feminists have argued. My reading of *The Prelude* encourages readers to stress those feminist insights that help us to see all voices – male and female – as more complex than merely 'masculine' or 'feminine'.

7. *A Poetics of Women's Autobiography: Marginality and the Fictions of Self-Representation* (Bloomington: Indiana University Press, 1987), p. 44.

8. See Nancy Chodorow, *The Reproduction of Mothering: Psychoanalysis and the Sociology of Gender* (Berkeley: University of California Press, 1978), p. 93. See also Carol Gilligan, *In a Different Voice: Psychological Theory and Women's Development* (Cambridge, Mass.: Harvard University Press, 1978), p. 156.

9. The often-quoted 'three people but one soul' phrase is attributed to Coleridge by J. Dykes Campbell, *Samuel Taylor Coleridge* (London: Macmillan, 1894), p. 75; see Robert Gittings and Jo Manton, *Dorothy Wordsworth* (Oxford: Oxford Univeresity Press, 1988), pp. 65–6. Coleridge did write to Godwin – of himself, Dorothy, and Wordsworth: 'tho' we were three persons, it was but one God', *CL*, 2: 775, a sentiment that expresses a very different psychological – and theological? – emphasis. Confusion about even this simple biographical attribution is only increased by Mary Moorman's claim that Coleridge's phrase was 'three persons and one soul', in her 'Introduction' to Dorothy's *Journals*, p. xi. Whatever the precise

quote, the point remains: Coleridge saw the three friends as more like a single person than three individuals; or rather, he *wanted* to see them that way.

10. See Ernest de Selincourt, *Dorothy Wordsworth: A Biography* (Oxford: Clarendon, 1933), p. 58. Coleridge could also be critical of his beloved friends' domestic arrangements when it suited him; to Thomas Poole on 14 October 1803, he wrote of William, 'I saw him more and more benetted in hypochondriacal Fancies, living wholly among Devotees – having every [*sic*] the minutest Thing, almost his very Eating & Drinking, done for him by his Sister, or Wife', *CL*, 2: 1013.

11. Derrida is here discussing Rousseau's 'Essay on the Origins of Language', in *Of Grammatology*, trans. Gayatry Chakravorty Spivak (Baltimore: Johns Hopkins University Press, 1976), p. 266.

12. Wolfson in Mellor, *Romanticism and Feminism*, p. 162; Levin in *Dorothy Wordsworth and Romanticism*, pp. 6–7. Compare Diane Long Hoeveler, in *Romantic Androgyny: The Woman Within* (University Park: Pennsylvania State University Press, 1990), who critiques Dorothy's 'symbolic role as internalized feminine "Other", because William's use of Dorothy in her dual role as "sister" not only informs the marriage metaphor that runs throughout his poetry, but illuminates his displacement of androgynous ideology', p. 84. My reading suggests that such a displacement of androgyny was less complete than it might at first appear.

13. Although the precise intertextual links between Dorothy's *Journals* and William's poems add support to my argument, they have been explored in extensive detail elsewhere. See, for example, Levin, *Dorothy Wordsworth and Romanticism*; Meena Alexander, *Women in Romanticism*; Gittings and Manton, *Dorothy Wordsworth*, and Moorman's introduction to Dorothy's *Journals*. Although we do not always know the precise details or chronology of composition, it is clear that William often used Dorothy's *Journals* as a spur to his own creative efforts and as a reminder of the details of their shared experience. Magnuson notes that Coleridge also used precise images from Dorothy's journal for the opening lines of 'Christabel', *Lyrical Dialogue*, pp. 120n–121n.

14. See *The Love Letters of William and Mary Wordsworth*, ed. Beth Darlington (Ithaca: Cornell University Press, 1981), p. 27. The fact that these letters were unknown to scholars and unavailable until 1977 reminds readers of one of the perils of psychobiography. While the letters do give us, in some sense, a 'new' Wordsworth: more passionate, more loving – more aggressively heterosexual? – than previously suspected, they serve as reminders of how much of any life is lost forever, in both textual and nontextual terms. For this reason, it is hard to agree with Darlington's conclusion: 'False images of William, Mary, and their marriage have gained currency in our time; these distortions need correction', p. 9. Whatever 'corrections' these love-letters might produce, they raise as many questions as they answer, particularly if we locate them in the context of 48 years of married life. Could there be a single 'correct' or 'stable' view of any

human relationship that lasted for over five decades? The most readers might hope for is texts that produce provisional rhetorical coherence while at the same time revealing textual gaps, sexualized slips of the tongue, and an always destabilizing dynamism.

15. See *Wordsworth's Art of Allusion* (University Park: Pennsylvania State University Press, 1988), p. 43.

16. Meena Alexander remarks on Dorothy's awareness of water as symbolic of maternity. One of Dorothy's commonplace books records details of a female water-deity described in Barrow's *Travels in China* and then points out that water is considered 'to be the primary element, and the first medium on which the creative influence begins to act' (Dove Cottage MS. 26, 41r–42v), in *Women in Romanticism*, pp. 111–12. Several of Wordsworth's poetic images assume a new significance if we see water as a figurative link between maternity and creativity: the sound of the Derwent that opens the 1799 *Prelude*, the water-carrying woman 'spot of time', the drowned man of Esthwaite, the bosom of the Winander boy's lake, the roar of waters on Snowdon, the Alps crossing (waterfalls, torrents, drizzling crags, raving streams). The mother of waters is also a mother of the poet's mind.

17. De Quincey's comment comes from *Recollections of the Lake Poets*, ed. David Wright (Harmondsworth: Penguin, 1970), p. 201. But, in this regard, see also Coleridge on Dorothy as a slave to William's 'minutest' wish', *CL*, 2: 1013.

18. Jacobus, *Romanticism, Writing, and Sexual Difference*, p. 215. Jacobus also notes that the 'function of *The Prelude*'s apostrophes is to constitute the voice of the poet: the function of its addresses to Coleridge (and to some extent, Dorothy) is to save it by domesticating it', p. 178. See also Marlon Ross, 'Naturalizing Gender: Woman's Place in Wordsworth's Ideological Landscape', *ELH* 53 (1986): 391–410 and Kenneth Johnston, 'Narcissus and Joan: Wordsworth's Feminist Recluse?', *SIR* 29 (1990): 197–221.

CHAPTER 6   COLONIZING CONSCIOUSNESS: CULTURE AS IDENTITY IN WORDSWORTH'S *PRELUDE* AND WALCOTT'S *ANOTHER LIFE*

1. 'Bibliography for 1973: The West Indies', *The Journal of Commonwealth Literature* 9: 2 (1974): 129. For criticism of *Another Life* see particularly Edward Baugh, *Memory as Vision: 'Another Life'* (London: Longman, 1978); Lloyd Brown, *West Indian Poetry* (Boston: Twayne, 1978); and Laurence Lieberman, 'New Poetry: The Muse of History', *Yale Review* 63 (1973): 113–36. Clara Thomas, in 'Commonwealth Albums: Family Resemblance in Derek Walcott's *Another Life* and Margaret Laurence's *The Diviners*', *WLWE* 21: 2 (1982): 262–8, notes that Walcott's Caribbean context compels him to 'go beyond his own racial past to record and commemorate the Carib Indians who held the land before the white men came, and who leaped from the rock at

Sauteurs rather than be enslaved', p. 265. J. A. Ramsaran analyzes the important interplay between Caribbean and Mediterranean sources in Walcott's poems, suggesting literary links to these autobiographical descriptions, in 'Derek Walcott: New World Mediterranean Poet', *WLWE* 21: 1 (1982): 133–47.

2. Baugh's essay appears in *Awakened Conscience: Studies in Commonwealth Literature*, ed. C. D. Narasimhaiah (New Delhi: Sterling Publishers, 1978), pp. 226–35. See also M. Travis Lane, in 'A Different Growth of a Poet's Mind: Derek Walcott's *Another Life*', *Ariel* 9 (1978): 65–78, who emphasizes differences between the Caribbean Walcott and the Lakeland Wordsworth.

3. Robert Hamner notes that 'Epitaph for the Young' (1949) includes many of the details of *Another Life* in a cruder, more imitative form, in his 'Introduction' to the Three Continents Edition.

4. My citations include page numbers from *Another Life*, 2nd edn (Washington, DC: Three Continents Press, 1982). Hamner provides a useful introduction and chronology in this edition. The poem also appears in its entirety in *Collected Poems: 1948–1984* (New York: Farrar, Straus & Giroux, 1986), pp. 141–294.

5. Lejeune, *On Autobiography*, p. 188. Brown argues that in Walcott's case 'the poet's growth or personal odyssey involves a fusion of the divided self into a unified consciousness without obliterating the distinctive nature of the experiences that he has inherited from either world' (*West Indian Poetry*, pp. 136–7). Wordsworth, not unexpectedly, dates a similar stabilizing fusion in his own poetic practice to the year 1798 – in April of 1843, he writes to a correspondent, 'as you are so intimately acquainted with my poems, and as no change has taken place in my manner for the last forty-five years', *LY*, 3: 1159. See Stephen Maxfield Parrish, *The Art of the Lyrical Ballads* (Cambridge, Mass.: Harvard University Press, 1973), p. 56.

6. Carol Jacobs, 'There's No Bitterness in Our Literature', *Sunday Guardian* (Trinidad), 22 May 1966, p. 9.

7. Hamner, p. xiii.

8. Gusdorf adds that when I see myself as a legitimate subject for autobiography, 'the recapitulation of ages of existence, of landscapes and encounters, obliges me to situate what I am in the perspective of what I have been', in 'Conditions and Limits of Autobiography' in James Olney ed., *Autobiography: Essays Theoretical and Critical* (Princeton: Princeton University Press, 1980), p. 38. Such a link between landscape and identity in colonial situations is well described by Michel de Certeau, in *Heterologies: Discourse on the Other*, trans. Brian Massumi (Minneapolis: University of Minnesota Press, 1986): 'land, serving as a reference point, in addition to preserving local representations and beliefs (often hidden beneath the occupier's system), is also a ballast and defense for the "own" [*le propre*] against any superimposition. It was, and is, a kind of palimpsest: the gringos' writing does not erase the primary text, which remains traced there – illegible to the passers-by who have manipulated the area for four centuries – as a silent sacrament of

"maternal forces", the forefathers' tomb, the indelible seal joining the members of the community together in contractual agreement', p. 229. I would extend this notion beyond the colonial situation to include a poet like Wordsworth, who finds a powerful source of artistic energy in 'silent' landscapes that can nevertheless 'speak' to him in powerful ways: 'and I would stand / Beneath some rock, listening to sounds that are / The ghostly language of the ancient earth', 1799, II, 356–8.

9. Gusdorf, in Olney, *Autobiography*, p. 30, adding that the autobiographer 'believes it a useful and valuable thing to fix his own image so that he can be certain it will not disappear like all things in this world'.

10. *Shelley's Poetry and Prose*, ed. Donald H. Reiman and Sharon B. Powers (New York: Norton, 1979), p. 96.

11. Meredith's 'Love in the Valley' is a sustained meditation on the problematic possibilities of recovering lost love; quoted from *The Pre-Raphaelites and Their Circle*, ed. Cecil Lang (Chicago: University of Chicago Press, 1975), p. 293. The line Walcott quotes introduces the conclusion to an early stanza in the poem:

> Darker grows the valley, more and more forgetting:
> So it were with me if forgetting could be willed.
> Tell the grassy hollow that holds the bubbling well-spring,
> Tell it to forget the source that keeps it filled.
>
> (37–40)

An autobiographer cannot ignore the sources of his identity any more than a well can forget the spring that continuously replenishes it with water. Consider, similarly, Edward Said's link between textual authority and the absent source of any text: 'the authority of any text, according to Renan, is tied to the realization that a text has outlived whomever participated in its original making', in *Beginnings: Intention and Method* (New York: Columbia University Press, 1985 [1975]), p. 217. Wordsworth and Walcott both outlive the earlier selves they describe, just as their autobiographical texts can outlive any self they might become.

12. See also John Pilling, *Autobiography and Imagination: Studies in Self-Scrutiny* (London: Routledge & Kegan Paul, 1981), who connects the autobiographical impulse in Wordsworth with an important strain in modern literature. According to Pilling, the author and the reader of modern autobiographical works that chart 'the growth of the poet's mind', 'coexist in a peculiar allegiance; for both of them the object (and the objectification) transcends the subject. This is, it seems to me, one of the special satisfactions to be derived from this particular branch of "post-Romantic" literature, and one of the most interesting evidences of the twentieth century's continuing struggle with the legacy of Romanticism. Just as many of the great figures of twentieth-century literature in traditional forms (Joyce, Eliot, Wyndham

Lewis, Ezra Pound, Paul Valery, Rilke) have sought to go beyond the self and proposed a modern version of "classicism", so – and precisely where one might least expect it – these modern "Preludes" are oriented outwards, in what Henry James very aptly calls an "act of life"', p. 119. Roger Rosenblatt sees a related phenomenon operating in minority autobiography. 'All autobiography is minority autobiography', Rosenblatt writes, insofar as every autobiographer feels unique and, to some extent, uniquely isolated. As a result, 'the autobiographer wishes the reader to be alone and counts on it because whatever else may separate them from each other, their states of loneliness are mutually recognizable. For the black autobiographer this is a central connection; he is after all not a minority in relation to his lonely reader. They are equal in the exchange', in 'Black Autobiography: Life as the Death Weapon', in Olney, *Autobiography*, pp. 169, 180.

13. Jerome McGann, *The Romantic Ideology: A Critical Investigation* (Chicago: University of Chicago Press, 1983), p. 91.

Bibliography

Alexander, Meena. 'Dorothy Wordsworth: The Grounds of Writing'. *Women's Studies* 14 (1987): 195–210.
————. *Women in Romanticism: Mary Wollstonecraft, Dorothy Wordsworth, and Mary Shelley*. Savage, Md.: Barnes & Noble, 1989.
Bahti, Timothy. 'Figures of Interpretation, The Interpretation of Figures: A Reading of Wordsworth's "Dream of the Arab"'. *SIR* 18: 4 (1979): 601–28.
Baker, Jeffrey. 'Casualties of the Revolution: Wordsworth and his "Solitary" Self'. *Yearbook of English Studies* 19 (1989).
Bakhtin, M. M. *Art and Answerability*. Ed. Michael Holquist and Vadim Liapunov. Trans. Liapunov and Kenneth Brostrom. Austin: University of Texas Press, 1990.
————. *The Dialogic Imagination*. Ed. Michael Holquist. Trans. Caryl Emerson and Michael Holquist. Austin: University of Texas Press, 1981.
Bate, Jonathan. *Romantic Ecology: Wordsworth and the Environmental Tradition*. London: Routledge, 1991.
Bate, W. J. *Coleridge*. Cambridge, Mass.: Harvard University Press, 1987 [1968].
Baugh, Edward. *Memory as Vision: 'Another Life'*. London: Longman, 1978.
Bewell, Alan J. *Wordsworth and the Enlightenment: Nature, Man, and Society in the Experimental Poetry*. New Haven: Yale University Press, 1989.
Bialostosky, Don H. *Making Tales: The Poetics of Wordsworth's Narrative Experiments*. Chicago: University of Chicago Press, 1984.
————. *Wordsworth, Dialogics, and the Practice of Criticism*. Cambridge: Cambridge University Press, 1992.
Bostetter, Edward. *The Romantic Ventriloquists*. Seattle: University of Washington Press, 1975 [1963].
Brown, Lloyd. *West Indian Poetry*. Boston: Twayne, 1978.
Butler, Marilyn. 'Plotting the Revolution: The Political Narratives of Romantic Poetry and Criticism', in *Romantic Revolutions: Criticism and Theory*. Ed. Kenneth Johnston et al. Bloomington: Indiana University Press, 1990
————. *Romantics, Rebels, and Reactionaries: English Literature and its Backgrounds 1760–1830*. Oxford University Press, 1981.
Byron, George Gordon. *Byron's Poetry*. Ed. Frank McConnell. New York: Norton, 1978.
Caruth, Cathy. 'Past Recognition: Narrative Origins in Wordsworth and Freud'. *MLN* 100 (1985): 935–48.
Chandler, James K. *Wordsworth's Second Nature: A Study of the Poetry and Politics*. Chicago: University of Chicago Press, 1984.
————. 'Wordsworth After Waterloo'. In *The Age of William Wordsworth*. Ed. Johnston and Ruoff. New Brunswick: Rutgers University Press, 1987.
Chase, Cynthia. 'The Accidents of Disfiguration: Limits to Literal and Rhetorical Reading in Book V of *The Prelude*'. *SIR* 18 (1979): 547–66.
Chodorow, Nancy. *The Reproduction of Mothering: Psychoanalysis and the*

Sociology of Gender. Berkeley: University of California Press, 1978.

Christensen, Jerome. *Lord Byron's Strength*. Baltimore: Johns Hopkins University Press, 1993.

Coleridge, Samuel Taylor. *Biographia Literaria*. Ed. James Engell and Walter Jackson Bate. Princeton: Princeton University Press, 1983.

————. *Collected Letters of Samuel Taylor Coleridge*. Ed. Earl Leslie Griggs, 6 vols. Oxford: Clarendon Press, 1956–71.

————. *The Notebooks of Samuel Taylor Coleridge*. Ed. Kathleen Coburn. New York: Pantheon, 1961.

————. *Poetical Works*. Ed. E. H. Coleridge. Oxford: Oxford University Press, 1969 (1911).

————. *The Poetical Works of Samuel Taylor Coleridge*. Ed. James Dyke Campbell. London: Macmillan, 1893.

————. *Specimens of the Table Talk of the Late Samuel Taylor Coleridge*. Ed. H. N. Coleridge. London: John Murray, 1886.

Collings, David. 'Coleridge Beginning a Career: Desultory Authorship in *Religious Musings*'. *ELH* 58 (1991): 167–93.

Cooke, Michael. *Acts of Inclusion: Studies Bearing on an Elementary Theory of Romanticism*. New Haven: Yale University Press, 1979.

Cooper, Andrew M. *Doubt and Identity in Romantic Poetry*. New Haven: Yale University Press, 1988.

Crawford, Rachel. 'The Structure of the Sororal in "Nutting"'. *SIR* 31 (1992): 197–211.

Culler, A. Dwight. 'Monodrama and Dramatic Monologue'. *PMLA* 90 (1975): 366–85.

Curran, Stuart. *Poetic Form and British Romanticism*. Oxford: Oxford University Press, 1986.

Danahay. Martin. *A Community of One: Masculine Autobiography and Autonomy in Nineteenth-Century Britain*. Albany: State University of New York Press, 1993.

de Certeau, Michel. *Heterologies: Discourse on the Other*. Trans. Brian Massumi. Minneapolis: University of Minnesota Press, 1986.

————. *The Practice of Everyday Life*. Trans. Steven F. Rendall. Berkeley: University of California Press, 1984.

de Man, Paul. 'Time and History in Wordsworth'. *Diacritics* 17: 4 (1987): 4–18.

de Selincourt, Ernest. *Dorothy Wordsworth: A Biography*. Oxford: Clarendon Press, 1933.

Derrida, Jacques. *Of Grammatology*. Trans. Gayatry Chakravorty Spivak. Baltimore: Johns Hopkins University Press, 1976.

Devlin, D. D. *Wordsworth and the Poetry of Epitaphs*. Totowa, NJ: Barnes & Noble, 1981.

Egan, Susanna. *Patterns of Experience in Autobiography*. Chapel Hill: University of North Carolina Press, 1984.

Eilenberg, Susan. *Strange Power of Speech: Wordsworth, Coleridge and Literary Possession*. New York: Oxford University Press, 1992.

Emerson, Ralph Waldo. *The Complete Essays*. New York: Random House, 1940.

Erdman, David V. 'The Dawn of Universal Patriotism: William

178   *Bibliography*

Wordsworth Among the British in Revolutionary France'. In *The Age of William Wordsworth*. Ed. Kenneth Johnston and Gene Ruoff. New Brunswick: Rutgers University Press, 1987.

———. 'The Man Who Was Not Napoleon'. *TWC* 12: 1 (1981): 92–6.

———. 'Wordsworth as Heartsworth; or, Was Regicide the Prophetic Ground of Those "Moral Questions"?' In *The Evidence of the Imagination*. Ed. Donald H. Reiman et al. New York: New York University Press, 1978.

Fay, Elizabeth. *Becoming Wordsworthian: A Performative Aesthetic*. Amherst: University of Massachusetts Press, 1995.

Ferguson, Frances. *Wordsworth: Language as Counter Spirit*. New Haven: Yale University Press, 1977.

Friedman, Geraldine. 'History in the Background of Wordsworth's "Blind Beggar"'. *ELH* (1989): 125–48.

Fruman, Norman. *Coleridge: The Damaged Archangel*. New York: Braziller, 1971.

Furet, François, *Interpreting the French Revolution*. Trans. Elborg Forster. Cambridge: Cambridge University Press, 1981.

Galperin, William H. *Revision and Authority in Wordsworth: The Interpretation of a Career*. Philadelphia: University of Pennsylvania Press, 1989.

Gagnier, Regina. *Subjectivities: A History of Self-Representation in Britain, 1832–1920*. Oxford: Oxford University Press, 1991.

Gassenmeier, Michael. '"Twas a Transport of the Outward Sense": Wordsworth's Own Account of his Visions and Revisions of the French Revolution'. In *Beyond the Suburbs of the Mind: Exploring English Romanticism*. Essen: Die Blaue Eule, 1987.

Gilbert, Sandra M. and Susan Gubar. *The Madwoman in the Attic: The Woman Writer and the Nineteenth-Century Literary Imagination*. New Haven: Yale University Press, 1979.

Gill, Stephen. '"Affinities Preserved": Poetic Self-Reference in Wordsworth'. *SIR* 24 (1985): 531–49.

———. *William Wordsworth: A Life*. Oxford: Clarendon Press, 1989.

Gilligan, Carol. *In a Different Voice: Psychological Theory and Women's Development*. Cambridge, Mass.: Harvard University Press, 1982.

Gittings, Robert and Jo Manton. *Dorothy Wordsworth*. Oxford: Oxford University Press, 1985.

Gravil, Richard. '"Some Other Being": Wordsworth in *The Prelude*'. *Yearbook of English Studies* 19 (1989).

Gusdorf, Georges. 'Conditions and Limits of Autobiography'. In *Autobiography: Essays Theoretical and Critical*. Ed. James Olney. Princeton: Princeton University Press, 1980.

Haney, David P. 'The Emergence of the Autobiographical Figure in *The Prelude*, Book I'. *SIR* 20 (1981): 33–64.

———. 'Incarnation and the Autobiographical Exit: Wordsworth's *The Prelude*, Books IX–XIII (1805)'. *SIR* 29 (1990): 523–54.

Hartman, Geoffrey H. *The Unremarkable Wordsworth*. Minneapolis: University of Minnesota Press, 1987.

———. '"Was it for this ...?": Wordsworth and the Birth of the Gods', in *Romantic Revolutions: Criticism and Theory*. Eds. Johnston et al. Bloomington: Indiana University Press, 1990.

————. *Wordsworth's Poetry: 1787–1814.* Cambridge, Mass.: Harvard University Press, 1987 [1971].

Heinzelman, Kurt. 'The Cult of Domesticity: Dorothy and William Wordsworth at Grasmere'. In *Romanticism and Feminism.* Ed. Anne K. Mellor. Bloomington: Indiana University Press, 1988.

Henderson, Andrea. 'A Tale Told to be Forgotten: Enlightenment, Revolution, and the Poet in "Salisbury Plain"'. *SIR* 30 (1991): 71–84.

Hodgson, John A. *Wordsworth's Philosophical Poetry, 1797–1814.* Lincoln: University of Nebraska Press, 1980.

————. '"Was It for This ...?": Wordsworth's Virgilian Questionings,' *TSLL* 33: 2 (1991): 125–36.

Hoeveler, Diane. *Romantic Androgyny: The Woman Within.* University Park: Pennsylvania State University Press, 1990.

Hollander, John. *The Figure of Echo: A Mode of Allusion in Milton and After.* Berkeley: University of California Press, 1981.

Holmes, Richard. *Coleridge: Early Visions.* New York: Viking, 1990.

Homans, Margaret. *Bearing the Word: Language and Female Experience in Nineteenth-Century Women's Writing.* Chicago: University of Chicago Press, 1986.

————. *Women Writers and Poetic Identity: Dorothy Wordsworth, Emily Bronte, and Emily Dickinson.* Princeton: Princeton University Press, 1980.

Hunt, Lynn. *The Family Romance of the French Revolution.* Berkeley: University of California Press, 1992.

————. *Politics, Culture, and Class in the French Revolution.* Berkeley: University of California Press, 1984.

Hyde, Lewis. *The Gift: Imagination and the Erotic Life of Property.* New York: Random House, 1979.

Jacobs, Carol. 'There's No Bitterness in Our Literature'. *Sunday Guardian* (Trinidad), 22 May 1966: 9.

Jacobus, Mary. *Reading Women: Essays in Feminist Criticism.* New York: Columbia University Press, 1986.

————. *Romanticism, Writing, and Sexual Difference: Essays on 'The Prelude'.* Oxford: Clarendon Press, 1989.

————. '"That Great Stage Where Senators Perform": Macbeth and the Politics of Romantic Theory'. *SIR* 22 (1983): 353–88.

————. *Tradition and Experiment in Wordsworth's 'Lyrical Ballads'.* Oxford: Clarendon Press, 1976.

Jay, Paul. *Being in the Text: Self-Representation from Wordsworth to Roland Barthes.* Ithaca: Cornell University Press, 1984.

Johnson, Hubert C. *The Midi in Revolution: A Study of Regional Political Diversity, 1789–1793.* Princeton: Princeton University Press, 1986.

Johnston, Brian. 'Revolution and the Romantic Theater'. *Theater Three* 4 (1988): 5–20.

Johnston, Kenneth R. 'Narcissus and Joan: Wordsworth's Feminist Recluse?' *SIR* 29 (1990): 197–221.

————. 'Reclaiming Dorothy Wordsworth's Legacy'. In *The Age of William Wordsworth.* Ed. Johnston and Gene W. Ruoff. New Brunswick: Rutgers University Press, 1987.

————. *Wordsworth and 'The Recluse'*. New Haven: Yale University Press, 1984.

Kearns, Sheila M. *Coleridge, Wordsworth, and Romantic Autobiography: Reading Strategies of Self-representation*. London: Associated University Press, 1995.

Kelly, George Armstrong. *Victims, Authority, and Terror: The Parallel Deaths of d'Orleans, Custine, Bailly, and Malesherbes*. Chapel Hill: University of North Carolina Press, 1982.

Klancher, Jon P. *The Making of English Reading Audiences: 1790–1832*. Madison: University of Wisconsin Press, 1987.

Knoepflmacher, U. C. 'Projection and the Female Other: Romanticism, Browning, and the Victorian Dramatic Monologue'. *VP* 22: 2 (1984): 139–59.

Kostenbaum, Wayne. *Double-Talk: The Erotics of Male Literary Collaboration*. New York: Routledge, 1989.

Kristeva, Julia. *The Kristeva Reader*. Ed. Toril Moi. New York: Columbia University Press, 1986.

————. 'The Ruins of a Poetics'. In *Russian Formalism*. Ed. Stephan Bann and John E. Bowlt. New York: Harper & Row, 1973.

————. 'Word, Dialogue and Novel'. In *Desire and Language*. Ed. Leon S. Roudiez. New York: Columbia University Press, 1980.

Lane, M. Travis. 'A Different Growth of a Poet's Mind: Derek Walcott's *Another Life*'. *Ariel* 9 (1978): 65–78.

Lang, Cecil, ed. *The Pre-Raphaelites and Their Circle*. Chicago: University of Chicago Press, 1975.

Lefebure, Molly. *Samuel Taylor Coleridge: A Bondage of Opium*. London: Gollancz, 1974.

Lejeune, Philip. *On Autobiography*. Minneapolis: University of Minnesota Press, 1989.

Levin, Susan M. *Dorothy Wordsworth and Romanticism*. New Brunswick: Rutgers University Press, 1987.

Levinson, Marjorie. *Wordsworth's Great Period Poems: Four Essays*. Cambridge: Cambridge University Press, 1986.

Lieberman, Laurence. 'New Poetry: The Muse of History'. *Yale Review* 63 (1973): 113–36.

Lindenberger, Herbert. *On Wordsworth's 'Prelude'*. Princeton: Princeton University Press, 1963.

Liu, Alan. 'On the Autobiographical Present: Dorothy Wordsworth's *Grasmere Journals*'. *Criticism* 26 (1984): 115–37.

————. *Wordsworth: The Sense of History*. Stanford: Stanford University Press, 1989.

————. 'Wordsworth and Subversion, 1793–1804: Trying Cultural Criticism'. *Yale Journal of Criticism* 2 (1989): 55–100.

Lukits, Steven. 'Wordsworth Unawares: The Boy of Winander, the Poet, and the Mariner'. *TWC* 19 (1988): 156–60.

Luther, Susan. '"A Different Lore": Coleridge's "The Nightingale"', *The Wordsworth Circle* 18 (1987): 91–7.

Magnuson, Paul. *Coleridge and Wordsworth: A Lyrical Dialogue*. Princeton: Princeton University Press, 1988.

Manning, Peter. *Reading Romantics: Texts and Contexts*. New York: Oxford University Press, 1990.

Mauss, Marcel. *The Gift: Forms and Functions of Exchange in Archaic Societies*. Trans. Ian Cunnison. Glencoe, Ill.: The Free Press, 1954.

McFarland, Thomas. *Romanticism and the Forms of Ruin: Wordsworth, Coleridge, and the Modalities of Fragmentation*. Princeton: Princeton University Press, 1981.

McGann, Jerome J. *The Beauty of Inflections*. Oxford: Oxford University Press, 1985.

————. *The Romantic Ideology: A Critical Investigation*. Chicago: University of Chicago Press, 1983.

Meisenhelder, Susan Edwards. *Wordsworth's Informed Reader*. Nashville: Vanderbilt University Press, 1988.

Mellor, Anne K., ed. *Romanticism and Feminism*. Bloomington: Indiana University Press, 1988.

Mitchell, W. J. T. 'Influence, Autobiography, and Literary History: Rousseau's "Confessions" and Wordsworth's "The Prelude"'. *ELH* 57 (1990): 643–64.

Modiano, Raimonda. 'Coleridge and Wordsworth: The Ethics of Gift Exchange and Literary Ownership'. *The Wordsworth Circle* 20 (1989): 113–120.

Morson, Gary Saul and Caryl Emerson. *Mikhail Bakhtin: Creation of a Prosaics*. Stanford: Stanford University Press, 1990.

————. *Rethinking Bakhtin: Extensions and Challenges*. Evanston: Northwestern University Press, 1989.

Newlyn, Lucy. *Coleridge, Wordsworth, and the Language of Allusion*. Oxford: Clarendon Press, 1986.

Nichols, Ashton. 'Dialogism in the Dramatic Monologue: Suppressed Voices in Browning'. *Victorians Institute Journal* 18 (1990): 29–51.

Nussbaum, Felicity. *The Autobiographical Subject: Gender and Ideology in Eighteenth-Century England*. Baltimore: Johns Hopkins University Press, 1989.

Parker, Reeve. '"Oh Could You Hear His Voice": Wordsworth, Coleridge, and Ventriloquism', in *Romanticism and Language*. Ed. Arden Reed. Ithaca: Cornell University Press, 1984.

————. 'Reading Wordsworth's Power: Narrative and Usurpation in "The Borderers"'. *ELH* 54 (1987): 299–331.

Parrish, Stephen Maxfield. *The Art of the Lyrical Ballads*. Cambridge: Harvard University Press, 1973.

Paulson, Ronald. *Representations of Revolution (1789–1820)*. New Haven: Yale University Press, 1983.

Pecora, Vincent P. *Self and Form in Modern Narrative*. Baltimore: Johns Hopkins University Press, 1989.

Pilling, John. *Autobiography and Imagination: Studies in Self-Scrutiny*. London: Routledge & Kegan Paul, 1981.

Pinion, F. B. *A Wordsworth Chronology*. Boston: G. K. Hall, 1988.

Prickett, Stephen. *Coleridge and Wordsworth: The Poetry of Growth*. Cambridge: Cambridge University Press, 1970.

Privateer, Paul. *Romantic Voices: Identity and Ideology in British Poetry,*

1789–1850. Athens, Ga.: University of Georgia Press, 1991.

Quigley, Austin. 'Wittgenstein's Philosophizing and Literary Theorizing'. *New Literary History* 19 (1988): 209–37.

Rader, Ralph W. 'The Dramatic Monologue and Related Lyric Forms'. *Critical Inquiry* 3 (1976): 131–53.

———. 'Notes on Some Structural Varieties and Variations in Dramatic "I" Poems and Their Theoretical Implications'. *VP* 22 (1984): 103–20.

Rajan, Tillotama. *Dark Interpreter: The Discourse of Romanticism.* Ithaca: Cornell University Press, 1980.

Ramchand, Kenneth. 'Bibliography for 1973: The West Indies'. *The Journal of Commonwealth Literature* 9 (1974).

Rehder, Robert. *Wordsworth and the Beginnings of Modern Poetry.* London: Croom Helm, 1981.

Richardson, Alan. 'Romanticism and the Colonization of the Feminine', in *Romanticism and Feminism.* Ed. Anne K. Mellor. Bloomington: Indiana University Press, 1988: 13–26.

Riffaterre, Michael. *Fictional Truth.* Baltimore: Johns Hopkins University Press, 1990.

Roe, Nicholas. *Wordsworth and Coleridge: The Radical Years.* Oxford: Clarendon Press, 1988.

Ross, Marlon. 'Naturalizing Gender: Woman's Place in Wordsworth's Ideological Landscape'. *ELH* 53 (1986): 391–410.

———. 'Romantic Quest and Conquest: Troping Masculine Power in the Crisis of Poetic Identity'. In *Romanticism and Feminism.* Ed. Anne Mellor. Bloomington: Indiana University Press, 1988.

Rousseau, Jean-Jacques. *Confessions.* Trans. J. M. Cohen. New York: Penguin, 1953.

———. *The First and Second Discourses and Essay on the Origin of Language.* New York: Harper & Row, 1986.

Ruoff, Gene W. *Wordsworth and Coleridge: The Making of the Major Lyrics: 1802–1804.* New Brunswick: Rutgers University Press, 1989.

Rzepka, Charles J. *The Self as Mind: Visions and Identity in Wordsworth, Coleridge, and Keats.* Cambridge, Mass.: Harvard University Press, 1986.

Said, Edward. *Beginnings: Intention and Method.* New York: Columbia University Press, 1985 [1975].

Sales, Roger. *English Literature in History: 1780–1830: Pastoral and Politics.* New York: St. Martin's, 1983.

Schama, Simon. *Citizens: A Chronicle of the French Revolution.* New York: Knopf, 1989.

Shapiro, Barbara. *The Romantic Mother: Narcissistic Patterns in Romantic Poetry.* Baltimore: Johns Hopkins University Press, 1983.

Shattuck, Roger. *The Innocent Eye: On Modern Literature and the Arts.* New York: Farrar, Straus, Giroux, 1984.

Simpson, David. *Wordsworth and the Figurings of the Real.* Atlantic Highlands, NJ: Humanities Press, 1982.

Siskin, Clifford. *The Historicity of Romantic Discourse.* New York: Oxford University Press, 1988.

Smith, Paul. *Discerning the Subject.* Minneapolis: University of Minnesota Press, 1988.

Smith, Sidonie. *A Poetics of Women's Autobiography: Marginality and the Fictions of Self-Representation*. Bloomington: Indiana University Press, 1987.

Spiegelman, Willard. *Wordsworth's Heroes*. Berkeley: University of California Press, 1985.

Starobinski, Jean. *Jean-Jacques Rousseau: Transparency and Obstruction*. Trans. Arthur Goldhammer. Chicago: University of Chicago Press, 1988 [1971].

Stein, Edwin. *Wordsworth's Art of Allusion*. University Park: Pennsylvania State University Press, 1988.

Stelzig, Eugene L. 'Coleridge in *The Prelude*: Wordsworth's Fiction of Alterity'. *TWC* 18 (1987): 23–7.

Stewart, Garrett. *Death Sentences: Styles of Dying in British Fiction*. Cambridge: Harvard University Press, 1984.

Stillinger, Jack. *Multiple Authorship and the Myth of Solitary Genius*. Oxford: Oxford University Press, 1991.

———. 'The Multiple Versions of Coleridge's Poems: How Many *Mariners* Did Coleridge Write?'. *SIR* 31 (1992): 127–42.

———. 'Textual Primitivism in the Editing of Wordsworth'. *SIR* 28 (1989): 3–28.

Swartz, Richard G. 'Wordsworth and the Politics of Ambition'. *Nineteenth-Century Contexts* 13: 1 (1989): 91–120.

Thomas, Clara. 'Commonwealth Albums: Family Resemblance in Derek Walcott's *Another Life* and Margaret Laurence's *The Diviners*'. *WLWE* 21 (1982): 262–8.

Thomas, Gordon. 'The *Lyrical Ballads* Ode: Dialogized Heteroglossia'. *TWC* (1989): 102–5.

Todorov, Tzvetan. *Mikhail Bakhtin: The Dialogical Principle*. Trans. Wlad Godzich. Minneapolis: University of Minnesota Press, 1984.

Tucker, Herbert. 'Dramatic Monologue and the Overhearing of Lyric', in *Lyric Poetry: Beyond New Criticism*. Ed. Chaviva Hosek and Patricia Parker. Ithaca: Cornell University Press, 1985: 226–46.

Turner, Victor. 'Liminality and the Performative Genres', in *Rite, Drama, Festival, Spectacle: Rehearsals Toward a Theory of Cultural Performance*. Ed. John J. MacAloon. Philadelphia: ISHI, 1984: 19–41.

Walcott, Derek. *Another Life*. Washington, DC: Three Continents Press, 1982.

———. *Collected Poems: 1948–1984*. New York: Farrar, Straus & Giroux, 1986.

Warminski, Andrzej. 'Facing Language: Wordsworth's First Poetic Spirits'. *Diacritics* 17: 4 (1987): 18–31.

Weiskel, Thomas. *The Romantic Sublime: Studies in the Structure and Psychology of Transcendence*. Baltimore: Johns Hopkins University Press, 1976.

Williams, Huntington. *Rousseau and Romantic Autobiography*. Oxford: Oxford University Press, 1983.

Wittgenstein, Ludwig. *Philosophical Investigations*, trans. G. E. M. Anscombe. Oxford: Blackwell, 1972.

Wolfson, Susan J. 'Individual in Community: Dorothy Wordsworth in Conversation with William'. In *Romanticism and Feminism*. Ed. Anne Mellor, 139–66.

————. *The Questioning Presence: Wordsworth, Keats, and the Interrogative Mode in Romantic Poetry*. Ithaca: Cornell University Press, 1986.

Wood, Nigel, ed. *The Prelude*. Buckingham: Open University Press, 1993.

Woodman, Ross. 'Wordsworth's Crazed Bedouin: *The Prelude* and the Fate of Madness'. *SIR* 27 (1988): 3–29.

Woodring, Carl. 'Shaping Life in *The Prelude*'. In *Nineteenth-Century Lives: Essays Presented to Jerome Hamilton Buckley*. Ed. Laurence S. Lockridge, John Maynard, Donald D. Stone. Cambridge: Cambridge University Press, 1989.

Wordsworth, Dorothy. *Journals of Dorothy Wordsworth*. Ed. Mary Moorman. Oxford: Oxford University Press, 1973.

————. *Journals of Dorothy Wordsworth*. Ed. E. de Selincourt. Oxford: Clarendon Press, 1941.

Wordsworth, Jonathan. *William Wordsworth: The Borders of Vision*. Oxford: Clarendon Press, 1982.

Wordsworth, William. *The Early Letters of William and Dorothy Wordsworth (1787–1805)*. Ed. Ernest de Selincourt. Oxford: Clarendon Press, 1935.

————. *The Five-Book Prelude*. Ed. Duncan Wu. Oxford: Blackwell, 1997.

————. *The Love Letters of William and Mary Wordsworth*. Ed. Beth Darlington. Ithaca: Cornell University Press, 1981.

————. *The Poetical Works of William Wordsworth*. Ed. Ernest de Selincourt and Helen Darbishire. 5 vols. Oxford: Clarendon Press, 1940–9.

————. *The Prelude: 1799, 1805, 1850*. Ed. Jonathan Wordsworth. New York: Norton, 1979.

————. *The Prelude, 1798–1799*. Ed. Stephen Parrish. Ithaca: Cornell University Press, 1977.

————. *Selected Prose*. Ed. John O. Hayden. New York: Viking Penguin, 1988.

————. *William Wordsworth*. Oxford Authors. Ed. Stephen Gill. Oxford: Oxford University Press, 1984.

Wu, Duncan. *Wordsworth's Reading: 1770–1799*. Cambridge: Cambridge University Press, 1993.

Yeats, W. B. *Essays and Introductions*. New York: Macmillan, 1961.

Young, Robert. '"For Thou Wert There": History, Erasure, and Superscription in *The Prelude*'. In *Demarcating the Disciplines*. Ed. Samuel Weber. Minneapolis: University of Minnesota Press, 1986.

————. 'The Eye and Progress of His Song: A Lacanian Reading of *The Prelude*', in *William Wordsworth's The Prelude*. Ed. Harold Bloom. New York: Chelsea House, 1986.

Index

adolescence, 68–9, 111
Alexander, Meena, 172 n.16
androgyny, 111, 123, 125, 128, 130
Arnold, Matthew, 135
Augustine, St., xv, 25
Ausonius, 10
autobiography, ix, xi–xii, xv–xvi, 3, 7,
    15, 21, 25, 27–8, 46–7, 59, 63-4,
    68–9, 75–6, 108, 130, 132–50
autography, 21, 27

Baker, Jeffrey, 160 n.16
Bakhtin, M. M., xi, xiii, 56–9, 63–4, 74,
    155 n.13, 160 n.1, 161 n.6, 162 n.13
Barthes, Roland, 151 n.3
Bate, W. J., 165 n.7
Baugh, Edward, 134
Beaumont, George, 24, 25
Beaupuy, Michel, 31, 48
Bewell, Alan, 152 n.4
Bialostosky, Don, 155 n.13
biography, 15, 21, 63, 130–1, 170 n.9
Bostetter, Edward, 156 n.14
Brown, Lloyd, 135, 173 n.5
Browning, Robert, 25, 58
Byron, (George Gordon) Lord, xi,
    12–13, 24, 27, 154 n.9, 156 n.13,
    161 n.5

Chaucer, Geoffrey, ix
Christensen, Jerome, 154 n.9
Chodorow, Nancy, xi, 109, 170 n.8
citizen, x, 30, 151 n.1
Coleridge, Samuel Taylor, xiii, 1–2, 4–5,
    12, 22–3, 26, 32, 36–7, 45, 55,
    78–101, 103–4, 109, 118, 143, 148,
    156 n.13, 165 n.7
  Works:
  'Dejection', 91, 96–8, 118, 166 n.11
  'Frost at Midnight', 20
  'The Nightingale', 15–21
  Osorio, 17
  'The Three Graves', 161 n.5
  'To William Wordsworth', 93–6
Crawford, Rachel, 167 n.2

Dahanay, Martin, 163 n.3
Darlington, Beth, 171 n.14
de Certeau, Michel, 157 n.2, 173 n.8

democracy, 30–1, 43–4, 48, 53, 64–5
De Quincey, Thomas, 23, 121, 122
Derrida, Jacques, 110, 117
Descartes, René, 63
Devlin, D. D., 162 n.11
dialogism, xiii, 1, 10–11, 22, 28, 56, 59,
    102
dramatic monologue, xiii, 25, 55, 56–77
dramatized speaker, xiii, 1, 14, 16, 22,
    25, 29–34, 49–50, 61, 64, 131,
    158 n.4

echo, 10–11, 15, 56, 61, 73, 77, 134
eco-criticism, ix, 163 n.3
Eilenberg, Susan, 155 n.13
elegy, 80–1, 94
Emerson, Ralph Waldo, 164 n.5
epic, 2, 26, 65, 104, 109, 126, 128, 129
epiphany, 66, 145–7
epitaph, 11, 14–15, 77, 121, 162 n.11
Erdman, David, 159 n.12

Fay, Elizabeth, xiv, 168 n.2
Fenwick, Isabella, 26, 105
Fleming, John, 7, 11
Fleishman, Avrom, 149
French Revolution, xiii, 17–18, 29–30,
    43–55, 121, 132, 157 n.1, 159 n.14,
    160 n.16
Friedman, Geraldine, 162 n.14
Furet, François, 30, 157 n.2

Gagnier, Regina, xv, 151 n.1
Galperin, William H., 166 n.9
Gassenmeier, Michael, 160 n.16
gift-exchange theory, xiii, 79–81, 96–8,
    100–1, 118, 164 n.5, n.6
Gill, Stephen, 3, 152 n.3, 162 n.12
Gilligan, Carol, 109, 170 n.8
Godwin, William, 22, 52, 118, 121
Graham, Robert, 37–8
Gusdorf, Georges, 144–5, 173 n.8,
    174 n.9

Hamner, Robert, 173 n.3, n.4
Haney, David, 154 n.10
Hartley, David, 22
Hartman, Geoffrey, xi, 57, 153 n.4,
    166 n.14